MW00587472

"This is an essential guide fo[r] who want to deconstruct the [harmful teachings linger]ing behind the faith they love. [Drawing on Dr.] Morgante's own life and the lives of others, critical analysis of what purity culture is and why it is harmful, and practical strategies for recovering from those wounds, this book will help readers more deeply know that their bodies were never the problem—only the stories told about them."

Dr. Hillary L. McBride, registered psychologist, podcaster, author of *The Wisdom of Your Body* and *Holy Hurt*

"In her debut book, Dr. Camden Morgante provides a refreshing, compassionate, and needed corrective to the harmful teachings of purity culture. This book is an essential resource for those who are working to untangle their faith from the destructive legacy around sexuality and embodiment that has been rampant within Christian spaces."

Aundi Kolber, MA, LPC, therapist, author of *Try Softer* and *Strong like Water*

"*Recovering from Purity Culture* by Dr. Camden Morgante is a well-written, well-researched, and compassionate guide for individuals coming out of purity culture who are looking for ways to renegotiate their experiences and faith in a way that feels authentic to them. Dr. Morgante offers her readers many therapeutic skills and tools to get them started on their own journey of recovery without requiring them to take on her own views and opinions. I highly recommend this book to anyone who is ready to recover from the impact that purity culture has had on them."

Dr. Laura Anderson, author of *When Religion Hurts You*

"Dr. Camden Morgante, in her book *Recovering from Purity Culture*, warmly invites readers into her office and charts a journey from the harms of purity culture, through faith deconstruction, to the rebuilding of one's sexual ethic. As a trustworthy and credible guide, Dr. Morgante offers a much-needed healing resource for countless individuals."

Mark A. Yarhouse, PsyD, Dr. Arthur P. Rech and Mrs. Jean May Rech Professor of Psychology at Wheaton College, director of the Sexual and Gender Identity Institute

"Reading Camden Morgante's book gave me renewed hope that the generation who grew up within purity culture could reclaim both their faith and their sexuality. Dr. Morgante takes a comprehensive and compassionate approach to various harmful effects of purity culture, giving readers the tools needed to identify how purity teachings negatively impacted them and to discover a 'values-congruent sexual ethic.' As such, *Recovering from Purity Culture* is a work of reconstruction. I highly recommend this book to anyone looking for a both/and approach to sexuality in a world of either/or answers."

Katelyn Beaty, author of *Celebrities for Jesus*,
editorial director of Brazos Press

"So many of us were deeply harmed by purity culture and don't know how to reclaim a healthy sexual ethic informed by consent and wisdom. Dr. Morgante doesn't give readers the 'right' answer but instead gives them tools to answer the question themselves."

Tim Whitaker, creator of The New Evangelicals

"Dr. Morgante exposes the dehumanization that both young men and young women suffered under the guise of spiritual wisdom, but she doesn't stop there. She untangles the webs of shame and self-hatred that purity culture myths brought into our lives and then courageously rebuilds a healthy sexual ethic that Christians so desperately need and hunger for. I am so grateful for this guidebook's assistance in unlearning and learning such tragically beautiful lessons here. Thank you."

Dr. Andrew J. Bauman, founder of the Christian Counseling
Center for Sexual Health & Trauma, author of *Safe Church*

"Surviving purity culture is no small task, and rebuilding our lives in its aftermath is often the hardest part. In these pages, purity culture survivors will find clear and compassionate guidance from someone who has been there and has the psychological expertise to provide a path forward."

Devi Abraham, cofounder and host of the
Where Do We Go from Here? podcast

RECOVERING FROM
PURITY CULTURE

RECOVERING FROM PURITY CULTURE

DISMANTLE THE MYTHS,
REJECT SHAME-BASED SEXUALITY,
AND MOVE FORWARD IN YOUR FAITH

DR. CAMDEN MORGANTE

BakerBooks

a division of Baker Publishing Group
Grand Rapids, Michigan

Published by Baker Books
a division of Baker Publishing Group
Grand Rapids, Michigan
BakerBooks.com

Printed in the United States of America

Library of Congress Cataloging-in-Publication Data
Names: Morgante, Camden A., author.
Title: Recovering from purity culture : dismantle the myths, reject shame-based sexuality, and move forward in your faith / Dr. Camden Morgante.
Description: Grand Rapids, Michigan : Baker Books, a division of Baker Publishing Group, 2024. | Includes bibliographical references.
Identifiers: LCCN 2024012133 | ISBN 9781540904263 (paperback) | ISBN 9781540904539 (casebound) | ISBN 9781493447053 (ebook)
Subjects: LCSH: Sexual ethics—Religious aspects—Christianity. | Spiritual life—Christianity.
Classification: LCC BT708 .M674 2024 | DDC 241/.664—dc23/eng/20240516
LC record available at https://lccn.loc.gov/2024012133

All client names and some identifying details have been changed. At times, client stories were combined to further disguise identities. Conversations with clients were re-created based on the author's notes, to the best of her knowledge. Nonclients who provided interviews all consented and agreed to include their stories in this book, some with a pseudonym. Interviews were edited or condensed for clarity.

This publication is intended to provide helpful and informative material on the subjects addressed. Readers should consult their personal health professionals before adopting any of the suggestions in this book or drawing inferences from it. The author and publisher expressly disclaim responsibility for any adverse effects arising from the use or application of the information contained in this book.

Some of the material in this book previously appeared on the author's website, DrCamden.com.

Portions of chapters 3 through 7 appeared in Camden Morgante, "5 Purity Culture Myths and Why They Are False Promises," *Christians for Biblical Equality*, May 28, 2019, https://www.cbeinternational.org/resource/5-purity-culture-myths-and-why-they-are-false-promises.

The author is represented by the literary agency of WordServe Literary Group, WordServeLiterary.com.

Baker Publishing Group publications use paper produced from sustainable forestry practices and postconsumer waste whenever possible.

24 25 26 27 28 29 30   7 6 5 4 3 2 1

To John, my gift of grace.

And to Grace Anne and Samuel,
our gifts of grace.

Contents

Contents

Foreword

I am not a purity culture survivor.

When I attended youth group in the 1980s, "being sold out for Jesus" wasn't about the state of one's hymen but instead was about being willing to go on the mission field and becoming comfortable giving your testimony to your friends at high school. Youth group was all about learning to evangelize, to be salt in the world, and to bring Jesus to the masses.

We had our own issues, but thankfully, I grew up before purity culture.

But while I was not raised in it, I did perpetrate it. When my oldest daughter, Rebecca, was thirteen, I bought her two things: a copy of Joshua Harris's *I Kissed Dating Goodbye* and a subscription to Focus on the Family's *Brio* magazine (the latter at her request). I was initially excited about the idea of saving dating until one was ready to marry and thought it might spare my daughters some of the heartache I went through in high school.

By the time Rebecca was sixteen, we had ditched that idea, so her sister Katie grew up rather unscathed. Even though Rebecca hadn't been "dating," she still had crushes. She still had heartache. And increasingly, I was finding that the people pushing purity culture were the same ones who were also denying my daughters—and myself—any role in the church beyond singing, bouncing babies, and making sandwiches for potlucks. We decided we needed a bigger faith, full of nuance, the Spirit, and even a bit of uncertainty, rather than legalism.

Over the next few years, though, we witnessed the effects of purity culture on those we loved in real time. We saw friends of theirs being date-raped and not being able to recognize it for what it was because of messaging eradicating the concept of consent. We heard one youth pastor tell a lovely but devastated teenager, "What did you expect dating a non-Christian?" We saw countless girls covering themselves in extra large clothing because they were so embarrassed about the size of their chests and didn't want to be stumbling blocks. We saw boys getting hooked on porn and thinking they were helpless to stop, because, after all, God made lust "every man's battle."

Today we're part of a growing movement, along with Dr. Camden, fighting for purity culture survivors—from the young women who had their sexuality stolen to the young men who were told they were sinning every time they noticed a girl's breasts. Along with my daughter Rebecca Lindenbach and our coauthor Joanna Sawatsky, I've conducted large studies on the effects of evangelical teachings on both women and men, and the results are not pretty. In the pages of this book, Dr. Camden will quote some of them, including the outsized burden of sexual pain disorders in evangelicalism and the huge orgasm gap between men and women.

As we've analyzed our results, a question keeps haunting us: *Why is it that those of us who know and love Jesus keep reaping such bad fruit?*

The answer is devastating: because the teaching at the heart of purity culture was bad. It didn't necessarily flow from bad intentions, but it was bad nonetheless because it wasn't focused on Jesus. And it's left a mess in its wake, a mess that thousands upon thousands of people now have to figure out how to clean up.

That's what Dr. Camden is going to guide you through in this book. She knows what she's talking about. She has experienced this bad fruit firsthand, and in her professional capacity she has helped others find healing.

Don't just read this book. Work through the exercises. You went to all the trouble to buy the book and pick it up, so honor yourself and your story and do the work. You'll emerge healthier.

Lighter. More peaceful. And, like Dr. Camden, I hope you'll also emerge knowing that it wasn't Jesus who was the author of the five purity culture myths that this book is going to deconstruct for you. Those weren't on him; they're on purity culture.

But that leaves another mess, doesn't it? If it was the church that taught this to us, then how can we trust the church again?

One of the hardest parts of my faith journey, as I've delved into the results of our teachings, is coming to terms with the fact that the church sometimes failed us. I know it's also done tremendous good, and I try to keep that in perspective. But when the harm is this great, and so many who perpetrated it won't admit it, it's hard to forgive. It's hard to feel welcome in the church or embrace it when there don't seem to be any amends being made.

But perhaps I've been looking in the wrong place for healing. I've been wanting those who taught this stuff to own up and apologize and acknowledge the hurt that's been done. That may not happen. Yet I believe that God is raising up new generations, especially Millennials like Dr. Camden and Gen Z that's coming next, who will bring healing where my Gen X brothers and sisters have failed. There's a movement going on—a shaking in the church and a desire for emotional health and wholeness even in our sexuality—that will not be quenched.

Quite simply, we don't have a choice. The crisis is too great. We need to fix this.

Now, Dr. Camden knows that many of you will question your faith as you start to unpack these purity culture myths that hurt you. I get it. I do. But I hope that in these pages, you can catch a glimpse of the real Jesus, who is okay with messy and who doesn't want to cover you in a blanket of shame. I hope you will see there's a chance to build a healthy sexual ethic that's not dictated to you but flows out of authentic searching. I hope you can see that health and Jesus are not polar opposites.

But wherever you land, I wish you healing.

Dive in. Do the work. And be free.

Sheila Wray Gregoire, founder of Bare Marriage
and award-winning author

Introduction

"Jesus wants the rose!"

In 2009, a megachurch pastor delivered this sermon at a Desiring God conference—the flagship organization of evangelical pastor John Piper. There, the pastor shared a sermon he'd once heard about sex. In that sermon, the speaker took a red rose and threw it out into the crowd of a thousand college and high school students, encouraging them to look at it, smell it, and touch its petals. Then, as the sermon wrapped up, the speaker called for his rose, which was now "completely jacked up . . . the petals are broken."

The speaker held up the rose, screaming, "Now who would want this rose?"

The megachurch pastor recounted the anger he felt hearing those words. Overcome, he shouted out, "Jesus wants the rose! That's the point of the gospel, that Jesus wants the rose!"[1]

The crowd cheered and applauded in response.

Yes, Jesus wants the rose.

But also maybe Jesus doesn't want his beloved image bearers to be compared to "jacked up" roses in the first place.

—————

These kinds of demonstrations were rampant in the late 1990s to early 2000s when the evangelical movement known as purity culture was at its peak. Youth leaders, teachers, parents, and Christian speakers on the conference circuit frequently used an object to, well, objectify us. For those of you, like me, who grew up immersed in purity culture, this is all too familiar.

The rose is a common symbol in purity culture object lessons. Typically, a young, married, male youth pastor or leader stands on stage in front of a large audience of teenagers, plucking petals off a rose one by one. Each petal represents a sexual indiscretion, making the rose less beautiful, less desirable with each loss. A rose stripped of all its petals represents the ultimate fall from grace: the loss of virginity.

"This is what you will be like if you have sex," he tells his audience as he removes petal after petal.

You were a rose, the illustration suggests, capable of offering love, purity, and partnership. But now? You are lacking. Each time you crossed the line, you lost a rose petal, a piece of your heart. Now, you are incomplete and tarnished. You are damaged goods. And because of that, you should be ashamed.

Whether it was a rose, a heart-shaped piece of paper torn into shreds, tape that lost its stickiness, a cup of water that had been spit into, or a chewed-up piece of gum, the message was clear. Sex irrevocably and wholly changes you. If you "give this gift" too early, you are no longer acceptable. You are unwanted and unclean.

But if you stay pure and don't give away pieces of yourself, these teachers suggested, God will bless you for your faithfulness. You will have an amazing marriage, a smoking-hot spouse, mind-blowing sex, and a beautiful family. You will prove your spiritual maturity through your virginity. You are a better Christian if you can just say no. As long as you obey God, he will reward you with everything your heart desires.

My parents gave me a copy of Joshua Harris's bestselling book *I Kissed Dating Goodbye* when I was eleven years old. They wanted me to follow the model of courtship laid out by the book, which they themselves had followed. This model involved avoiding dating but entering into a courtship type of relationship with the intention of marriage, usually guided by one's parents, church leaders, and faith community. According to courtship teachings, I would be spared the pain of heartbreak and preserve my purity by dating only one person, who would eventually become my husband. Some forms of courtship also emphasized saving any physical affection for the wedding day, such as sharing your first kiss at the wedding altar.

At age fourteen, I received a True Love Waits ring and eagerly signed my pledge card along with an estimated 2.5 million American teenagers:

> Believing that true love waits, I make a commitment to God, myself, my family, my friends, my future mate, and my future children to a lifetime of purity including sexual abstinence from this day until the day I enter a biblical marriage relationship.[2]

I wore my True Love Waits ring for almost a decade. During those years, I had my first serious relationship while in college. He was my first kiss and my first love. We maintained sexual boundaries in our affection, tried to put God at the center of our relationship, and prayed together before dates that we would not "give in to temptation." I trusted that my boyfriend was The One. I was immersed in the "ring by spring" culture of our Christian college, which idolized marriage and where it was the norm for nineteen- and twenty-year-old couples to meet and marry within a year.

I assumed my boyfriend and I would follow a similar formula. Throughout our almost three-year relationship, I sincerely believed we would get engaged and then marry after we graduated. Yet we never discussed practicalities like where we would live, our finances, or how our future education and career goals would align. Serious conversation about the future was discouraged in purity culture—after all, emotional intimacy might arouse physical intimacy—so instead we danced around the details, and I never got the clarity and assurance I needed to make this life-altering decision.

Right before our senior year, my boyfriend unexpectedly ended our relationship. As with most breakups, the reasons were complicated. We both had hurt each other in profound ways, which I truly regret. But still, I was shocked. What I expected was marriage; ultimately what I got was heartbreak.

To say I was devastated is an understatement. Not only did I suffer relational disappointment, but I was also spiritually disillusioned. Where was the fairy-tale marriage God promised me if I stayed pure? I had done everything right by intentionally dating and remaining a virgin—why didn't God bring me The One? I saw countless other friends get engaged, some who'd had sex with their spouse or other partners before marriage. *Why did God bless them*, I wondered, *when clearly I was more spiritually mature?*

After graduating from college, I spent over seven years of my twenties single and yearning for marriage. I felt ashamed for being single, jealous of my married friends, and angry at God. During this season, I also went to graduate school to get my doctorate in psychology, hoping to help others with my passion for marriage and relationships. As I began seeing therapy clients for the first time, I was rocked by stories of church harm, abuse, trauma, and grief—many types of suffering that I had not experienced in my privileged life as a white, heterosexual, middle-class, well-educated woman. Clients shared how confused they felt about sexual morals in our culture. I was shocked when I learned in my doctoral human sexuality class that rigid religious beliefs, such as those perpetuated by purity culture, were a direct cause of some sexual disorders. I heard stories from friends and clients about how disappointing sex was in marriage. I worked with therapy clients who blamed themselves for their own sexual abuse and no longer saw themselves as worthy. Their stories and experiences, along with my own prolonged singleness and unfulfilled desires for marriage, left me questioning my faith. Eventually, I stopped going to church for a while and felt distant and distrusting of God—a process that I now refer to as my faith deconstruction.

Looking back, I largely attribute my deconstruction to the teachings of purity culture, patriarchy, and legalism. Over time, I gained distance and perspective from the ideology in which I was raised. I began to identify how so much of what I had been taught by purity culture were myths. I studied and eventually wholeheartedly endorsed egalitarian theology—which promotes gender equality and mutual submission rather than a hierarchy with men at the top—and embraced my identity as a Christian feminist. My theological studies in grad school aided my search for biblical truth. Yet through this deconstruction process, I maintained an identity as a Christian.

Even with distance, purity culture can leave undeniable, long-lasting traumatic effects in our bodies. Purity culture promised us relationships free of heartbreak, but it left many of us with disillusionment. If we are single or if our marriages don't turn out to be fairy tales, then what? Purity culture promised us mind-blowing, carefree marital sex, but it can create disembodiment, shame about past sexual experiences, and disappointment when sex doesn't live up to those expectations. Purity culture promised us a strong faith built on virginity and pleasing God, but for many, it triggered religious trauma and doubts. It became clear to me that this trauma can continue to live on in our bodies long after we no longer believe purity culture in our minds.

After finishing my doctorate and earning my license as a psychologist, I met my now-husband, and we married when I was almost thirty.[3] Once we solidified our dating relationship, we had many talks about our faith and beliefs, including our sexual values and my strong support of gender equality. It was a blessing and a relief to find a Christian man who not only respected my beliefs but was open to exploring them with me.

However, when it came to my sexual ethic, I realized that the reasons given for sexual purity in my teens and early twenties didn't hold true anymore. I questioned, *Why should I wait?* I found that the reasons for abstinence I'd learned from public-school sex education—mainly to avoid teen pregnancy and sexually transmitted infections (STIs)—were no longer relevant to me. But purity culture and the Church's[4] lack of sex education had also failed me. They promised that I'd only have to remain a virgin until God brought me my prince—probably my first love in my late teens or early twenties. Assuming that we would all get married young, they never spoke a message of sexual values beyond the college years. There had to be a more compelling reason and purpose for waiting—a *deeper why*—to sustain me through my adult years when "true love waits" and "because the Bible says so" didn't resonate anymore.

Over the years, my faith had become deeply entangled with my sexual purity. Now, the Church's overemphasis on sexual purity as a mark of a true Christian felt shallow and shortsighted. Surely there was more to base my faith on than "being a good girl" and receiving rewards from God. As I sought to navigate a new way forward, I quickly realized I needed two things: a more robust sexual ethic *and* a more robust faith. I needed a theology that could move past the false promises of purity culture and stand up to the challenging questions I had. I wanted to embrace nuance and uncover the vast gray between the black-and-white answers of purity culture legalism.

And I wanted to do it all while still holding on to my relationship with Jesus.

Becoming a psychologist not only prompted my faith deconstruction; it also provided me with many tools to assist in the reconstruction of my faith and sexual ethic. Purity culture did not provide me with sex education—but my psychology classes in human sexuality and training in sex therapy did. Patriarchy did not empower me to use my voice, gifts, and strengths as an equal person in marriage and church—but my research in feminist psychology and egalitarian theology did. And legalism did not give me the skills to ask hard questions, accept ambiguity, and find sources of truth—but my training in the integration of spirituality and therapy did.

Not everyone has the opportunity (or desire) to pursue an education in psychology or even the resources to seek professional therapy. I see it as my mission to use the privilege of my education to pass on to others the skills and tools I've learned. This mission has propelled and sustained me in the writing of this book in order to help others uncover the harm done by purity culture and to finally find a path forward in their recovery.

————

If you've lived through purity culture, you know quite clearly what it is and how it has hurt you. But how do you heal from it? How can you create a healthy path forward? In this book, I aim to provide you with that *how*. I want you to not only discover how purity culture affects you but also learn how to overcome those effects. As a mental health professional, I want to use the tools I've gained in my education to help you reject toxic beliefs, understand trauma, and recover from the sexual shame caused by purity culture. I offer you the same techniques and strategies I teach my therapy clients and Purity Culture Recovery Coaching clients to allow you to dismantle the myths of purity culture and begin to reconstruct your faith and sexuality.

There are many excellent books on sexuality—both Christian and secular—some of which I recommend in appendix 2. This book, however, is not intended to be an all-encompassing view of Christian sexuality. You will not find here an extensive sexual manual with tips for treating sexual dysfunctions. Also, while I do give general guidelines on how to reconstruct your sexual ethic and teach your kids about sex, this book is not a how-to guide for parenting. Nor will we unpack sexual "hot topics" of interest to many Christians today, such as sexual and gender identity, masturbation, pornography, abuse, and sexual addiction. These topics are important. In particular, I acknowledge that LGBTQ+ Christians have been deeply hurt by purity culture and the Church. I also know that beliefs about LGBTQ+ theology vary widely, even among the readers of this book. While I admit the purpose and scope of this book and my own expertise are limited on all these topics, I hope the resources in the appendixes and notes will be helpful for your further study.

In this conversation, we need to hear from diverse perspectives about how to reconcile purity culture and faith. Many of purity culture's loudest critics are those who have left the faith. But as a Christian who still values an ethic of premarital sexual abstinence (yet no longer adheres to legalism and strict gender roles), I struggled to see myself in their stories. And I know I am not the only one.

Those raised in the '90s purity culture of True Love Waits rings, Silver Ring Thing events, and "Just Say No" campaigns are now adults. We are ready to critically look back on the movement that shaped our sexuality in our adolescent and college years and examine its effects on our adulthood. We are single adults, wondering why the promises of purity did not deliver our "happily ever after" and floundering in our confusion about our beliefs. We are women made to feel like damaged goods after sexual mistakes or sexual trauma. We are married adults, struggling to enjoy sexual intimacy with our spouses after years of denying, squelching, and stifling any sexual desires or urges. We are starting our own families or launching kids into adolescence, worried about how or what to teach them about sexuality. We are all looking for a better way forward.

―――――――――――

On the first day of teaching a college psychology class, I tell my students to expect to hear something they disagree with in every class. Likewise, I expect that you will find places in this book where you disagree with me. You will not find many black-and-white answers here; instead, I will encourage you to explore the gray areas, search for sources of truth (including the Bible), and develop more robust beliefs. Some of you may feel I go too far and others, not far enough. As someone who identifies on the middle path in my faith—too conservative to be progressive and too progressive to be conservative—I am familiar with criticism on both sides.

The main purpose of this book is not to argue for a particular sexual ethic or theology of sexuality. While it will be necessary for us to venture into theological territory on our healing journey, I am not a theologian. I intend to mostly stay in my lane as a psychologist. My goal isn't to change your mind or ask you to prescribe to my own personal ethic. Instead, it's to provide you tools and techniques to change toxic beliefs and find healing by integrating the mind and body. I want to inspire critical thinking so you can discern what you believe and how you want to live out those beliefs.

No matter what, I want to be clear with you, my friend and reader. I am writing as a Christian primarily to other Christians who believe that the Bible is a source of truth and authority in our lives. I personally hold to a traditional sexual ethic of sex within a covenantal marriage. I have reconstructed my sexual ethic with much care, study, discernment, and searching, and I trust that you have done (or will do) the same with your sexual ethic. I am sympathetic to those along the journey of deconstruction who are unsure if the Bible is a trusted source or who question if they are still a Christian at all. You are welcome here too. I hope you feel a spirit of generosity, openness, and empathy in my words. While we may be coming from different places at times, we are all in this recovery process together. And I am hopeful this book can be a helpful resource to any reader, both those who share my sexual ethic and faith orientation and those who ultimately do not.

I encourage you to use this book to think through the messages and lessons you were taught about sexuality, some of which may be unconscious, and examine how those have affected you. In turn, I hope you come away with new insights, greater clarity, and most importantly, a toolbox of techniques, exercises, and skills that you can apply to your own healing. While this book will be an excellent guide for purity culture recovery, it cannot diagnose any mental health condition or replace professional mental health services. Unlike in therapy, where I can tailor my approach or interventions to each client's needs, this book cannot speak to every person's unique situation.

From my heart, I want you to know that your safety and healing are my top concerns. I understand that the topics in this book may be triggering to some readers. Please take the tools at your own pace and stop if you become triggered, flooded, or overwhelmed.[5] Give yourself permission to pause and process with a safe and trusted friend or a therapist. If you have a history of trauma or mental health problems, sexual dysfunction, or problems with sexual compulsivity, I encourage you to seek more support. You will find resources for seeking professional help in appendix 1.

To help us move through this journey, this book is divided into three sections. Section 1 introduces the construction and history of purity culture. Purity culture affects us in three main areas: faith, sexuality, and relationships, including our relationship to ourselves and our mental health. Here, we will examine these problems as well as what recovery looks like in each.

Section 2 will dismantle the myths and false promises of purity culture as well as their damaging effects. We will identify five prevalent myths perpetuated by purity culture and consider real stories and examples of the impact of these messages. You'll learn practical strategies drawn from psychology to replace the myth with a new perspective.

In Section 3, we will reconstruct. You will find insight on how to rebuild your faith and sexual ethic, strategies to become more comfortable with your sexuality and to overcome common sexual problems in your marriage, and techniques for reducing shame. I also offer some basic guidelines and principles for setting a foundation to teach your children about their bodies and sex.

Throughout each chapter, you will find reflection questions to help you pause, ponder, and metabolize the information you're learning. Also, at the end of each chapter, you will find "Tools for the Journey"—the skills, exercises, and techniques I teach my clients. These tools are drawn from evidenced-based practices such as cognitive-behavioral therapy, dialectical behavior therapy, and somatic and mindfulness-based therapies.[6] In order to support integration and wholeness, each tool will focus on four areas: (1) the body: our physical sensations, actions, and behaviors; (2) the mind: our thoughts and beliefs; (3) the heart: our emotions and feelings; and (4) the soul: our spiritual connection to God, to what is holy, sacred, and divine.[7] I view these exercises as a particularly important piece of this journey—skills I would share with you in person if you were sitting across from me in my office. I encourage you to dive into these exercises and invest time and energy into your healing. Consider journaling your responses to the reflection questions and applying the techniques to your life situation. By integrating your mind, heart, body, and soul into the work, you can truly experience lasting and authentic change.

My hope is that this book will give you valuable knowledge and tools to rebuild your faith and sexuality. If it feels comforting, I hope you'll invite Jesus into this journey with you too. He cares about all of you—body, mind, heart, and soul—and he wants you to experience healing and be set free from these lies. And please hear it from me: you are worth doing this work. No matter what you have done or what has been done to you, you are so much more than a "jacked-up rose." Purity culture may have stolen a lot from you. It may have left you exactly where it left me: with years of disillusioned faith, broken relationships, shame in your sexuality, and toxic beliefs.

But you *can* heal from the trauma.

You can go forward in faith and freedom.

Now, let's find the path together.

Constructing Purity Culture

1

Surviving Purity Culture

As a survivor of sexual violence *and* purity culture, I could more easily resolve the trauma in my body stemming from my experiences of sexual violence than from purity culture.

Dr. Laura Anderson, *When Religion Hurts You*[1]

Michelle and Jack are a couple I worked with in therapy. In their late thirties and married for almost twenty years, they told me they met in college and were the "poster children" for the courtship model of *I Kissed Dating Goodbye*. They waited to kiss until their wedding day and were looked up to in their church as a model couple because of it. Early in their marriage, they began leading their youth group and teaching young men and women to do what they'd done: save themselves for marriage and stay pure.

Two decades later, Michelle and Jack had experienced years of painful sex, low sex drive, and disconnection. Michelle felt "locked up" sexually and admitted that 90 percent of the sex in their marriage had been out of obligation or duty. She struggled with body shame and a lack of any sexual desire. A loving husband, Jack did not want Michelle to feel obligated to have sex, so he stopped initiating. Still, he missed the affection and connection with his wife. He was also trying to reconcile this lack of sex with the sexual entitlement he was taught as a male.

In that season, the couple was trying to disentangle their marriage from the patriarchal gender roles they'd learned growing up. They both felt their faith had suffered because of this, so they had stopped going to their church. Michelle no longer felt safe in a church that preached male authority and suggested that wives had to give their husbands sex to keep them from cheating. Jack wrestled with feeling like he and Michelle "followed the rules" and "did things the right way," yet they were still struggling.

Despite their attempts to reinvigorate their love life, Michelle couldn't get over her shame and Jack couldn't get over his guilt and frustration. When they started seeing me, they hadn't had sex in months. In our work together, we began to realize that the majority of the problems in their relationship, sexuality, and faith were due to purity culture.

As they describe it, they are purity culture survivors.

Defining Purity Culture

What do you remember learning about sex in church?

Did you learn that good Christians save sex for marriage? If you don't, you will be damaged goods, right?

Were you taught that God would bless you with an amazing marriage and sex life as long as you waited?

Did you hear that men can't control themselves sexually, so it's up to women to dress modestly, set boundaries, and stay pure?

If you heard these messages—especially if, like me, you heard them as a teenager in the 1990s and 2000s—then you likely grew up in purity culture.

In 1994, the Southern Baptist–sponsored organization True Love Waits held a rally in Washington, DC, which twenty-five thousand youths attended. They displayed 210,000 abstinence pledge cards on the National Mall. It was a stunning demonstration. There was a mass of young people spread across the DC landmark believing they would save themselves from all kinds of pain by promising to have sex with only one person: their future spouse.

At its core, purity culture is an evangelical movement that peaked in the 1990s to 2000s that attempted to persuade young people to abstain from premarital sex. Many other faiths[2] preach a similar ethic of premarital abstinence. Yet it was not only the belief in premarital sexual abstinence—what was called "purity"—that defined the movement. It was also the *culture*—the purity pledges and rings, purity balls and rallies, and books. It was object lessons involving damaged roses, chewed gum, cups of water with spit in them, and other shaming metaphors.

It's important to note that many of the teachers of purity culture had good intentions, wanting young people to avoid the dangers of early sexual activity and to value the sacredness of sex. But what may have started with good intentions turned into a tool of control, particularly of women's sexuality. Fear and shame were the twin swords used in the battle against promiscuity and the war to control and subdue women.

The execution of these teachings left destructive and unanticipated consequences. We were left with pride and judgmentalism when our pastors taught us that virgins are more spiritually mature than nonvirgins. We experienced entitlement and disillusionment when the purity books promised us a fairy-tale marriage if we stayed pure. We felt disappointed when we had difficulty "flipping a switch" on our wedding night or if sex was frustrating and painful rather than pleasurable. We felt shame for being "damaged goods" if we did have premarital sex, went "too far," or even if we experienced sexual trauma at the hands of someone else. And we were set up for inequality, making women the gatekeepers of men's sexuality and robbing men of the opportunity to learn sexual self-control.

In the wake of several cultural movements, many Christians now readily acknowledge the problems and harm that came from traditional religious teachings about dating, marriage, and sexuality. The scars we're left with do not disappear as we get older or even if we marry. Many of us are deeply impacted by the #MeToo and #ChurchToo movements, by the way allegations of sexual assault and harassment have been covered up in the Church and blame heaped on the victims. We are outraged at the way Church teachings have perpetuated modesty culture and rape culture. We are angry that the LGBTQ+ community has been ostracized and ridiculed. We are concerned when we see former Christian idols "deconverting"—that is, walking away from church and faith entirely.

Because of the damage purity culture has caused, many critics denounce anything resembling a traditional Christian sexual ethic.[3] Instead, a new sexual ethic centered on consent, authenticity, and personal expression has taken its place. This can, at first, feel like a safe and liberating replacement for purity culture. Yet sometimes, this ethic exchanges one form of legalism for another by continuing an all-or-nothing mindset. As one author concludes, "There is no way to hold on to any part of purity culture without simultaneously being a part of the problem. . . . The baby [purity] and the bathwater [purity culture] both must go."[4]

For many of us, this isn't tenable. Here is my definition of purity culture: the myths, messages, and cultural movement to persuade Christians to avoid any sexual activity prior to marriage, often using and resulting in shame and fear as a method of control. Despite surviving my own purity culture experience, I still personally believe in a Christian sexual ethic of premarital sexual abstinence and sexual faithfulness in a covenantal marriage, and I don't believe that this sexual ethic itself is harmful. The control and lack of choice of purity culture—that is what is harmful. That's what we must discard.

As gender essentialism (the belief that men and women are essentially and inherently different and those differences are designed by God) and patriarchy (the belief that men are the head and leaders of society and women are the subordinates) creeped into mainstream theological beliefs about gender,[5] purity culture began to creep into Christian theologies about sexuality. The two have become so entwined that we have difficulty separating God's truth from what is cultural, man-made myth. But instead of attempting to disentangle them and search for nuance, the dominant approach has often become getting rid of both the bathwater—purity culture—and the baby—a Christian sexual ethic or sometimes even Christianity altogether.

It doesn't have to be that way. We can heal from purity culture and hold on to our faith. Deconstruction does not have to mean deconverting. It can mean shaping a sexual ethic that aligns with our values and beliefs without the weight of shame and control hovering over us.

> **REFLECT**: How did you experience purity culture?

Purity Culture and Trauma[6]

Although we share many similarities, everyone who grew up in purity culture will have unique experiences. From my own clinical work, research, and listening to others' stories, I believe that purity culture can cause trauma for some people.

Here's what I mean: trauma is not the event itself but our nervous system's reaction to the event.[7] It is the feeling of helplessness, powerlessness, and fear—a complete loss of control—that characterizes trauma. We typically think that trauma is caused by single incidents (sometimes called "big T" traumas), such as sexual assault, natural disasters, combat trauma, and witnessing violence. To be sure, these events are traumatic and can lead to a diagnosis of PTSD.[8]

But trauma can also be caused by a series of smaller events (or "little t" traumas)—for example, bullying, social exclusion, loss of community or significant relationships, and emotional abuse. There may not be a single incident but multiple smaller events that cumulate and lead to a traumatic response in the body.[9] In fact, Dr. Francine Shapiro, the creator of eye movement desensitization and reprocessing (EMDR) therapy, one of the most evidenced-based treatments for PTSD, defines trauma as any event that has a lasting negative effect on the self.[10]

Many who grew up in purity culture may experience it as a series of "little t" traumas.[11] Trauma is largely dependent on our early childhood experiences and the negative core beliefs that developed from them.[12] For many, the origins of purity culture started in early childhood, meaning these beliefs are deeply entrenched.

Research has found that multiple "little t" traumas lead to increased distress that causes significant damage, even if they don't officially meet the criteria for a PTSD diagnosis.[13]

This is the body's response to trauma. And these effects continue to live on in our bodies long after we no longer believe purity culture in our minds. The myths of purity culture cannot simply be "turned off" in the mind because the trauma of those teachings is stored in the body. *The body keeps the score.*[14] Trauma is embodied, meaning that we cannot resolve the effects of it by simply changing our beliefs.

In the case of purity culture, even long after my clients leave high school sex ed and the purity books of their teens, their bodies and hearts still react to these messages. Think back to Jack and Michelle. Michelle *knew* sex was for her too, but her body still tensed up and her heart still carried shame and anxiety about sex. Her husband Jack *knew* sex was a learned skill that doesn't happen overnight, but he still felt angry and disappointed at how their sex life turned out.

Some of my clients, like Michelle and Jack, have even identified as a "survivor of purity culture." Using this language of "survivor" may seem extreme to you, as it's often a term used for "big T" traumas. And by no means do I invalidate the impact from these forms of trauma. But as the opening quote by trauma therapist and trauma survivor Dr. Laura Anderson illustrates, sometimes the effects of multiple events—like from a whole *culture*—are more insidious or take longer to resolve than the effects of a single incident. So, for some, the term "purity culture survivor" validates the long-lasting and far-reaching effects of purity culture on their bodies, minds, hearts, and souls. It is not a single incident they can leave in the past. It still feels very real and present today.

Does everyone who grew up in purity culture have trauma from it? No; trauma is subjective,[15] so not everyone will identify purity culture as a traumatic event or have a traumatic response in their bodies. If you had a positive experience of purity culture, I am happy for you. There are parts of it that I acknowledge were good too.[16] But "the neutral-to-positive experiences of some do not invalidate the negative experience"[17]—even trauma—of others.

Even if it does not result in trauma, there is a high correlation between purity culture and later mental health problems.[18] Misunderstandings about the heart—the metaphorical source of our emotions—lead to not only a divorce of mind and body but also a divorce from the heart. If all we learn about our emotions is "the heart is deceitful" and "desperately wicked,"[19] then how are we to pay compassionate attention[20] to them? How are we to befriend our emotions and see what message they might be trying to send us? This denial and suppression of the heart—of our emotions—can lead to them becoming more overwhelming and distressing, thus turning into stored trauma in the body. And that trauma tends to create problems in three areas: faith, sexuality, and relationships.

How Purity Culture Affects Faith

Can you picture that scene from *Willy Wonka and the Chocolate Factory* in which spoiled Veruca Salt dances around the factory, demanding a golden goose? Her indulgent father promises to get her one as soon as they get home, but that's not good enough for Veruca.

"Don't care how, I want it now!" she sings as she gives a litany of demands.[21]

Throughout my twenties, I was a bit like Veruca. Instead of a golden egg, I wanted a husband. And like a spoiled little girl in a magical chocolate factory, I demanded it from my Father, convinced that he owed me one because I had followed the rules.

"I want it now!" I insisted, while metaphorically shaking my fists at the heavens.

As I've shared, the false promises of purity culture directly contributed to my faith disillusionment and subsequent deconstruction when I found myself unexpectedly (and undesirably) single for many years. I had upheld my end of the bargain, but God had not upheld his. Purity culture had promised me that by remaining pure and taking "delight in the LORD," my good Father would want to give me "the desires of [my] heart."[22] When that didn't appear to be happening, I struggled with anger toward God, broken trust in his goodness and sovereignty, and a waning faith.

A follower of my work shared a similar story with me.

"I have realized how much damage purity culture has caused in my life," she said. "It led to a lot of disappointment in my faith, shame, and struggles with self-acceptance and self-worth. But the worst effect of purity culture is that it made me question the goodness of God. For years I felt like I couldn't trust God anymore."

This is the unanticipated harm of purity culture—the disillusionment in our faith that results from believing in blessings promised by man and not by God. No wonder purity culture has been called the "sexual prosperity gospel."[23] It promises us a reward from God as long as we hold our end of the bargain. The prosperity gospel, popularized by some pastors and televangelists, promises wealth, health, and happiness for those who live a good Christian life, mainly through financial giving and service to the church. Most Christians know this isn't true. Yet when it comes to purity, many of us have bought into this false gospel. When we do everything God asks and we don't get the promised reward, then what?

When I asked my social media audience what prompted their faith deconstruction, the overwhelming majority named purity culture and patriarchy as the reasons.[24] By setting us up for disappointment through unbiblical claims of sexual prosperity, purity culture causes trauma to our faith.

REFLECT: How did purity culture affect your faith?

How Purity Culture Affects Sexuality

Over and over again in my education, I read research about the positive effects of religion. People who self-identify as religious tend to live longer, have better overall health, and report greater happiness. They tend to have stronger community ties. Even when it comes to marriage and sexuality, religious people generally report greater frequency of sex, more sexual satisfaction, and greater marital commitment. The research consistently shows that overall, religion is good for your health.[25]

Except when it comes to purity culture.

In my doctoral class on human sexuality, I learned about sexual pain disorders. One disorder, vaginismus, is characterized by vaginal spasms that make intercourse painful or even impossible. Unlike most sexual dysfunctions, which tend to have physical causes, vaginismus is directly linked to a restrictive religious upbringing.

In other words, research shows that religion can hurt us sexually.

The *DSM-5*, our current nomenclature for diagnosis, renames vaginismus as "Genito-Pelvic Pain/Penetration Disorder," but the associated causes remain. In fact, the *DSM-5* notes that "inadequate sexual education and religious orthodoxy" may be predisposing factors for sexual pain disorders.[26] Fifteen percent of women report *recurrent* sexual pain during intercourse, and three out of four women will have sexual pain at some point in their lifetime.[27] Of course, I can't help but wonder how many of these women were raised in a restrictive "religious orthodoxy."

Studies have found that people who come out of purity culture have similar sexual problems as people who have experienced sexual trauma.[28] Moreover, a study of evangelical women found that when women believe the myths of purity culture, they have lower rates of orgasm and sexual desire, higher rates of sexual pain, and lower sexual satisfaction overall.[29] This is supported by other empirical research indicating a connection between purity teachings and sexual dysfunction.[30] When women have guilt and shame about their bodies and sex from religion, they tend to have lower sexual desire and less sexual satisfaction.[31]

The proof is there. Purity culture affects our sexuality as a whole—our sense of ourselves as sexual beings. It creates a sense of sexual shame, repression, and anxiety about sex regardless if one is single or married, sexually active or not. Purity culture teaches us to divorce our minds from our bodies. Our bodies themselves—and especially our genitals—are the source of our shame. They are sinful, bad, and prone to temptation. It's better to focus on our minds and having right beliefs than attend to our bodies and our lived experience in these bodies, right? As we know now, that erroneous teaching disconnects us from ourselves. And with that, it casts our sexuality in a shroud of shame.

REFLECT: How did purity culture affect your sexuality?

How Purity Culture Affects Relationships

One of my coaching clients, Tiffany, was a married mother of five who grew up in purity culture. Tiffany came to me not for problems around intimacy or sexual shame—the typical issues I see—but because of her intense anxiety about platonic male-female friendships. Tiffany worried that any amicable feelings of affection or connection with men, such as good, healthy male friends from college, must be sexual or romantic. So she felt guilty about enjoying keeping in touch with these friends. She didn't trust men and worried that any interaction with men had sexual undertones.

"In relationships with men, you're either married to them or nothing. Anything in between is unsafe," Tiffany told me.

Purity culture mars relationships—in opposite-sex friendships as in Tiffany's story, in marriages, and with ourselves. Women in particular learn to distrust their instincts and ignore their bodies, which can have devastating effects. The myths of purity culture often pit women and men against each other. Women are responsible for gatekeeping men's sexuality—putting the brakes on before marriage and being "joyfully available" after marriage—so men aren't tempted to sin. And men are taught to look at women as "stumbling blocks" in their "battle" for purity. Women are dangerous temptations, but they are also the source of sexual satisfaction.

With these so-called truths hanging over us, it's no wonder we see a trail of confusion and broken relationships left in the wake.

REFLECT: How have you seen purity culture affect your relationships with others? How about with yourself?

How Do We Heal?

Father Richard Rohr says, "We do not think ourselves into a new way of living, we live ourselves into a new way of thinking."[32]

When I first read this quote, everything fell into place for me. It made sense why my clients like Michelle and Jack were having a hard time enjoying sex in their marriage—even twenty years after they got married. It made sense why so many of us are still trying to escape the effects of purity culture.

Traditional therapy approaches assert that all you have to do to fix problems is to change your thoughts. Then you can change your feelings. But my purity culture clients usually come in already knowing what they *should* believe. They know purity culture was full of lies, and oftentimes they already know what the *right* thoughts are. But they can't seem to make their hearts and bodies catch up; they can't seem to get their feelings and actions on the same page with their new beliefs. Their souls feel disconnected from God too—from any sense of their sexuality as sacred and spiritual.

Because of the disconnection in purity culture, because of how it severs our relationship to our sexuality, feelings, and faith, we have to pay attention to our beliefs, emotions, embodied experience, and spirituality. Instead of changing our thoughts to change our emotions, we use our new beliefs—what we *now* know to be true—and live them out in our hearts and bodies. To heal from purity culture, we have to get our head, heart, body, and soul aligned.

Trauma therapist and author Aundi Kolber says, "We cannot logic ourselves into safety or out of trauma."[33] We need to "show, don't tell"—showing our bodies, hearts, and souls the truth through our lived experience rather than just telling our minds what we should believe. We need a new understanding—true, helpful beliefs—*and* a new experience—bodily, emotionally, and spiritually—in order to change.[34] According to psychologist and researcher Dr. Hillary McBride, "The deepest and most lasting change happens when we have new experiences and then integrate them into the larger story of our lives. . . . Embodied experience is undeniably the most powerful channel of change."[35]

This is exactly what happened with my clients. Jack and Michelle began to find unity between their bodies and beliefs. For Michelle, living into her new belief that she mattered too meant she took more time for self-care and to attend to her body through massage, yoga, and relaxation exercises. Acting out his new belief that intimacy was more than just sex meant Jack paid attention to other ways to connect with Michelle, such as trying new activities together, sharing their thoughts about the books they were reading, and taking on more parenting and household responsibilities. And they both found a way to feel connected again to God and their spirituality, including finding a safe church home.

For Tiffany, intellectually she understood that not all relationships with men were sexual, that not all men were unsafe and untrustworthy. But she needed a new experience—an embodied and emotional experience of these new beliefs. This required not just deconstructing the harmful and untrue beliefs. She also worked on living the truth through situations that disconfirmed her previous beliefs and confirmed the new ones, such as making friendly conversation with a male barista and experiencing that interaction as safe and nonsexual. Tiffany learned to pay attention to her body and what feelings or sensations came up for her and to nonjudgmentally validate and accept those feelings.

Over time, my clients found healing through living out their new beliefs in their bodies, hearts, and souls. And over time, I believe we can all do the same.

Tools for the Journey

Mind   Heart   Body   Soul

Dialectical Thinking

In dialectical behavior therapy (DBT),[36] one of the foundational skills is called "walking the middle path." We do this through dialectical thinking, or embracing both/and instead of either/or.

Dialectical thinking is the opposite of polarized, all-or-nothing thinking. It is about finding the synthesis between two seemingly opposing ideas. It is embracing nuance in the gray areas and rejecting black-and-white answers or extremes.

Purity culture only taught us to think in an absolute, right or wrong way. Dialectical thinking helps us bring openness and flexibility to our thinking patterns.

I believe it is also consistent with the way Jesus taught. Jesus was full of paradox, both welcoming people and calling them to change, both forgiving sins and requiring repentance, both offering grace and speaking truth. Jesus often said, "You have heard it said . . . but I say . . ." And as believers, we live in the "already, but not yet."

See if you can identify which is a black-and-white, either/or statement and which is a dialectical, both/and statement. Suggested answers are available in the endnotes.[37]

1. You are either pure or impure, a virgin or not.
2. As Christians, we are made pure through Jesus regardless of our sexual past.
3. "There is no way to teach children or young adults to be abstinent until marriage without effectually teaching purity culture."[38]
4. You can heal from purity culture and still hold on to a Christian sexual ethic.
5. Deconstruction means you're no longer a Christian.
6. Questioning your beliefs can lead to a deeper, more nuanced faith.

Writing Your Story

1. Write your purity culture story in a journal. You might use the reflection questions throughout this chapter to guide you. Where did your story start? Where are you today?

2. What have you tried for healing? What successes have you experienced? Where do you still feel stuck?

3. As you are writing, be mindful of your body's response. Observe any tension, tightness, or clenching in your body. Try to see if you can sit with and breathe into those sensations and allow them to pass.

4. What emotions come up for you? Do you notice an urge to cry or to avoid?

5. Notice any points of spiritual disconnection, such as times in your story when you felt distant, angry, confused, or hurt by God or a spiritual community.

6. When you finish, look back over your story and pay attention to the process of writing. Was there a time you had to stop writing? Was there a part of your story you left out? At any point, did you zone out? What might those reactions mean? They may point to areas where you still need healing.

2

Toxic "Christian" Cultures

Patriarchy wasn't what God wanted; patriarchy was a result of
human sin.

Dr. Beth Allison Barr, *The Making of Biblical Womanhood*[1]

The scene opens with girls dressed in ball gowns, some with tiaras
and elbow-length gloves, some with long-stemmed roses. The men
are in tuxedos with boutonnieres.

This isn't a prom or a ballroom dance recital. It is a purity ball.

As depicted in the 2008 documentary, *The Virgin Daughters*,[2]
purity balls took place across the United States in the 1990s to
2000s—the height of the purity movement. Girls as young as five
participated in these ceremonies, publicly committing their virginity to their fathers until they married.

Purity balls, perhaps one of the most disturbing rituals of purity culture, illustrate each of what I call the five myths of purity
culture.

- *The Spiritual Barometer Myth*: Your worth, identity, and
  spiritual maturity, especially for women, is your virginity.
- *The Fairy-Tale Myth*: If you remain pure, God will bless
  you with a loving spouse and marriage.

- *The Flipped Switch Myth*: Your sex life will be instantly pleasurable and satisfying if you wait until marriage.
- *The Gatekeepers Myth*: Men are more sexual and can't control themselves, therefore it is up to women to enforce boundaries before marriage and meet their husband's sexual needs after marriage.
- *The Damaged Goods Myth*: If you have premarital sex, you are broken and damaged.

I call these "myths" because, although widely taught in both overt and subtle ways, none of these beliefs are biblical.

You may not have experienced a purity ball, but I bet you remember wearing a T-shirt over your bathing suit on youth group trips, being encouraged to save your first kiss for your wedding day, or hearing that marriage is your highest calling.

To heal from purity culture, it is crucial that we separate what is biblical from what is cultural. Because purity culture—the myths, messages, and false promises used to persuade young people to abstain from sex until marriage—isn't biblical. As we'll see, purity culture was a reaction to historical-cultural events, not biblical teachings. And the root of this and other toxic so-called Christian teachings is patriarchy.

History of the Purity Movement

The virtue of chastity has been around since biblical times. The belief in sexual abstinence outside of marriage is a widely held one across cultures, religions, and time periods. So what makes something a part of "purity culture" rather than just "purity"?

Purity culture largely began in the 1990s. Many other books on the subject[3] have provided a thorough analysis of the historical, political, and cultural events that shaped the purity movement. What most historians and authors agree on is that the purity movement was not biblical but a reaction to historical-cultural and sociopolitical events. The following chart summarizes these events and the events within Christianity that shaped purity culture.

Historical Events

	Historical-Cultural Events	Events within Christianity
1940s to 1960s	Traditional family structure, men returning from World War II, baby boom	Billy Graham crusades
1970s	Feminist and sexual revolutions, legalization of abortion, invention of the birth control pill, rise of women in the workforce, rise in divorce rates	*The Act of Marriage* published, Moral Majority and religious right
1980s	AIDS crisis, rise in other STIs, rise in teen pregnancy rates, average age at marriage begins to increase	*Passion and Purity* published, Focus on the Family expanded
1990s	Cohabitation increases	True Love Waits established, *I Kissed Dating Goodbye* published, rise in Christian Nationalism, first purity ball
2000s	Increased government funding for abstinence-only education in schools, invention of the internet and rise of internet pornography	*Wild at Heart* and *Every Man's Battle* published
2010s	Legalization of gay marriage, proliferation of social media, smartphones, online dating, election of Donald Trump	*Pure* published, public criticism of purity culture heightens
2020s to present	#MeToo movement, COVID-19 pandemic, Atlanta massage parlor shooting, Josh Duggar convicted for child sexual abuse material, racially motivated murders of George Floyd and many others, overturn of *Roe v. Wade*	#ChurchToo movement, multiple church sexual abuse scandals, Ravi Zacharias sex scandal, greater rise in Christian Nationalism, religious deconstruction rises as church rates decline, rise of "religious nones"

While a thorough description of these events is beyond the scope of this book (and beyond my expertise), can you see the correlation? How each of the historical-cultural and sociopolitical events snowballed into the reactive events within Christianity? The

#ChurchToo movement was a needed addition to the #MeToo movement. The Moral Majority and the religious right were reactions to the feminist and sexual revolutions in the 1970s. Abstinence-only education in schools in the 2000s was a reaction to the rise in teen pregnancy rates in the 1980s and facilitated by the rise in Christian Nationalism, which promoted Christian ideals in politics and public policy.

While purity culture exists in some form throughout the decades, it is not until the 1990s to 2000s that modern purity culture, which many of us are healing from, was popularized. In my therapy practice, I mostly see women and couples from Gen X (born 1965 to 1979) to Gen Z (born 1995 to 2012). But the generation most affected are Millennials like me (born 1980 to 1994),[4] the ones raised at the height of the movement.

Abstinence-Only Education

"Don't have sex, because you will get pregnant and die!"

Most Millennials remember this iconic quote from the movie *Mean Girls*.[5] The sex education the students in the movie received was not unlike the abstinence-focused sex education we learned in public schools: full of scare tactics and lacking the skills teens and young adults needed to make values-informed decisions.

Abstinence-focused sex education grew exponentially between 1996 and 2006, particularly during the George W. Bush administration, and was significantly reduced after 2010.[6] The weight of scientific evidence finds that these programs were not effective in delaying intercourse until marriage or improving sexual risk behaviors (such as multiple partners or contraceptive use). Furthermore, a 2019 study asserts that abstinence-focused programs "inherently withhold information about human sexuality and may provide medically inaccurate and stigmatizing information."[7] This can lead to a lack of appropriate sexual health knowledge and education.[8]

Religion-focused virginity pledges, an integral part of purity culture, also proved largely ineffective. In 2005, the peak of purity culture, 23.8 percent of a national sample of twelve to seventeen-year-olds had signed a virginity pledge (with females more likely than males to be pledge signers).[9] Multiple research studies on the effectiveness of these pledges found that they did not prevent premarital sex, although they may have delayed first sexual intercourse by an average of eighteen months. But when pledgers did have their first sexual intercourse, they were less likely to use protection.[10] Consequently, purity pledging did not reduce the rates of teen pregnancy or STIs.[11]

In a 2013 study of college students (ages eighteen to twenty-four), researchers found that 88 percent of participants who took a virginity pledge had intercourse prior to marriage, whereas 99 percent of nonpledgers did.[12] The research suggested that those who waited until marriage did so for religious reasons. But for the other nearly nine out of ten, the pledge failed.

Interestingly, the research also observed that when participants' religious commitment was high—measured as an internalized commitment to their faith and sexual ethic versus just church attendance—they were more likely to stick with their pledge.[13] Therefore, abstinence pledges may have provided encouragement and support for those who had already chosen abstinence, but they didn't convince anyone to be abstinent if the genuine desire or commitment wasn't already there.[14]

You may be a part of the estimated 12 percent who took a virginity pledge and did wait for marriage to have sex (most of my clients are). Or perhaps your pledge "failed." Either way, the truth is the same: purity culture failed you. It failed us all—an entire generation of Christians who were "sacrificed on the altar of abstinence."[15]

> REFLECT: What was your experience of formal sex education? If you made a virginity pledge, do you remember why?

Minority Groups

Purity culture even failed those it ignored. It assumed and targeted a specific demographic: white, evangelical, heterosexual, able-bodied Christians. Other critics have helpfully pointed out how purity culture was built on white supremacy,[16] the belief that white people are superior and should hold power and privilege over other groups. Marginalized groups such as the LGBTQ+ community and people of color were ignored, shunned, or even demonized.

I spoke with Brittany Broaddus-Smith, a Christian sexologist, about her experience of purity culture as a Black woman. Broaddus-Smith explained that Black women suffer from the weight of the religious trauma of purity culture and the weight of systemic racism.[17] "What femininity looks like in purity culture is not always afforded to Black women," she stated. "Chastity, inherent purity, innocence—those are not qualities associated with Black bodies."[18]

Black females are sexualized at an early age.[19] "If you're a little girl who hits puberty early or has a shapely body, there is a presumption that you are 'fast,'" Broaddus-Smith shared. "You don't want to be accused or presumed of sinning, because this brings shame to your family, your church, and your community."

Broaddus-Smith explained the distinction between purity culture and "respectability politics" for Black women. "To present ourselves professionally and prevent harm, we have to behave a certain way around white people. There are rules around decorum, dress, language, and 'taming our hair.' What would a respectable or honorable person do or not do? Respectability forces us to contort to fit into these boxes, trying to undo the perceived, inherent unworthiness and overt sexualization of Black women. If we conform, we can get closer to white purity culture ideals."[20]

Author Bridget Eileen Rivera, who identifies as a queer Christian, explained that queer people didn't exist in purity culture at all. "The structures that maintain purity culture are built on the assumed, sole starting point of heterosexuality," she told me.[21] Same-sex attraction or LGBTQ+ identity was not acknowledged as a reality for many of the youth who were hearing the promises of heterosexual marriage and great sex. This "romance idolatry"[22] set queer Christians up for disappointment.

Neither Black women nor queer people are a monolith, and clearly other marginalized groups will have different experiences of purity culture. Linda Kay Klein, author of *Pure*, a groundbreaking exposé of purity culture, says, "The virus of religious sexual shaming does not affect us all in the same way. White women . . . will never *really* understand the way in which racism and sexism interact and impact women of color in this country."[23] I cannot do justice to the effects of purity culture on marginalized groups in this space; however, I believe it is important to recognize the ways they too have been hurt in the conversation and culture along the way.

Five Toxic "Christian" Cultures[24]

Out of the toxic belief system of purity culture in the Church came several other belief systems that I call "toxic 'Christian' cultures." They are toxic because they are harmful and untrue. None of them are biblical. I call them "cultures" because they are embedded into the fabric of evangelical Christianity and the Church. All of these cultures either developed as a direct result of purity culture teachings or build on each other to lead to purity culture. Therefore, in order to deconstruct purity culture, we have to deconstruct them all.

Modesty Culture

Modesty was a hot topic when I was in youth group. Books and ministries like *Secret Keeper Girl* focused on promoting high modesty standards for girls so they would not tempt boys. We were taught that our worth was on display. Our value was determined by shorts that were at least fingertip length, straps that were three fingers wide, and clothing that was loose enough to hide our curves. And don't even mention a two-piece bathing suit! Modesty culture leads to body shame and a sense that our bodies are inherently wrong, sinful, and can cause others to "stumble." It makes girls responsible for boys' lust instead of empowering each sex to be responsible for their own thoughts and actions.

Rape Culture

Rape culture is the natural result of a modesty culture that blames women for men's actions. Rape culture is not only a part of the Church; it has poisoned our secular culture as well. But many activists have astutely pointed out how purity culture can promote rape culture.[25] In fact, research reviewing Christian dating books revealed themes supportive of rape culture, such as the teaching that women are responsible for sexual violence perpetrated by men.[26] We hear rape culture any time a woman is blamed, questioned, or held responsible for her sexual assault and an offender is given a free pass:

"Well, what was she wearing?"

"He's a man; he couldn't help himself!"

"She should have known better than to be alone with him."

The truth is a victim is never responsible for their sexual assault, no matter what they wear, where they were, or whom they were with. No one is to blame but the perpetrator (and the systems that are complicit in the abuse). Yet rape culture blames women and gives perpetrators (almost always men) a free pass.

Courtship Culture

The Duggar family of TLC's *19 Kids and Counting* and Joshua Harris's *I Kissed Dating Goodbye* brought the idea of parent-arranged marriages and courtship back into trend in the 1990s and 2000s. Purity culture goes hand in hand with courtship culture because one way to avoid premarital sex is to not date—or to have a chaperoned, heavily monitored courtship process.

The truth is dating can be healthy, a topic we will explore more in chapter 10. Not all dating has to lead to marriage, but because of the idolization of marriage, we weren't allowed to date for any other reason. Thus, courtship culture became the way forward for many.

Marriage Culture

There's nothing inherently wrong with marriage. Marriage can be a beautiful gift. I am grateful for my husband, and I love being married. But toxic marriage culture idolizes marriage. Being married is given privileged status in evangelical Christianity, while other relationship statuses such as single, divorced, or widowed are often discriminated against.

Marriage culture assumes that married people are more spiritually mature or have more leadership potential than unmarried people. Churches tend to cater to the needs of couples and families and seclude them together, while unmarried people are lumped in with the youth. And there is often no place for those who are divorced or widowed. They may feel judged or isolated from the rest of the church community.

Like purity culture, marriage culture assumes marriage is an eventuality, not merely a possibility,[27] for every believer. Marriage is the pinnacle of adulthood and will make you holier. This breeds pride for those who are married and shame for those who are not.

But the truth is we are all valuable members of the body of Christ. Marriage does not make you more spiritually mature, capable of leadership, or holier. Marriage is not the ultimate goal of a Christian's life. Serving and honoring God is—and that can happen whether single or married.

Purity Culture

Purity culture contains elements of all these other toxic Christian cultures—the idolization of marriage, a distrust of dating, an overemphasis on women's clothing, and blaming women but exonerating men for sexual sin or violations. Purity culture, like the other four toxic cultures, is not biblical. As author and theologian Zachary Wagner says, "Purity culture isn't simply an extreme version of historic Christian sexual ethics. It is a perversion of Christian sexual ethics. It's not too Christian. It isn't Christian enough. . . . A vision of sexuality rooted in guilt and shame is not a Christian vision of sexuality."[28]

> **REFLECT**: How did any of the mentioned toxic "Christian" cultures affect you?

Patriarchy

Underlying all the toxic cultures is patriarchy.

Patriarchy is the belief that men are superior to women and should rule over them as the leaders and the head. It's rooted in the idea that women are in need of protection and provision. Men make the decisions; women are subordinate and submissive. Women are denied autonomy and agency unless men are acting on their behalf.

What is the result of modesty culture? Men can control women through their clothing.

What does rape culture lead to? It absolves men of responsibility for their crimes and puts the blame on women.

Why is courtship culture "biblical"? Because men (especially fathers) make all the dating decisions and women follow.

Why is marriage culture so prevalent in the Church? Because women gain value and status if they are married to a man.

What is the outcome of purity culture? It controls sexuality (particularly women's) through myths and false promises about premarital sex.

With cultural changes such as birth control, the feminist movement, and higher rates of women in the workforce, women began having more freedom on their own and became less dependent on men as a result. But if you could indoctrinate women to believe their sexuality is dangerous, to believe they are responsible for men's sexual sin, that their virtue and desirability as partners is largely tied to their purity, and that their fathers need to control their dating choices, then you've developed another way to subdue and subordinate them—one that is so insidious, it comes under the cover of benefit and protection for women, one that is sanctified by its similarity to the Christian virtue of chastity.

Beliefs about gender roles exist on a spectrum from patriarchy to extreme feminism or matriarchy.[29] I expect that most of my readers will fall along the continuum from those who believe that men and women are equal in value but have different roles in the home and church, to those, like me, who believe that men and women are equal in value *and* role.[30] I am not anti-men; I yearn for both men and women to work alongside each other toward a more just and equal church that reflects God's heart for us. Regardless of your stance or mine, my hope is that, from across different views, we'll find areas of agreement in how purity culture is unbiblical and toxic and how we can move forward from it.

The problem is we cannot simultaneously heal from purity culture and promote patriarchy. We cannot support a culture that subordinates women to men. We cannot subscribe to a belief system that puts men in charge of women's sexuality, yet blames and holds women responsible for men's sexual sin.

Purity culture is both a systemic problem and an individual one.[31] While our focus here is on the individual and personal experience of healing, there are systemic changes that also must be made to overcome purity culture. So if we want to fully dismantle the myths of purity culture and rebuild healthy faith and sexuality, we have to pluck out the roots of patriarchy in ourselves and in our systems.

Tools for the Journey

Thought Record, Part 1

One place to begin is to see how patriarchy and other toxic cultures have impacted our own thoughts, emotions, and actions. Thought records are an essential skill in cognitive-behavioral therapy (CBT)[32] to analyze and then change our beliefs.

We'll be constructing (and deconstructing) your thought record throughout the book. For this step, let's focus on identifying your beliefs and where they come from.

1. On a piece of paper, draw three columns. In column one, write down all your beliefs that came from purity culture. You can come back to this and add more later as you think of them. If you're stumped, consider the three main areas that purity culture affects: sexuality, relationships, and faith.

2. In column two, reflect on where that belief comes from—who or what is the source? Parents, pastors, peers, books? Ask yourself, Is it biblical, cultural, or both?

3. In column three, consider why that person or source may have taught you this belief. What were their intentions? Were they simply passing on what they were told? Did they think it was true or right? Or was there another motive? Ask yourself, Who benefited from your believing this?

4. Notice what emotions come up for you as you do this exercise. It's normal to feel anger, sadness, grief, and even compassion. Allow your feelings and see if you can validate them. Use containment (see the next exercise) if you feel overwhelmed.

Example

Belief	Source	Why?
I need to cover up so I don't cause men to stumble.	Youth pastor Modesty event for girls Book for young girls Some of it was biblical, but mostly cultural	They wanted to hold women responsible for men's behavior and give men an out. They may have genuinely believed men couldn't control themselves. This was a narrow interpretation of the Bible's teachings on modesty.

Containment

At times, the journey of healing from purity culture may feel overwhelming. It is important to take breaks from this hard work to allow our bodies to return to a calm state and to help us go about our day.

I want to give you skills so you can mindfully and purposefully choose to put this work aside when you need to refocus your attention on other tasks. These skills can also be used if you feel triggered or overwhelmed at any point, giving yourself permission to distance from any disturbing thoughts or emotions.[33] This helps restore safety to your body and regulate your nervous system when you are outside your window of tolerance.

Whatever method you choose, you are in control of your pain. You choose when to put it away and when to address it. Instead of avoidance or suppression, containment is an intentional way for you to engage in the work of healing at times you choose.

- Visualize yourself building an imaginary wall between yourself and your problems.
- Mentally take a vacation from your distress. Imagine leaving the problems on the ground and taking an airplane to a safe, peaceful, and calming place.
- Intentionally choose times to "clock in" for your healing work, then visualize "clocking out" when that time is up. You may even symbolize this through a ritual, such as lighting a candle.
- Visualize building a container for your problems. The container should be strong, sturdy, and have a lid that closes and locks. Yours

might be a file box, a safe, or a chest. Imagine placing your pain in the container, closing and locking it, and then putting it away. You could put the container on a shelf—you know it exists, you can see it, but you are choosing to put it away for a while. Or you may need to imagine sending it farther away—throwing your container in the ocean, sending it up into the sky, or burying it underground or in a cave.[34]

Deconstructing the Myths

3

Myth #1

The Spiritual Barometer Myth

Why do we like Walmart? Because it's cheap, easy, and accessible. But do we carry ourselves like we are easy and accessible too? A Walmart girl has low value . . . and she resolves to give pieces of herself away recklessly. . . . But a Dolce and Gabbana girl carries herself differently.

Mo Isom, *Sex, Jesus, and the Conversations the Church Forgot*[1]

I loved my True Love Waits ring. I asked my parents for it when I was fourteen, and they gladly complied. Having it gave me value—a tangible display that I was worth waiting for. It gave me purpose—that I would please God by following his rules. It gave me identity—that I was a virgin. And it gave me pride—showing I was a better Christian because I was pure.

I dreamed of when I could give my husband that purity ring on our wedding day while Rebecca St. James's song "Wait for Me" played in the background. With it, I was giving him the greatest gift by being a virgin. It didn't matter as much if he was, because virginity was too high of an expectation for males, I thought. By remaining pure myself, I would keep our marriage bed from becoming defiled, have no sexual baggage, and be able to enjoy pure, shame-free sex.

I wore my purity ring like a badge of honor for almost ten years. I only stopped because I began seeing clients as a graduate student intern, and the ring left them inquisitive about my marital status. One male client—a faith leader with an admittedly colorful past—even noticed the words "true love waits" on my ring and commented that I must be judging him because of his sexual past.

I probably was. Because to me, that purity ring was more than just a symbol of my pledge; it was a symbol of my spirituality. It was the barometer for my faith.

The Spiritual Barometer Myth sets the stage for the other purity culture myths because it gives a purpose to purity. This myth states that your spiritual maturity and even the status of your salvation are based on how far you've gone sexually. Your purity, whether you are a virgin or not, becomes the measure—the barometer—of your spiritual life, a way to judge how good a Christian you are compared to others.

The purity ring is the ultimate symbol of the Spiritual Barometer Myth. English professor and author Dr. Karen Swallow Prior explains that a symbol represents something else and comes laden with meaning. Wearing something on your body—furthermore, something you tend to wear every day—is one way to identify yourself to the world. But of course, any symbol has limitations. For example, a red rose is a symbol of love, but it is not love itself. The purity ring was meant to represent waiting until marriage, but it is not purity or spirituality itself. Yet it became the outward sign or expression of one's purity and, therefore, one's value and identity.

Prior cautions, "Getting symbols right is more than a mere literary exercise because symbols shape our understanding or misunderstanding of reality. Getting it right can be a matter of life or death."[2]

In the case of purity culture, this is true. The purity ring symbolized one of two things: spiritual life or death.

Uncovering the Myth

"I don't know where it came from, but I learned that having pre-marital sex was the unforgivable sin."

Many of my clients and other people I interviewed for this book repeated this refrain. Premarital sex was the worst sin, and anyone who did it was clearly not a real Christian. The Spiritual Barometer Myth taught us that, especially for women, our virginity or purity was a marker of our status as believers. Indeed, purity rings were almost exclusively marketed to females. And purity balls were solely for young girls and their fathers—the keepers of their virginity. Author of *The Scarlet Virgins*, Rebecca Lemke clarifies: "It wasn't as if someone came out and said, 'You are only worth as much as your virginity,' but through the implications of bad analogies and attitudes, many of us got this message."[3]

Still, men weren't exempt from the Spiritual Barometer Myth. Zachary Wagner, author of *Non-Toxic Masculinity*, notes that for young men in purity culture, the strength of their walk with God was determined by how they were doing sexually or, more specifically, how many times they had masturbated that week.[4] Journalist Jon Ward tells the story of meeting with a small group of men in his early twenties to talk about how often they looked at porn and masturbated. The entire focus of this weekly discipleship group was sexual behavior. Ward goes so far as to say that "if I had to point to anything that made my years of intense religiosity a psychologically painful time, it was [these meetings]."[5] The intense hyperfocus on holiness, defined as avoiding masturbation, led Ward to years of depression, a warped view of sex and sexuality, crushing shame, and self-loathing.

According to historian Dr. Samuel Perry, this is an example of sexual exceptionalism,[6] the tendency for evangelicals to make sexual behaviors such as premarital sex, pornography, and mastur-bation, the worst or "unforgivable sins." There is additional shame and stigma for Christians who experience same-sex attraction or identify as LGBTQ+. Purity culture made sexual purity the essence of Christian discipleship. Boundaries were only sexual ones. Purity was synonymous with sexual virginity, which was synonymous with our spiritual maturity.

I was active in my high school youth group and made great friendships there. Several of us girls (and again, none of the boys) had purity rings. My virginity pledge was well known; in fact, I did not seriously date or kiss anyone in high school. A friend of mine was examining my and my friend Kylie's rings one day. He commented that hers was a lot heavier than mine.

"It must be because of the weight of her sins," he said sarcastically.

Neither Kylie nor I said anything; we probably laughed it off. Today, I have a lot to say. Because now I know that smug remark personified the Spiritual Barometer Myth.

At the time, purity and Christianity had become so enmeshed, I did not know if you could have one without the other. My entire faith was built on virginity. This sexual exceptionalism leads to an idolization of virginity and judgmentalism. "When virginity becomes tied to our standing with God, especially for women, this out-of-proportion and unbiblical pressure creates a whirlwind of shame and pride."[7]

Personal Assessment:
Does the Spiritual Barometer Myth Affect You?

Read through these statements. Mark 0 if you disagree, 1 if you are neutral or unsure, and 2 if you agree. Add up your score at the end. Scores will range from 0 to 10, with higher scores indicating greater belief in the myth.

You may want to answer this from your present vantage point to see what beliefs continue to affect you. Or you might pick an earlier age or stage in your development (perhaps adolescence or young adulthood) and answer the questions as you would have at that stage.

1. Christians who are virgins before marriage are stronger in their faith. _____

2. Premarital sexual abstinence is a sign of spiritual maturity. _____

3. If someone claims to be a Christian but I know they had premarital sex, I start to question their status as a believer. _____

4. I feel good about myself, and I know God is proud of me when I abstain from premarital sex. _____

5. One way to tell if someone is a true Christian or not is if they are a virgin before marriage. _____

To take an electronic version of the assessment, visit www.drcamden.com.

Discovering the Effects

"Virginity is an idol in purity culture that must be dethroned."[8]

The idolization of virginity claims it is the best gift you have to give to your spouse. I heard this many times growing up (and still do). While making a choice to remain abstinent until marriage is honorable, what about the value of other "gifts" in marriage? Isn't the lifelong commitment you're making to your spouse the greatest gift? How about unconditional love? What about forgiveness, acceptance, and supporting each other "for better or for worse"? Do these not hold the same value?

When I first told my parents I was dating my now-husband, my mother's first question about my new love interest was not about his personality, how we met, how he treated me, or even where he was from or what type of work he did.

"Is he saving himself for marriage like you are?" she asked outright.

Bypassing my problem with the term "saving himself," I was struck that virginity was what she considered the most important criteria in a man I would date. Whether she realized it or not, virginity—purity—had become an idol. And like any idol, the promise of purity culture is one that will always fail.

Purity culture sets up a works-based religion that seeks to ensure blessing and prevent pain through moralism. Moralism is making religion about being a good person, often setting up a contract between us and God. Pastor and author Meredith Miller explains, "Contractual moralism is appealing. It asserts that one can control their happiness through their right behavior. . . . God is happy if you are good and less happy if you are not good."[9] So it was for me. I believed God was more pleased with me because of my virginity; therefore, I was a better Christian.

While purity culture, including the Spiritual Barometer Myth, deeply harmed me, it is important for me to acknowledge that I actively participated in it. I was a proponent of purity culture and perpetuated its myths, especially this one, to others. For the ways I judged, condemned, and gossiped about others because of their sexual experiences, I am truly regretful. I repent of the sinful pride that made me believe I was a better Christian or deserving of "blessings" because of my sexual choices. For me, acknowledging that I am not only a survivor of purity culture but also complicit in it is part of tearing down the idol I'd built around it. It's part of cultivating humility.

> REFLECT: Have you ever judged or condemned others because of their sexual choices? Examine yourself and consider if you need to repent or make amends.

Recovering the Truth

Humility is the antidote to any form of pride.

For some, cultivating humility and resolving the pride and judgmentalism of the Spiritual Barometer Myth may mean developing a more expansive sexual ethic that supports sex outside of marriage. For others, humility comes from a more expansive understanding of sexual sin—accepting that we all have areas of sin or shortcomings and no sin is worse than another. Sexual sin exists, yes, but it is not "exceptional." We can also have empathy, knowing that there is a myriad of reasons for people's choices, including their upbringing, biology, self-esteem, and attachment style. Because it is not my job to analyze or judge others' sexual behavior, I do not need to rank their sins—and therefore their spiritual maturity—against my own.

The dialectic here is that while we are to cease judging,[10] we are called to have wise discernment. "Discernment . . . isn't the same as judgmentalism or condemnation. To discern is . . . to be willing to name what is true and what is not."[11] However, godly discernment requires a posture of humility too. Jesus said to discern good teachings from bad ones by their fruit: "Every good tree produces good fruit, but a bad tree produces bad fruit. A good tree cannot produce bad fruit, and a bad tree cannot produce good fruit."[12] When I examine the fruit of purity culture in my life and others, I do not see much good fruit. Again, I am distinguishing here between "purity" and purity culture. Yes, there is good fruit in a Christian sexual ethic. But the fruit of the purity movement itself is rotten.

Cultivating the fruit of the Spirit—love, joy, peace, patience, kindness, goodness, faithfulness, gentleness, and self-control[13]— can also put the Spiritual Barometer Myth in perspective. Yes, abstinence may fall under the fruit of self-control or faithfulness, but humility is a part of the fruit of kindness and love.

Another dialectic in the Christian tradition is that all of us are impure because we are all sinners in need of God's grace.[14] *And* all of us are made pure through Christ[15] regardless of our past. Therapist and author Jay Stringer explains, "If you are a Christian, you must remember that the issue of purity has already been addressed once and for all in the death of Jesus. . . . Your purity has already been accomplished and applied to your identity."[16]

Therefore, the biblical call to purity is more than just sexual abstinence. Purity is not something we attain or achieve through our behavior; it is a state granted to us as Christians. This cuts through the moralistic, works-based, prideful nature of the Spiritual Barometer Myth. I do not "earn" my purity; it is accomplished through the work of Jesus. My identity is not in being a virgin before marriage; my identity is in Christ. My purpose is not to be pure; it is to love and follow God with all my heart, soul, body, and mind.

Many of my clients have found it helpful to reconceptualize purity as the virtue of chastity—the spiritual discipline of living a life aligned with God's heart for our sexuality. Spiritual disciplines are practices that align our feelings, actions, and minds to God's will.[17] They are "exercises that train us in the Christian life" and "form in us the habits, skills, and strengths of faithful followers of Christ."[18] You may be familiar with the spiritual disciplines of prayer, giving, or solitude. We engage in these practices to cultivate spiritual virtues—fruit of the Spirit that empower us to live a godly life. We do not do it for an end result—as a means to an end. Likewise, we do not do it out of pride—to make ourselves look good. The purpose is the practice. Spiritual disciplines draw us closer to the heart of God, conform our will to his, and deepen our intimacy with him.

Chastity is a lifelong pursuit; it does not end with marriage. It encompasses a full stewardship of our sexuality, yielding our choices to God, as we offer our bodies as living sacrifices to him in a spiritual act of worship.[19] Theologian Dr. Beth Felker Jones explains that chastity through either abstinence in singleness or fidelity in marriage is a way that Christians express the faithfulness of God:

> Sexual ethics are essential because faithful sex testifies to the power and the character of the God who saves. . . . In both marriage and singleness, Christian bodies are testimony to the faithfulness of God. . . . Faithful marriage—like faithful singleness—becomes a training ground for discipleship.[20]

> REFLECT: What is your experience with spiritual disciplines such as giving, fasting, prayer, solitude, and silence? How might you practice humility as a spiritual discipline?

The fruit of the Spiritual Barometer Myth is pride and judgment when we believe the lie that we are "holier than thou" because of our virginity. The truth may lie in the lifelong spiritual discipline of chastity. Stewarding our sexuality, whether married or single, in a way that is faithful to God cultivates humility.

Despite my dream as a teenager, I did not give my purity ring to my husband on our wedding day. I felt content with the choices both he and I had made, but I no longer placed my identity and virtue in virginity. I recognized that the gifts we were pledging to each other in marriage—love, commitment, faithfulness, trust, and humility—were much greater than our sexual status on just one day. And those fruits continue to be gifts today.

Tools for the Journey

Kernel of Truth

One of the questions I get asked when I speak about purity culture is "Are these really myths?" A myth is a widely held but false belief or idea. But myths tend to be believed because there is some element of truth to them. In DBT, we call this looking for the "kernel of truth." It is a way to examine and try to make sense of a behavior, thought, or belief that seems unexplainable.

As strongly as I believe that the myths of purity culture are false, I also believe that there may be a small kernel of truth to each of them. (How is that for a dialectic?) Discerning this kernel of truth can help us avoid all-or-nothing thinking. By playing the devil's advocate, we can acknowledge what is true and disentangle it from the parts that aren't.

Look back at the beliefs you wrote down in your thought record. What parts can you quickly discard as myth or lie? Now, discern what parts might be true or biblical. What is the kernel of truth? If you are unsure, how can you explore this belief more?

Thought Record, Part 2

Cognitive-behavioral theory proposes that like a triangle, our emotions, thoughts, and behavior are all connected. If we can change one part of the triangle, we can change the whole shape of the triangle, and thus change our experience.

When my clients begin therapy, they usually want to change their emotions—they want to feel less depressed, anxious, and shameful and more joy and pleasure. But we can't directly change emotions by telling ourselves to stop feeling this way any more than we can tell our heads to stop feeling the rain falling on it on a stormy day. Instead, we have to indirectly change our emotions through an embodied experience.

We are going to build on the thought record you created in the previous chapter by recognizing the connections between your beliefs, emotions, and behavior—body sensations, urges, and actions. Repeat the beliefs you listed in part one of your thought record. Then add a column for emotions—what emotion does this belief bring up for you? Then add behavior—what sensations in your body do you feel? What do you have an urge to do? What do you do?

Example

Belief	Emotions	Behavior (Body Sensations + Actions)
I'm a better Christian because I did not have sex before marriage.	Pride, then guilt	Fullness in my chest, proud body posture Heaviness when I feel guilt I look down on others and constantly compare myself. I judge people, then feel bad for doing it.

4

Myth #2

The Fairy-Tale Myth

From the moment I wrote my "shopping list for HIM," I never dated a guy for a second time unless he met the criteria on that list. . . . I am happy to say that eventually God did bring me a man into my life who was everything I dreamed of in that list. It was really neat to write "You are everything" across the list and present it to him one day. One day you will probably find the special one God has created just for you. Until then, pray for him.

Dannah Gresh, *And the Bride Wore White*[1]

When I was thirteen, I read the book *And the Bride Wore White*. The author encouraged readers to compose a list of every criterion they wanted their future husbands to have. She had created such a list herself on a "rugged piece of rose-colored stationery"—and God had blessed her with a spouse who fulfilled all her desires.

It was a guarantee for us too, as long as we waited. The book even promised that "if you will wait, then you'll make babies with great celebration." (But those who don't wait could get chlamydia, the author warns, which may lead to infertility and "no babies. Ever."[2])

I eagerly created my two-page, front and back, list, trusting that if I remained faithful to God's teachings about sexual abstinence, he was sure to bless me with a loving Christian husband and a fairy-tale marriage. I wrote letters to my future husband, wondering who he might be and what he was doing at that time. I prayed for him, asking God to help my husband stay pure despite all the temptations in the world.

I no longer have that list of "future husband criteria," but I do remember that brown hair and tan skin were features I longed for. (More than twenty years after composing this list, I am married to a blond, pale-skinned man.) I also vividly remember the pain of singleness when I so desperately wanted marriage. Because I had an intense desire to be married, I was certain God wanted me to be married as well. I felt entitled to love and happiness because I followed the rules. My religion said God would grant me the desires of my heart. Yet I continued to wait, longingly, as friend after friend got married, and my promised husband was nowhere in sight.

My faith began to crumble.

The fairy tale I'd been promised was shattered.

Uncovering the Myth

The Fairy-Tale Myth is another belief system born out of purity culture. It implies that if we stay pure, God will grant us our desired fairy-tale ending complete with the perfect spouse, marriage, and sex life. The 1990s were full of purity culture books touting this myth. *When God Writes Your Love Story*, *I Kissed Dating Goodbye*, and *Before You Meet Prince Charming* all promised, sometimes implicitly and sometimes explicitly, that if a Christian girl remained pure, prayed for a Christian husband, and avoided casual dating, she was sure to find The One. (Interestingly, purity culture emphasized more the promise of great sex than the promise of a spouse to Christian boys.) Our youth pastors encouraged us to hold out sexually until the blessing of an early and satisfying marriage. As long as we waited to have sex, they assured us, God would bless us with a good Christian husband that met every one of our heart's desires.

Critics of purity culture recognize the prevalence—and the problems—of this myth. In *Making Chastity Sexy: The Rhetoric of Evangelical Abstinence Campaigns*, author Dr. Christine J. Gardner notes that the fairy-tale narrative of courtship and marriage, particularly popular with female-focused purity groups, can exacerbate problems in their faith for women struggling to wait for God to send them their spouse.[3] Rachel Joy Welcher, author of *Talking Back to Purity Culture*, agrees that purity culture's promise of marriage, sex, and children to those who wait is an empty promise, for purity cannot guarantee a happy marriage or even marriage at all.[4]

For LGBTQ+ Christians, Bridget Eileen Rivera explains they can be "devastated when they are told their whole lives that marriage is the wonderful reward God is going to give them, but then they hear, 'Actually, no, you're not allowed those things. Your reward for being pure is celibacy,' which isn't appealing in a culture that idolizes sex and marriage." Queer Christians are led to believe "everyone else has a happy and wonderful sex life and marriage to look forward to except you. This is your cross to bear; this is the miserable, lonely existence God has given you. And that isn't viable."[5]

The Fairy-Tale Myth leaves gaps in our theology for people for whom marriage or children are not a reality: those who experience long-term singleness, infertility or child-free by choice, or queer Christians who choose to remain celibate. What reason do these groups have for abstinence, if marriage (or children) is not on the horizon? If for some, it never will be?

Of all the purity culture myths, I was personally most affected by this one. I devoured purity books, sure that by waiting for my "Boaz" and refusing to date "bozos," God would bring me The One. But instead of getting married young right out of college to my first and only love, I spent the majority of my twenties single after my devastating breakup.

Not only did my belief in this myth lead to my intense anguish and despair over those years; it also brought on anger toward God, jealousy toward friends, and ugly pride in myself. I stood as a bridesmaid for six friends while single, and I regret I was not able to be a joyful supporter of some of them due to my own envy and bitterness. I constantly compared myself to others and felt "less than" and left behind.

I didn't know then what I know now: the Fairy-Tale Myth failed me, setting me up for false expectations and arbitrary timelines. And this isn't just my story. Many other Christians raised in purity culture have waited for a spouse much longer or have never gotten married or had children despite a deep longing for both. I also know there are people who choose to remain single and those who find themselves single but do not struggle with intense longings for marriage. I believe that singleness is a valid and valuable life station—one that is not less than marriage. But for those of us raised with the Fairy-Tale Myth as our guide, these realities didn't seem possible.

Personal Assessment: Does the Fairy-Tale Myth Affect You?

Scoring guidelines: 0 = disagree, 1 = neutral or unsure, 2 = agree

1. If a Christian abstains from premarital sex, God will bless them with a loving marriage.
2. Being a virgin when you marry means God will give you a long and happy marriage.
3. God will give you your desire for a spouse if you submit to him and his teachings on purity.
4. When I see friends who had premarital sex get married, I wonder how God could bless their marriage.
5. I wonder why my friend is still single when she's done things the right way and is still a virgin.

Add up your score. The higher the score, the greater the belief in the myth.

Discovering the Effects

The problem with the Fairy-Tale Myth is that it reduces God to a fairy godmother who grants our wishes as long as we do the right thing. It twists our relationship with God into a transaction: staying pure equals a dream spouse. It puts if-then clauses on our relationship with God: "If I am a virgin, then God will give me a prince." We feel entitled to a fairy-tale marriage; our obedience to God should earn us the reward of marriage like a child doing chores earns screen time.

Yet we cannot deny our suffering when we don't get the "happily ever after" that was promised to us. What happens when we do remain sexually abstinent and the "reward" is nowhere in sight? Inevitably, this false promise runs out of steam.

Does God promise a spouse if we remain pure? Does he promise to grant us our wishes, like a genie in a bottle, if we don't sleep around? We feel like jilted grooms at the altar, waiting for our runaway bride who we think our matchmaker God promised us. We think God has abandoned the commitment he made to us—the commitment to deliver the future we hoped for based on terms we created.

My thirty-eight-year-old friend Carrie is single and a virgin. She explained that the Fairy-Tale Myth has ultimately left her disillusioned. "I delighted myself in the Lord, and he was supposed to give me the desires of my heart. But following what I was supposed to do, upholding my end of the bargain, didn't bring me what I wanted."

Carrie continued, "I feel like God hasn't upheld his end of the bargain. And I feel like it's a bargain he drafted in the first place."

Purity culture sold us on a bargain God never intended. And we might be so caught up in this false belief in a prize for the hard work of abstinence that we feel angry and entitled when it doesn't come to pass. We may question the goodness and trustworthiness of God. We neglect the whole point of the gospel and miss out on the chance of a genuine relationship with Christ when all we want from him is to play by the rules of the sexual prosperity gospel.

Most significantly, the Fairy-Tale Myth sets up our relationship with God as a formula with guaranteed outcomes. We don't have the ability to control God's actions through our own behavior. Yes, certain choices we make can influence the course of our lives. But God does not reward us for making wise choices by giving us a spouse. We don't have to behave or perform a certain way as if to hold God to his end of the bargain. As I have said, there is no bargain. And this posture of entitlement increases our resentment and disillusionment when our demands are not fulfilled. God never promises an easy life full of all the pleasure we desire and none of the problems we fear. As Welcher says, "We create opportunities to be disappointed with God when we put our hope in things he never promised."[6]

How the Fairy-Tale Myth Affects Singles

Author Joy Beth Smith describes the shame of singleness in the church: "After years of wondering what kind of character deficiency or unknown flaw would cause the Lord to keep a husband from me, I realized it doesn't really work that way. That's turning the God of the universe into a Coca-Cola machine that exists to dispense happiness."[7]

Part of our shame comes from a poor understanding of and value for singleness. In 1 Corinthians 7:8, Paul suggests that singleness is preferable to marriage. Many well-meaning older people in the church will offer platitudes to comfort single people: "It's just a season, just wait; you won't be single for long!" Or "The right man is just around the corner!" But singleness is not a season; it is a valid life path that God calls all people to at some point in their lives.

He also calls some people to singleness for a prolonged time or even a lifetime. When we attach phrases like "season" or "waiting period," it's easy to live life on hold rather than experience the fullness of life that God wants for us. We might miss out on valuable personal growth and introspection. We might miss out on the joy and the promise of God's presence in our suffering. We might miss out on being a blessing and help to others. When we ask, "Why me?" we might miss out on what God wants to teach us through our circumstances.

Purity culture treats singleness as if it's the years of college classes we must slog through and endure before we get the hard-earned prize of the MRS degree. Instead, we can view singleness as an equally legitimate vocation to marriage. They are unique callings, and neither one is better than the other.

> **REFLECT**: If you are single, what feelings do you have about that? How is singleness both a struggle and a joy?

How the Fairy-Tale Myth Affects Marriage*

The promise of a fairy-tale marriage can also lead to disillusionment for those who find that marriage does not bring them the automatic sense of joy and fulfillment they thought would await them. Many are shocked that the "in love" feelings of infatuation do not last (on average, research suggests only two years). Fanning the flames of romance and passion past "the butterflies" is hard work—past children and bills and laundry and aging and career changes and health issues. At its extreme, this myth may even lead some Christians to stay in an abusive or harmful marriage much longer than they should. After all, if your marriage was a reward for sexual abstinence, why would you reject this reward, even if it is harming you and your spouse is unwilling to change or seek help?

Nicole, a thirty-year-old single mother of three, told me bluntly, "I blame purity culture for my divorce."

Nicole explained that she and her former husband met at a church camp. They got married at age twenty even though they didn't know each other well, and according to Nicole, "there was no depth." She looked past this, however.

"I was told by my pastor's wife before we married that I cannot rely on my husband to meet my emotional needs. We were never taught what it means to be emotionally healthy."

Over time, various life changes, including having children, led to a decline in sex in Nicole's marriage. Their sex life was nothing like what the Fairy-Tale Myth had promised, and it continued to deteriorate. Then, when she was eight months postpartum, things got much worse.

---

* Content warning: This section describes an incident of marital rape.

"We went camping, and he pressured me to have sex. It was nonconsensual . . . me lying there crying, asking him to get off of me. And afterward, I told him I felt used, and he got mad at me and just shut down."

When I asked gently—wanting her to feel empowered to use whatever words she felt were appropriate—whether she would call this experience marital rape, she was unequivocal.

"Yes," she declared. "And that happened a lot. For the next six to eight months, I just laid like a starfish . . . totally detached, no emotional connection. And I was set up for that."

After about five years of marriage, Nicole told her husband she couldn't be married to him anymore and that their marriage had been sexually abusive. Since her divorce, Nicole said she has been trying to navigate life and figure out who she is.

Nicole's story may seem like an extreme case, but unfortunately, it's not the first of its kind I have heard. The Fairy-Tale Myth pressures young adults to marry—many before they are ready and without adequate preparation. This can lead to unhappy marriages, or as in Nicole's case, even unhealthy and abusive ones. When it comes to marriage, the poor theology of this myth creates unrealistic expectations that most marriages can't live up to. It can set women up for potentially abusive and unsafe situations. And it causes disillusionment to fester and grow.

> **REFLECT**: If you are or have been married, how do your expectations of marriage compare to the reality?

Recovering the Truth

To recover from the Fairy-Tale Myth, we must trade the entitlement of the sexual prosperity gospel with the gospel of grace. The definition of grace is an *undeserved, unearned, and unmerited gift of kindness, goodness, or mercy.* In the Christian's case, grace also includes God's forgiveness and eternal life.

I wrote my doctoral dissertation on relational grace in couples. The two years I spent studying grace, teaching it to couples, and

74

reflecting on it in my research profoundly changed me.[8] Grace became more than just a vague theological concept; for me, it became a transformative experience. As someone who has struggled with placing my value in my accomplishments, the idea that I cannot earn or merit grace had a deep impact on me. It healed me of much of my perfectionism and achievement-based worth. And it helped me reconcile the disappointment I had in my singleness.

The truth is, we are not guaranteed a fairy-tale marriage or even a spouse. In fact, Jesus guarantees that in this life, we will have trials and challenges.[9] He is not withholding good things from us to punish us. He is not waiting until we are "ready" or "seek him first." Our desires may never go away, and that's painful. We all live with unmet desires and longings in our lives, but "the Christian life is not a life of following rules to earn rewards. The Christian life is a life of grace—full stop."[10] The goal should be the same whether we are married or single: to love God and live in relationship with him.

After my breakup, in my seventh consecutive year of singleness, I wrote this truth on an index card and reviewed it daily: "I am single because this is God's best for me. I am living God's best for me right now." With that truth in sight, my faith shifted from an if-then formula to "even if."

God is gracious, faithful, and loving . . .

Even if we desperately want a spouse and never find one.

Even if our hearts are broken over and over again.

Even if we marry and our marriage is difficult.

Even if we do not have the children we long for.

Even if, God is good.

This doesn't mean that we deny our pain or don't work to change undesirable circumstances. In singleness and in marriage, we can acknowledge our ambiguous grief[11] when life doesn't turn out like we expected. We can practice validating our emotions, grieving our losses, and accepting that we can have both struggle and joy, both contentment and sorrow. We don't have to discount our feelings, avoid them, or pretend they don't exist. Look at your pain with nonjudgment.

Then give yourself grace.

A turning point in my disillusionment came when a mentor encouraged me to "seek God, not the things of God." I realized I was pursuing a relationship with God as a means to an end— marriage. I wanted the gifts of God, not the glory of God. I had to shift my goal. I began to believe that pursuing a relationship with God was worth it, regardless of my relationship status. That God was good and worthy of my trust and devotion even if I never found a husband. And that the point of following Jesus, which for me includes practicing chastity, is not to get a fairy-tale reward. Jesus is the reward.

Welcher puts it this way:

> Marriage is not the goal of purity. Family is not the goal. Sex is not the goal. God and his glory are the goal of purity. Practicing purity is a form of worship, another way we get to praise God through obedience with our bodies, hearts and thoughts. . . . We are called to purity because we are called to be like Jesus.[12]

REFLECT: Do some research on the promises of God. Are there any promises or guarantees in the Bible related to sexuality or relationships? Whether married or single, reflect on these promises of God when you are doubting.

It is discouraging to see the years go by where we have to attend one more wedding without a date or one more baby shower as the only nonparent in the room. It is painful to go on blind dates, each ending in disappointment. It is hurtful when friends dismiss the loneliness we feel in marriage. So yes, we must acknowledge and validate our grief and pain from these unmet desires.

And we must not grow weary of trusting God. If we believe that our God is good and loving, we can trust that he is with us even in our pain. We can be secure that he will "never leave [us] or forsake

[us]."[13] We can trust God's promises in Scripture rather than purity culture's false promise of a guaranteed spouse or marital bliss.

Though we are not entitled to any "rewards" for "following the rules," we have the greatest gift in the form of God's grace—his unending love and forgiveness. We don't have to be disillusioned by a bargain God never intended. We can trust in his goodness and faithfulness. While I can't explain why God chooses to lead some of us to marriage (or some of us later in life than we would like) while others remain single, I do know this: his grace is with all of us.

Tools for the Journey

Validation

Validation is the skill of calling a thought or feeling *valid* and real; there are legitimate reasons for why you feel or think the way you do. You may not like your feeling, but you can understand that there is valid evidence leading to it. Likewise, you can validate someone else's experience even if you don't agree.

Invalidation is what many of us grew up with: "You shouldn't feel that way . . . there's no reason to cry . . . it's wrong to get angry . . . it's bad to think that." Invalidation questions and even judges our reality, and over time, it can make someone doubt themselves and ignore their intuition.

Validating your thoughts and feelings is crucial to healing the trauma from purity culture, which is often invalidated by well-meaning religious communities. It's also imperative that we learn *both* how to respond to invalidation from others with assertive responses that reclaim our voice and stand up for ourselves, *and* how to respect and validate the other person's perspective as much as possible. (See the both/and there?)

Change the following examples of *invalidating* statements into *validating* ones. I've done the first examples for you.

Validating yourself:

- I shouldn't feel this way. → Even though I don't like feeling this way, it makes sense because of the beliefs I was taught.
- I should be happy for my friend getting married. It's a sin to be jealous or angry. → _____
- There must be something wrong with me for being single. → _____
_____

Validating others:

- "Purity culture didn't harm me. It wasn't that bad." → I'm glad you had a positive experience with purity culture. Many people, however, myself included, have suffered long-lasting harm from purity culture.
- "Just trust God. I'm sure he'll bring you a spouse when it's the right time." → _____

- "You're so blessed. You shouldn't complain about your marriage." →

Thought Record, Part 3

Deconstruct the Fairy-Tale Myth. Let's expand the thought record technique and take it a step further.

1. Draw four columns. In column one, list your thoughts and beliefs related to the Fairy-Tale Myth.

2. In column two, include how these beliefs affect you emotionally and physically. Do they lead to anger, disappointment, and entitlement? How do you experience these beliefs in your body?

3. In column three, list the evidence that supports this myth and the evidence against this myth. Pretend you are two opposing lawyers arguing in court for why this myth is true and why it is false. Basically, why should you believe this myth and why should you not believe it?

4. In column four, write more helpful and healthier thoughts to replace the myth. What might God speak to you as truth?

Use your truth statements in column four whenever you find the beliefs in column one coming up. Repeat the truths to yourself, and meditate on them to make them stick.

Example

Beliefs about the Fairy-Tale Myth	Effects	Evidence	Truth
I deserve a spouse if I stay pure.	Angry at God, jealous of married friends Tense, clenched fists, tightening in my stomach	*For*: My youth pastor growing up taught me this. All the books I read as a teenager promised me a spouse. *Against*: Nothing in the Bible promises marriage. I have several Christian friends who are still single.	I want to be married, but God doesn't owe me a spouse.

5

Myth #3

The Flipped Switch Myth

> God's perfect plan is that you enjoy sexual intercourse exclusively
> within your marriage. . . . The great sex you and your husband will
> enjoy someday will be free from painful consequences or guilt—
> and well worth the wait!
>
> Shannon Ethridge and Stephen Arterburn, *Every Young*
> *Woman's Battle*[1]

"Sex is great! Sex is great! Sex is great!"

The audience of teens repeated this chant as strobe lights and green lasers flashed across the stage. The twentysomething speaker led the crowd in cheering before following with an admonishment: "Sex is great . . . in the context of marriage." Married for four years, he held up his left hand as proof while the screen captured a close-up of his wedding ring and the "Hallelujah Chorus" played.

This scene opened an abstinence event by Silver Ring Thing as depicted by Dr. Christine J. Gardner in her book *Making Chastity Sexy*. A communications professor, Gardner explored three evangelical abstinence groups to understand the arguments and strategies they employed to persuade young people to abstain from premarital sex. She consistently found that evangelical sexual abstinence campaigns—purity culture—used the promise of delaying gratification now for a greater prize of love and sex in the future. Historically, she noticed that the rhetoric changed from "just say no" to "just say yes" to sex in marriage. The most persuasive abstinence message "reduced sex to a persuasive tool to sell abstinence";[2] if teens said no to premarital sex, they were guaranteed sex that was "well worth the wait" once they were married.

The evangelical purity movement is not the only one that perpetuates this myth. When I watched the Netflix TV show *Bridgerton*, which takes place in England during the Regency era, it wasn't hard to make connections between nineteenth-century London and twenty-first-century purity culture. While the similarities are too numerous to detail here, one that stood out to me was the women's complete lack of sexual education and knowledge prior to marriage and their rapturous, ecstatic wedding night with their more experienced husbands. Despite lacking a basic understanding of sex and procreation and having been prohibited from being alone or having any physical contact prior to marriage, the women on the show had no trouble "flipping a switch" to have euphoric sex.

And yes, purity culture promised us the same thing.

Uncovering the Myth

The Flipped Switch Myth is one of the most recognizable myths of purity culture. Although I am the first to give it this name, many of my clients say a variation of this statement: "It's like before you're married, sex is bad, and then after you get married, you just flip a switch and it's great!"

Their expectations are not coming out of nowhere. The purity culture books and teachers we learned from in our youth all promised the reward of great sex in marriage—as long as you waited.

Lady in Waiting, my favorite book as a teenager, taught us that "God gives true sexual fulfillment to the lady who waits for this

Gift. . . . The wonder and joy of this intimate act is maximized through purity before marriage."[3]

And the Bride Wore White furthered its promise of a fairy-tale marriage with fairy-tale sex: "If you will wait, then it will be exciting! . . . It will be a blast."[4]

Shelly Donahue, a former public-school teacher who created a national abstinence curriculum that was taught in forty-eight states and seven foreign countries, said this: "[Sex in marriage] could be like fireworks for you someday. . . . But if you open the door to sexual activity right now in high school and college, you know what kind of sex you settle for? Squirt gun. . . . I want you to love sex because sex is awesome! Just not right now."[5]

Is teenage sex "fireworks"? Likely not. Yes, there are practical, emotional, and spiritual reasons for delaying sex or waiting until marriage for sex. But promising great sex if you wait—and horrible sex if you don't—just isn't reality, as many purity culture survivors discover.

A satisfying sex life is not a guarantee because a couple remained abstinent before marriage. A lousy sex life is certainly not an absolute because a couple was sexually active prior to marriage. Purity culture set Christians up for disappointment and failure when it offered false promises, without emphasizing the work, communication, and patience needed for fulfilling intimacy.

On an episode of *The Love Hour* podcast, Melissa and Kevin Fredericks invited me to talk about the broken promises of the purity movement, particularly the Flipped Switch Myth. Melissa was a twenty-year-old virgin when they married, and even after being married seventeen years, Melissa still felt "bamboozled."

"I have found that I still struggle with that switch. Even though I've read books, listened to podcasts, and talked to experts, I still hold on to this lie from purity culture. Unraveling it continues to be a struggle for me today."

Melissa felt like she had to go into "battle mode" in her mind to combat these lies, often taking her out of her body during sex. "I have this narrative about what I'm allowed to do and what is not allowed," she explained. "Even indulging in pleasure can still feel off-limits."

To say the Flipped Switch Myth affected Melissa's marriage, sexuality, and faith would be an understatement. "I couldn't even bring myself to talk about sex before I was married. Then you put this ring on, and you're supposed to freely enjoy sex! But then what if you don't?"

Eventually, she started to wonder. "Why did I do everything right if this is the outcome? I felt like I read the terms and conditions and I fulfilled my portion, and this is a breach of contract. This is not what I expected."[6]

Personal Assessment: Does the Flipped Switch Myth Affect You?

Scoring guidelines: 0 = disagree, 1 = neutral or unsure, 2 = agree

1. Once you marry, sex will be enjoyable, pleasurable, and rewarding—if you waited.
2. Virginity is the most important gift you can give your spouse on your wedding day.
3. Having a great sex life in marriage is a reward after all these years of waiting.
4. People are bound to have sexual problems in their marriage if they had premarital sex.
5. God will certainly bless my faithfulness in waiting by giving me great sex in marriage.

Add up your score. The higher the score, the greater the belief in the myth.

Discovering the Effects

Like Melissa and Kevin, some couples struggle to flip the switch in their brain that takes sex from "off-limits" to "go for it." What many purity culture survivors are greeted with on their wedding night is not mind-blowing orgasms and shame-free intimacy. How do they feel when their reality doesn't live up to the promised fantasy?

Here is what some of my interviewees and clients said about their experiences:

- "Sex still seems bad. It went from being dirty and the worst sin to now being something I'm supposed to enjoy and always be ready for."
- "All of a sudden everything that was so wrong my whole life was now allowed. It was hard to flip the switch. I still felt like sex was wrong or dirty."
- "I still feel guilty, like we're not supposed to be doing this thing."
- "The way I remember it is don't have sex before marriage, and when you get married, it's like this switch in your head is supposed to flip and [sex] is great."
- "I read [a purity culture book] all about these steps you take so you don't have sex before you're married and how in the end it's going to be so perfect, and the reward is going to be so wonderful. . . . Then two nights ago I was in bed crying because sex is so much harder than that."

No matter their experience, these stories all have one thing in common: disappointment.

Effects in the Mind and Body

When I taught a human sexuality class at a Christian college, my students were shocked to learn that it is not unusual for couples to wait days or even weeks to consummate their marriage. "But isn't everybody 'getting it on' as soon as they say I do?" was the students' reaction. In theory, yes. But in reality, not necessarily. Many couples find that a lack of comprehensive sex education before marriage leads to being unprepared for marriage and sex or to unrealistic beliefs or expectations—something they don't realize until they're in the moment.

A month after she got married, one of my friends shared, "We weren't able to have sex on our honeymoon. We still haven't. It is just too painful." And as we know, she's not alone in her experience. Beliefs can't just be turned off in our minds, because the effects of these beliefs are stored in our bodies. Once we get married, our minds may know that sex is holy, but do our bodies know? It can be confusing when what was sinful and guilt-inducing one day is supposed to be intimate and pleasurable the next.

The inability to flip a switch in one's body is one of the precursors to sexual dysfunctions such as low sex drive, erectile dysfunction, and sexual pain. Remember, psychologists have found that one of the probable causes of vaginismus, a sexual pain disorder making intercourse painful or impossible, is a strict, religious upbringing with condemning messages about sex.[7] You are *twice as likely* to have vaginismus if you were raised in evangelical purity culture.[8]

When Hanna got married, she expected sex to hurt the first time, but when she was in pain every time after that, she assumed this was just what sex is supposed to be like. Finally, after one year of marriage, she went to her doctor and was diagnosed with vaginismus.

Hanna told me, "I realized my body was rejecting penetrative sex because of purity culture. My brain could not switch from 'sex is bad' to 'sex is good' when we walked down the aisle." She felt disappointed that sex wasn't what she expected. "I remember telling God, 'I did everything right; why is this happening to me?'"

Now a podcast host and advocate for sexual health, Hanna realizes her sexual pain was not her fault. It came from a belief system that trained her body to react negatively to sex—and her body could not catch up with her brain once she was married. "I grew up believing sex was the worst sin," she said, "so of course my body paid the price for it."[9]

This is why I am skeptical of the rise of "Christian influencers" online who tout the sexual benefits of waiting for marriage.[10] Of course, it's fine to believe that sex is worth the wait for marriage; I personally affirm this too. But these influencers continue to perpetuate the Flipped Switch Myth when they guarantee sex will be great . . . *if* you wait.

This is not to say that sexual inexperience or abstinence before marriage always leads to a dismal sex life. Some couples don't experience significant sexual struggles in marriage—good for them. But bragging about your honeymoon sex on social media is furthering this myth. We can be honest about our personal decision and positive experience with waiting. But if we want to help others avoid the disappointment that comes from the Flipped Switch Myth, we also need to acknowledge that many other Christians who wait don't experience the "reward."

Effects in the Heart and Soul

When we can't flip the switch, we might experience continued guilt, anxiety, and shame around sex. We may feel disconnected from the sacred aspects of sex, continuing to feel that sex is dirty rather than holy.

Some people don't wait for marriage and have great sex. This can create jealousy, resentment, and doubts of "What's wrong with me?" for those who do wait. When they hear stories from their friends of how great sex is, yet are struggling to flip the switch themselves, it can feel unfair.

Other couples I've worked with who did have sex before marriage often found that their sex life wasn't as great after marriage. For them, the question became "What happened? Was this punishment for not waiting?"

I don't believe God arbitrarily punishes us for "breaking the rules." However, there can be natural consequences (or results) for our decisions. A natural result of waiting for marriage is that you are less experienced and may be less educated when it comes to sex. It may take you longer to figure out sex in your marriage. A natural result of not waiting is that sex may not be as exciting as it once was. There can be a "been there, done that" feeling.

For both couples who do and don't have sex before marriage— especially those who grew up in purity culture—I've noticed another culprit for this decline in sexual interest: the fact that sex is no longer "off-limits." What was once exciting, taboo, and something that you had to be sneaky about now feels like a duty or obligation, hardly the exciting and "sexy" way we expected it to feel. In this too there is a sense of disappointment.

> REFLECT: If you are married, how has the reality of sex compared to the promise? Have you experienced disappointment? If you are single, how can you have accurate expectations of sex in marriage?

Recovering the Truth

So what can we do? How do we overcome this disappointment brought on by the myths of purity culture?

The truth is that sex is a learned skill that requires work, regardless of whether you waited or not. Sex won't "just come to you." Like everything in marriage, it takes mutual responsibility, teamwork, and communication to have a satisfying sex life. And like all skills, we can improve over time as we gain more experience and knowledge. I believe sex education is the number one way Christians can prepare for or enhance their intimacy in marriage.

Fortunately, I received sex education and training in sex therapy in my doctoral program before I got married. Considering that most of us coming out of purity culture did not have adequate sex education, it is now my mission to give others the sex education they likely never received. While there is so much to learn about sex, we're going to spend time focusing on four key lessons.

Ready? Then welcome to Sex Ed 101!

Lesson #1: Communication

Sex requires communication—with God, your spouse, yourself, and sometimes with professionals.

God can bless your marriage and your sex life. You can pray and invite God into your marriage and ask him to grow your intimacy in all areas.

But you can also be an active participant in your own sex education. You and your spouse can educate yourselves by reading and discussing books like this one together, taking courses, listening to podcasts, and even seeing a licensed mental health professional, sex therapist, or marriage coach if you need additional support. If you are engaged and preparing for marriage, talk about expectations ahead of time and commit to being beginners together. If you are single and not sexually active, you can take steps to educate yourself and embrace your sexuality as a single person.

All of this will help you work on your sexual communication. Your spouse may know you inside and out, but I guarantee they don't know how to please you sexually *unless* you communicate.

Lesson #2: Frequency

There is no seventy-two-hour rule.

Contrary to what some Christian marriage books and pastors have said, there is no physiological, psychological, or spiritual reason for the prominent teaching that Christian couples need to have sex every three days.

You and your spouse can determine the frequency that is right for you, which may be more or less than seventy-two hours. The average sexual frequency for married couples varies depending on the state of the marriage, health issues, stage of life, and other responsibilities.

Frequency is not the best measure of the sexual health of a marriage. When I see a couple for sex therapy, I do ask about frequency, but I am more concerned about the couple's overall sense of pleasure, mutuality, and satisfaction. As sex educator Dr. Emily Nagoski says, "Pleasure is the measure," not frequency.[11]

If there are physical or relationship issues preventing you from enjoying a fulfilling sex life, please seek additional help. Otherwise, don't let anyone pressure you into thinking sex has to occur at a certain frequency. Come to a mutual decision about what works for your marriage and let that be your standard.

Lesson #3: Pleasure

One word the purity books rarely mentioned: clitoris. But this is one of the most important parts of sexual anatomy.

For women, having an orgasm from intercourse is the exception rather than the norm. Only about 10 to 30 percent of women can orgasm from intercourse alone—and even then, it usually takes some clitoral stimulation too.[12] The only physiological function of the clitoris is sexual pleasure, and for most women, this is their pleasure center. Yet pastors and male authors often present a male-centric view of sex focused on penis-in-vagina intercourse.

I believe part of the reason for the overfocus on intercourse as the "main event" is due to purity culture. Many couples who have not had intercourse before marriage have engaged in other sexual activities, including ones resulting in orgasm such as oral or manual stimulation. Because purity culture doesn't define this as "sex," couples can become fixated on sex as intercourse. Other forms of stimulation which tend to be more pleasurable and orgasmic for women are downplayed and minimized, especially in marriage once intercourse is "allowed."

This is also why it is generally rare for both spouses to orgasm at the same time during sex. Because women typically need clitoral stimulation and men need penile stimulation, many couples find that simultaneous orgasm eludes them.

The problem in all of this? The sexual activities outside of the so-called main event aren't secondary; for many women, they *are* the main event.

As you navigate this aspect of sex, remember this: God created us to experience pleasure in this way. He made our bodies differently to draw us outside of ourselves and attend to each other's desires. Use the natural differences in your bodies and sexual responses to bring you closer together as you mutually explore intimacy. Learn other ways to experience pleasure and orgasm besides intercourse. If you and your spouse want to experiment with simultaneous orgasm or orgasm for the wife during intercourse, go for it! But if you don't, it is not something to experience shame over. Invite God into your sexual intimacy and ask him to guide you to greater knowledge and understanding of each other's body.

Lesson #4: Pain

I heard horror stories about the pain of intercourse when I was younger. The scare tactics of purity culture taught us that intercourse would break the woman's hymen,[13] and she would never be the same. Sexual pain was unavoidable and "just the way it is" for virgins. Married friends would describe how painful sex was, how they ached and throbbed later, and how they bled. Bleeding was almost a badge of honor—a sign of one's virginity likely from earlier times when they needed to confirm paternity of an heir.

If you experience sexual pain, know that you are not alone. And more than that, know you do not have to keep suffering. God has provided tools for your healing and wants you to be free of the shame and pain that inhibit sexual intimacy with your spouse.

Seek out professional help. In the meantime, expand your sexual repertoire to include pleasurable, nonintercourse activities. Focus on what you can enjoy during this process and work together with your spouse to enhance intimacy.

> **REFLECT:** Which of the Sex Ed 101 lessons helped you the most? In which area do you want to seek out additional help, resources, and tools?

Contrary to what the Flipped Switch Myth taught us, few couples who grew up in purity culture are chanting, "Sex is great!" on their wedding night. To move past disappointment, sexual dysfunction, and guilt, we have to empower ourselves with sex education. We have to learn to communicate with our spouses about our sexual desires and patiently work on our sexual skills.

And when we do, we'll find a path forward that doesn't end in disappointment.

"Educating myself has been *the* biggest help in overcoming these myths," Melissa told me, affirming the importance of sex education in helping her through her own personal hurdles with sex in marriage. "I feel empowered as a woman to own my sexuality. A lot of books frame sexuality in the lens of your husband's needs, and you end up feeling like an object in your husband's sex life instead of an active participant in your own sexuality. Now, I recognize that sex is also for me."

Tools for the Journey

Sexual Communication

With your spouse, decide on a distraction-free time to schedule a conversation about your sexual intimacy. Set aside about thirty minutes. If it feels more comfortable for you or you need more time to process, you might take time to reflect on these questions privately before talking together.

Take turns asking and answering these questions of each other. After each set of questions, check in with each other. Observe the physical and emotional effects of the conversation. Can you keep going? Are either of you feeling overwhelmed or need a break? If so, honor that need and schedule a time to follow up.

Start with positive affirmation:

1. What do you like about our sex life?
2. What I love about your body is _____.
3. I appreciate that you _____.

Questions about sexual satisfaction:

1. How satisfied are we with our sexual intimacy?
2. What would make our sexual satisfaction greater?
3. What is your favorite place to be touched? How do you like me to touch you? Is there a place you prefer I don't touch?
4. How satisfied are we with our sexual pleasure? Are we both experiencing pleasure?

Questions about sexual frequency:

1. How often are we sexually intimate? How often would we like it to be?
2. How do you like me to initiate sex? How do you like me to decline sex?
3. What are some ways we can increase our sexual frequency (if we both want to)?

4. Is there a preferred day or time to have sex? Do we want to schedule sex? Or do we prefer spontaneity?

Questions about sexual positions and activities:

1. What is your favorite sexual position and why?
2. What is a sexual position or activity you love to do? What is something you are not comfortable with or don't enjoy?
3. Is there a sexual position or activity you want to try?
4. Are there any sexual positions or activities that you have said yes to in the past but no longer want to do?

Questions about problem areas:

1. Are we experiencing any sexual problems or difficulties?
2. Do we experience any sexual pain or discomfort?
3. What, if anything, has been inhibiting our sexual desire?
4. What, if anything, has been inhibiting our sexual pleasure?
5. Do we need to consult professional help or resources for these problem areas?

If it feels comfortable for you, end the conversation by praying with your spouse, asking God to bless your marriage and your sexual intimacy.

6

Myth #4

The Gatekeepers Myth

Your wife can be a methadone-like fix when your temperature is rising. . . . [Wives,] once he tells you he's going cold turkey [from using pornography], be like a merciful vial of methadone for him.

Stephen Arterburn and Fred Stoeker, *Every Man's Battle*[1]

Michelle Duggar, the mom of *19 Kids and Counting* fame, made headlines in 2015 with her advice to newlyweds: "Wives should be joyfully available to meet [their] husband's special needs. Be willing to say, 'Yes, sweetie, I am here for you' . . . even though . . . you may not feel like he feels."

Michelle claimed this was "the best advice I have ever received." No matter the circumstances, she encouraged wives to smile and say, "I'm going to meet that need because I know it's a need for you."[2]

The Duggars also advocated for strict boundaries prior to marriage. In her memoir, *Counting the Cost*,[3] Jill Duggar Dillard recounts how, as a child, she was taught that showing any skin is "defrauding" your brother in Christ. The time she spent with her fiancé had to be chaperoned by one of her siblings so the couple would not fall into temptation, meaning the couple spent no time alone until their wedding night.

The phrase "joyfully available" has become a joke in my marriage, one that thankfully my husband does not hold me to. But this phrase perfectly captures the Gatekeepers Myth of purity culture. The message in it is loud and clear.

Women, you are the gatekeepers of men's sexuality. Before marriage, you are responsible for stopping the sexual progression, setting boundaries, and dressing modestly so you don't cause men to "stumble." And after marriage, you must always meet your husband's sexual needs so that you don't tempt him to turn to pornography or infidelity.

Men, you are sexual deviants who can't control yourselves. Your mind is debased, and your hyperactive sexual desire is an unavoidable part of being male—in fact, it is sanctified.

As Zachary Wagner states in his excellent book *Non-Toxic Masculinity*, "Purity culture dehumanizes women and girls by oversexualizing their bodies. It dehumanizes men and boys by oversexualizing their minds."[4]

A woman I interviewed for this book said, "Purity culture makes me angry for what it does to women, but it makes me sad for what it does to men." I couldn't have said it better myself. Yes, the Gatekeepers Myth dehumanizes us both.

Uncovering the Myth

As we've explored, purity culture is rooted in patriarchy. You cannot separate one from the other. Patriarchal culture, and thus purity culture, teaches that women are less sexual and don't want or enjoy sex as much as men. Sex is primarily to meet men's sexual needs and urges, and women must respond to their "wifely duties" cheerfully, willingly, and, well, joyfully. They were created to be "penis homes."[5] Wives should give their husbands sex "without complaint" because "the Bible says you should not withhold sex for long periods of time." Wagner puts it bluntly: "If men are sex machines, women are machines for sex—objects of seduction toward sexual sin or the fulfillment of men's sexual urges."[6]

My friend Sarah visited a church in which they advertised two gender-specific groups for high school youth. The boys' group was called "Man Up!" and the girls' was "Purposed for Purity." Based on these titles alone, we can presume that masculinity is broader; there's more to being a man than just not having sex. On the other hand, women's main purpose is purity. Like we've said, purity balls, purity rings, and other symbols of the abstinence movement are almost exclusively marketed to females. I had dozens of female friends with True Love Waits rings through high school and college but did not know a single male friend who had one. All this emphasis on sexual purity for women alone sets us up for inequality in the conversation about and experience with sex.

And just imagine the shame for those who don't conform to these rigid gender stereotypes, including men with a lower sex drive and women with a higher one, and people who don't identify as heterosexual or cisgender. No matter where we fit into this space, it leaves us feeling like something is wrong if we don't conform to these molds. By emphasizing purity in an unbalanced way to both young men and young women, purity culture treats us all with inequality. It shames and silences both men and women if they don't conform to traditional sexual stereotypes. And it can perpetuate sexual dysfunction and marital distress.

Personal Assessment:
Does the Gatekeepers Myth Affect You?

Scoring guidelines: 0 = disagree, 1 = neutral or unsure, 2 = agree

1. Men are more sexual than women, so wives must be prepared to meet their husband's sexual needs.
2. Women have to be careful about modesty, so they don't tempt men and cause men to lust.
3. Purity is an important part of what it means to be a Christian girl or young woman and part of a young woman's purpose.

4. Sex is mostly about physical pleasure for men and emotional bonding for women.

5. It's harder for men to control their sexual urges, so it's up to young women to enforce sexual boundaries when dating.

Add up your score. The higher the score, the greater the belief in the myth.

Discovering the Effects

The Gatekeepers Myth weaves an intricate web of inequality from the clothes we wear to the relationships we have to the way we see our own sexual needs and desires. Here are some of the main areas affected by this inequality.

Modesty

"Modest is hottest."

Those of us who grew up in purity culture likely heard this phrase. Perhaps you, as a good youth group kid, even wore it on a T-shirt (high-necked of course!). Young girls and women were told that they are temptresses, inciting lustful passions in young men and causing them to "stumble." The solution? Girls were to pursue modest dress and a humble, meek demeanor—to have a gentle and quiet spirit. Rules such as only wearing shorts that meet the "fingertip rule," one-piece bathing suits with a T-shirt over it, and no tank tops or V-necks were common and expected in Christian schools and youth groups. (Interestingly, I never heard a message of male modesty. How about you?)

In case you haven't heard the truth, let me be clear: clothing choice should not be about what the opposite sex thinks. The problem with a phrase like "modest is hottest" is that it still makes clothing about others (usually men). It still sends the message that you're trying to appear "hot" and acceptable by someone else's standards.

As we know, it is a slippery slope from modesty messages to rape culture. When you blame a woman for a man's lust based on what she is wearing, you take the onus off the man completely. When you couple that with the belief that men cannot control their sexual urges, this too easily transforms into blaming a survivor for her own sexual assault because of something like her clothing or behavior. Though most of purity culture exemplifies a double standard, it is especially apparent here, in standards of modesty.

Boundaries and Obligation

The Gatekeepers Myth teaches that all men have high sex drives, look at women primarily for their sexual functions, and can't be held responsible for their sexual desires. If men can't control their urges, and women are less sexual, then, at least for purity culture proponents, the math is simple: it is up to women to set boundaries and be the gatekeepers of men's sexuality. They are to blame for men's lust and are there to meet men's sexual needs. They are responsible not only for their own boundaries and sexual desires but also for those of their male counterparts.

This message was coined the "obligation sex message" by Sheila Wray Gregoire, Rebecca Gregoire Lindenbach, and Joanna Sawatsky.[7] Their groundbreaking research analyzed popular evangelical teachings on sex such as the opening quote for this chapter. Their subsequent book *The Great Sex Rescue* demolishes the Gatekeepers Myth. Here are some of their disturbing findings:

- Believing the "obligation sex message" was correlated with increased rates of vaginismus, lower orgasm rates, and lower marital satisfaction.
- Believing that "all men struggle with lust" was correlated with lower libido and orgasm rates for women, lower trust in marriage, and lower marital satisfaction.
- Believing that a woman should have frequent sex with her husband to keep him from watching porn (being "a methadone-like fix") was correlated with lower orgasm rates, higher rates of sexual pain, and lower marital satisfaction.[8]

In reality, this purity culture teaching on boundaries and obligation couldn't be further from the truth. Men and women are both responsible for sexual boundaries and communicating consent—before and after marriage. It's not *her* responsibility; it's *ours*. When purity culture heaps this undue burden solely on women, it doesn't just shame women and rob them of their agency. It also robs men of the opportunity to learn crucial skills such as self-control and delayed gratification. These are skills they could carry on into marriage to enhance mutuality.

Boundaries and consent are important before and after marriage. Purity culture promised as long as you were married, sex was "pure." Not so. Sex can take place in marriage without being pure if it is coerced, manipulated, one-sided, and without mutual respect and love. Women (and men) have to be able to say no. And with that, they have to experience saying no as safe. When they can, it provides a corrective experience that disconfirms the old belief that they aren't allowed to say no. As Gregoire says, "Without the ability to say no, we can never truly say yes."[9]

Desire and Pleasure

The concept of "brakes and accelerators," popularized by Emily Nagoski's landmark book on women's sexual health, *Come as You Are*, can be helpful for understanding sexual desire. According to Nagoski, sexual desire is fueled by a dual-control model of both brakes (turn-offs) and accelerators (turn-ons). Common brakes can be physical, emotional, relational, or personal, such as triggers of past trauma. Accelerators might be physical touch, expressing feelings, emotional closeness, environment, sexual fantasies or daydreams about one's spouse, or sexual stimuli through any of the five senses. Increasing sexual desire involves both taking your foot off the brakes and putting the "pedal to the metal."[10]

It is common to have "discrepant desire" in marriage, in which one spouse has a naturally higher sex drive than the other. There is no gender rule when it comes to sex drive (although on average, men do report more sexual desire). Knowing this, there are two primary types of desire: spontaneous (also called initiating) desire and responsive desire. Spontaneous desire arises, you guessed it—spontaneously. This is what we typically think of when we talk about sexual desire. You get a sexual thought, urge, or image, and then you have a desire or hunger for sex. Sexual desire *leads to* seeking out sexual arousal. By contrast, in responsive desire, you become more open or receptive to sex only after engaging with sexual stimuli or pleasurable activity. Sexual desire *follows* arousal and pleasure. The desire is a response to your environment or your spouse's desire.[11]

Spontaneous desire more commonly occurs in men while responsive desire is more common in women.[12] Neither one is good or bad, right or wrong. But as usual, our culture prioritizes the typical male experience and downplays the typical female one.

Rather than leaning into arbitrary gender rules about desire, we can get curious about our expectations of sex and what is getting in the way of our goals. Instead of judging ourselves, we can respect and work with natural differences in how we experience desire. We can explore our personal pleasures and desires as well as those of our spouse without shame, pressure, or fear together, as equals.

> **REFLECT**: Which of these aspects of inequality affects you the most?

Recovering the Truth

Instead of this hyperfocus on sex to meet all intimacy needs, we can elevate other types of intimacy and make sure sex is *mutually* pleasurable and connecting. The message of sexual responsibility should be given to both women and men equally, as the tasks of respecting boundaries and consent, attending to desire and pleasure, and increasing intimacy are the jobs of both sexes. To bust the Gatekeepers Myth, we must strive for mutuality when it comes to several aspects of the way we see sex and relationships.

Increasing Desire and Pleasure

My client Molly told me she was "just not a sexual person." She had chronic low sex drive, believed that sex was for her husband, and could not enjoy her own sexual pleasure. We explored the meaning of her statement that she is "just not a sexual person" and found that this wasn't the case. It was a false belief that came from repressing her sexuality and sexual desire because it was seen as wrong or sinful in her purity culture days.[13]

Still, she, like many, had to work to accept her sexuality and notice her sexual desire. To do so, Nagoski recommends making the most of responsive desire. Increase nonsexual touching and affection with your spouse and see where that takes you. Create the right context for responsive desire to grow. What environment gets you in the mood?

Doing things like this helped Molly learn to confidently claim her identity as a sexual person, which meant believing that her desire, pleasure, and experience mattered too. Instead of shaming herself for experiencing mostly responsive desire, she learned to maximize it. Molly found that she could explore desire and observe if it grew. When she didn't have the energy or interest in intercourse, she could suggest another sexual (or sensual) activity that sounded good. Molly learned to communicate with her husband about what got her in the mood for sex and what brought her pleasure. She also practiced sensual mindfulness skills[14] to tune into her body sensations and enhance pleasure and orgasm. These skills allowed her to take advantage of any moments of spontaneous desire and maximize times of responsive desire too.

> **REFLECT:** Have you ever said you are not a very sexual person? What does that mean to you?

Rewriting Scripts

In sex therapy, a sexual script is a way of behaving and relating to each other sexually. Who initiates, when and where sex happens, how you initiate, how the sexual encounter transpires, what positions you take, and what happens before, during, and after a sexual encounter are all parts of sexual scripts.

Purity culture teaches rigid beliefs about how sex should happen. For example, the husband should always initiate. It should be at nighttime, in a bed. You can only have sex in one or two acceptable positions. "Sex" means you have intercourse until the man orgasms, and then it's over. These are not universal scripts, but ones that my clients have often picked up on from either purity culture or broader sexual norms. And research has shown that having sexual scripts that tell you to follow a limited range of sexual behaviors to be "appropriate" or successful is linked to decreased sexual and relationship satisfaction.[15]

For those of us recovering from purity culture, rewriting that script with more mutual and inclusive thought is so important. This might mean going outside the norms of "proper sex" that you learned. Please hear me on this: I am not suggesting anyone violates their values or agrees to activities they find demeaning, painful, or objectifying. Neither spouse should pressure or coerce the other one into doing something they find unacceptable. It is important that you claim your sexual agency and set boundaries for your health, comfort, and safety.

But there is so much freedom that God wants us to experience within a safe, trusting, covenantal marriage: freedom from shame, repression, expectations, and rigid gender stereotypes. So the question you might consider is this: Can you expand your script *and* stay within your sexual values? Whatever that means for you, choose to rewrite the script in a way that serves both partners equally.

Expanding Intimacy

How can you and your spouse expand the definition of intimacy beyond just intercourse or even physical intimacy?

You may have been taught that sex is a biological "need" for men and the primary, if not only, way they feel loved. This belief can cripple men in their ability to express love and experience intimacy in other ways. Many of my clients have paired belonging and attachment—a hardwired, biological need—with intercourse. But the truth is sex is not a biological *need* like hunger, thirst, and sleep. All of us can live without sex; we cannot live without water, food, or some type of belonging. Sex is important, but it is not an obligation.

Intimacy isn't just sex; it's anything that makes you feel close and connected to another person. Many couples with inequalities in their sex life, whether differences in desire or pleasure, discount these other forms of intimacy. But when we increase intimacy in other areas, what often follows is helpful to both parties. Typically, the higher desire spouse feels more "filled up" with love and connection, thus decreasing the pressure on the other spouse to have more sex. And the lower desire spouse often finds their sexual desire grows, as their marriage has a greater environment of closeness and attention.

Ruth and Mitchell are a married couple who worked with me to rewrite their sexual scripts and enhance their connection and intimacy. Mitchell had a higher drive and felt loved and desired when sexually intimate with his wife. The only way he knew to feel close and connected was to have intercourse. Previously, Ruth had always said yes—even when she didn't want to—because of the Gatekeepers Myth. But now Ruth had gained confidence and given herself permission to say no. When she declined, Mitchell felt rejected and inadequate.

Together, we worked on Ruth continuing to advocate for herself and set boundaries while expanding their intimacy beyond sex. I coached them on enhancing other areas of intimacy (see the Circles of Intimacy tool at the end of the chapter). When Mitchell noticed and felt loved from these other forms of connection—talking and taking walks together, back rubs and weekends away—he put less pressure on sex to meet all his intimacy needs, which in turn put less pressure on Ruth sexually.

By working on increasing intimacy in all areas—emotional, spiritual, intellectual, social, and physical—we can get closer to healing the inequality of the Gatekeepers Myth and reaching the mutuality of healthy, God-honoring sex.

The truth is, sexual integrity in all forms is the responsibility of both men and women.

Men, you are not sexually depraved and incapable of controlling your urges and impulses.

Women, you are not the gatekeepers, responsible for boundaries in dating and for being "joyfully available" and a "vial of methadone" in marriage.

Whereas the Gatekeepers Myth created inequality and reinforced gender stereotypes and rigid sexual scripts, mutuality creates space for the health and honoring of yourself, your spouse, and God.

Tools for the Journey

Rewriting Scripts

Write a typical script of a sexual encounter between you and your spouse, as if you were writing stage directions and lines for actors in a play. What is the setting (time and place)? What are you wearing? Who does what? What do you each say? Then what happens? How does it progress, and how does it end?

Now, rewrite the script, thinking "outside the box" but still within both your values. Get outside purity culture but respect your and your spouse's boundaries. Consider changes to the script such as who initiates and how, what you do, the setting, the ambiance, and the progression of the sexual encounter.

During this exercise, pay attention to your thoughts ("I could never do that!"; "That sounds fun.") and emotions (curiosity, interest, arousal, desire, disgust, or shame). Share your scripts with your spouse and look for areas of overlap, new ideas, and suggestions you both want to try. Make sure you mutually agree on any new ideas!

Circles of Intimacy

Following are the main dimensions of intimacy and common activities in each category. Read through the list with your spouse. Add to it and create your own additional ideas for intimacy. Decide if there is anything you want to take off your list. Remember, intimacy is anything that makes you feel close and connected to your spouse. Let's expand beyond intercourse to include other forms of closeness and pleasure.

Circles of Intimacy

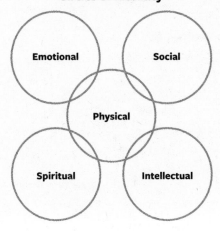

Physical

Hugs

Kissing

Cuddling

Holding hands

Back rubs or massages

Taking a bath or shower together

Sensual touch

Nonintercourse sexual activity

Sexual intercourse

Emotional

Speaking each other's love language

Sharing goals and dreams together

Talking about our day

Supporting each other

Working through a problem or conflict together

Being there for each other

Saying I love you and words of affirmation

Spending quality time together

Reminiscing on past memories

Spiritual

Praying together

Reading the Bible together

Going through a Bible study or devotional together

Attending church

Talking about the sermon

Discussing our spiritual lives

Praying for each other

Serving at our church or community

Meditating together

Social

Socializing with friends or family

Engaging in mutual hobbies

Taking trips

Engaging in family activities

Hosting dinners or parties

Going out on dates

Trying new restaurants or activities

Playing games or puzzles

Watching movies, sports, the arts, and so on

Intellectual

Reading and discussing a book

Attending a lecture or training

Discussing new ideas

Listening to a podcast

Taking a class or course together

Learning a new skill

7

Myth #5

The Damaged Goods Myth

> Suppose you made a beautiful birthday cake . . . and found your beautiful cake with a piece missing. . . . The cake is ruined. How will your future husband feel if you have already given pieces of your heart to others and can offer him only a partly-eaten cake?
>
> Sarah Mally, *Before You Meet Prince Charming*[1]

In 2002, fourteen-year-old Elizabeth Smart was kidnapped from her home at knife point. In every parent's worst nightmare, Elizabeth was missing for nine months as she was held captive in the woods by a man, who claimed to be a religious preacher, and his wife. During this time, Elizabeth was repeatedly raped by her captor.

Elizabeth was fortunately found and returned home to her family. Her captors were found guilty and sentenced for their crimes; the male captor is currently serving a sentence of life in prison without parole. But Elizabeth was profoundly affected by the trauma of her capture, kidnapping, and repeated rapes.

This trauma was exacerbated by the messages of purity culture.

A member of the Church of Jesus Christ of Latter-day Saints, Elizabeth received abstinence-only sex education prior to her kidnapping. In a 2014 speech at Johns Hopkins University, Elizabeth shared that she remembered a purity culture object lesson—that those who have premarital sex are worthless, old pieces of chewed-up gum.[2] It was this lesson, in fact, that deterred her from trying to escape.

"I thought, 'Oh my gosh. I'm that chewed-up piece of gum,'" Smart told the college audience. "Nobody re-chews a piece of gum. You throw it away. And that's how it is to feel like you no longer have worth, you no longer have value. Why would it even be worth screaming out? Why would it even make a difference if you are rescued, if your life still has no value?"[3]

Why would she believe this? Why would any of us believe this? As heartbreaking as her words are, if we buy into the Spiritual Barometer Myth, that our status as virgins determines our identity and value, then the reverse must be true too. If we engage in premarital sex or sexual activity, or even if we are sexually abused, then we must be damaged goods, right?

Uncovering the Myth

The Damaged Goods Myth declares that you are soiled and damaged goods if you have premarital sex. As we've seen, purity culture used many illustrations to underscore this myth. One purity book suggested that having premarital sex makes you a "trashable Styrofoam cup" compared to a "valuable, priceless teacup."[4] Some youth group purity rallies passed around a cup of water and had everyone spit into the cup, which symbolized the impurity that comes from having sex with multiple partners. In another demonstration, a heart-shaped piece of paper was passed around, and the youth were invited to tear off pieces of it, representing the pieces of your heart that you give away each time you have sex.

I Kissed Dating Goodbye starts off with a bride and groom at the altar on their wedding day. Suddenly, several women in the congregation, one by one, stand up and join the groom, lining up beside him. The groom is forced to explain to his bewildered bride that he has given part of his heart to each of these past girlfriends.

Thus, his dating "baggage" joins the couple in their wedding vows, tarnishing the sacredness of the moment.

The rhetoric of the Damaged Goods Myth continues today. As I was writing this chapter, a host of a podcast on "biblical masculinity" with twenty thousand followers on X called college women who have casual sex "well used mattresses."[5] I don't know about you, but for me, it's hard to imagine this is what Jesus wrote in the sand when talking to a woman about her sexual sins.[6]

The message of each of these illustrations is clear: you won't be whole, clean, and pure if you have premarital sex. You will present a tarnished and ruined self on your wedding day. You won't have your whole heart to give away to your future spouse; you will be forced to present them with torn-up pieces of it instead.

Of all the purity culture myths, I believe this one is the most harmful.

> **REFLECT:** What were the subtle and not-so-subtle ways that you were taught the Damaged Goods Myth?

Personal Assessment: Does the Damaged Goods Myth Affect You?

Scoring guidelines: 0 = disagree, 1 = neutral or unsure, 2 = agree

1. You won't have your whole heart to give to your future spouse if you aren't a virgin.
2. Having premarital sex leads to sexual difficulties in your later marriage.
3. Every sexual experience you have before marriage hurts you when you marry.
4. You are no longer pure if you have premarital sex.
5. Even if it's not unforgivable, you can't "undo" losing your virginity. You are forever changed.

Add up your score. The higher the score, the greater the belief in the myth.

Discovering the Effects

No purity culture survivor is immune to the shame of the Damaged Goods Myth. Whether we're married or single, male or female, virgin or not, shame affects us all. In fact, shame is so pervasive and toxic that I've dedicated an entire chapter to address what it is and how to heal it (see chap. 12). For now, though, let's look at three specific areas affected by the Damaged Goods Myth.

Sexual Abuse

Sexual abuse survivors like Elizabeth Smart live with the shame from this myth. Shame is a common symptom of PTSD,[7] but purity culture and rape culture add the burden of religiously based shame after a sexual assault. Many women do not report their sexual assault because they feel broken or to blame, or they worry about others' reactions. One survivor shared, "I went to my church to report the abuse and was told I need to repent of it and forgive the perpetrator to be sexually healed."[8] Sadly, the response of a survivor's family or religious community can leave searing pain that outlasts the effects of the assault itself.

My heart breaks for the sexual assault survivors I have worked with as a therapist or know personally. Sexual abuse is always spiritual abuse[9] because trauma of any kind cuts to the core of who we are as embodied beings. It dishonors the image of God in us.

If you are a survivor of sexual abuse, I hope you believe in your whole being that you are not to blame for what was done to you. The shame and guilt do not belong to you; they belong to the perpetrator(s) and the systems that allowed the abuse to occur, maintained it, and hid it. Although the road to recovery from trauma can be long and painful, I believe God wants to be your partner on your healing journey. Please seek out a licensed, trauma-informed therapist[10] who can also partner with you as you work through the shame of sexual abuse.

Virginity

Purity culture is obsessed with virginity; it idolizes it. Often purity and virginity were synonymous, meaning anyone who was a virgin was pure and anyone who was not a virgin was impure. And because of sexual exceptionalism, sexual sins are the biggest sins and often seem "unforgivable."

My friend Carrie explains, "I grew up believing that sex was the one sin you couldn't undo. You can return something you stole, you can tell the truth after a lie, you can stop overeating or gossiping. But once you have sex, you're no longer a virgin. Once given away, you cannot take it back."

Dr. Richard Beck, psychologist and author of *Unclean*,[11] is an expert on the psychology of purity. One aspect of the psychology of purity is the appraisal of permanence; that is, that the loss of purity is understood to be permanent and unrecoverable. This is why the loss of sexual purity may be seen as the worst sin. It cannot be undone.

Several women I interviewed for this book noted that after their loss of virginity (whether consensual or forced) or after a painful divorce, they had multiple casual sex partners. "I felt terrible about what I was doing, and I knew I needed to stop," one woman told me. "I was out of control. But after my divorce, I felt so ashamed. I wasn't a virgin anymore, so what did it matter?"

Another example of the obsession with virginity was the hymen. The hymen, a membranous tissue that surrounds the vaginal orifice, was historically thought to indicate whether a woman was a virgin. If her hymen tore and she bled on her wedding night, she was a virgin. If her hymen was already torn or missing, she was not. However, research concludes that the hymen is not a reliable indicator of virginity, as it can become worn down through a variety of activities besides intercourse.[12] The condition of the hymen certainly should not be taken as a measure of a woman's purity, spirituality, or value as a marriage partner.

Purity culture put so much emphasis on virginity that many critics now claim virginity is a social construct perpetuated by patriarchy. Others have tried to reclaim the original definition of "virgin" as a fierce, independent woman who is not attached to a man; a woman who is "one-in-herself."[13]

Some Christians propose the concept of "secondary virginity," a state of restored purity in one's heart after premarital sex.

Co-opting language from evangelical conversion experiences, the person is a "born-again virgin" after repenting of their sexual sins.

If this concept is meaningful for you, I respect that. I believe God forgives and restores all of us. But I still worry this puts too much emphasis on virginity as one's worth. We don't need a restored hymen;[14] we need wholeness in our minds, bodies, hearts, and souls.

Whether you think virginity is a meaningless social construct or identify as a "born-again virgin," the truth is that your worth and value are not in your virginity. "Virgin" can simply be a term that refers to someone who has not had sexual intercourse; it is only when we attach virginity to one's status or worth that it becomes a tool of condemnation and judgment. Jesus does not look at our genitals to judge us; he cares for our hearts.[15] When we assign a value to "virgin" or "nonvirgin," we harm and shame others and ourselves.

Soul Ties

"Soul ties" is a particularly fear-inducing part of this myth and is especially prevalent in the Black church or Pentecostal traditions.[16] According to this teaching, having sex (or any physical intimacy) bonds you to the other person. This bond cannot be undone and could create extreme pain if you break up because it could limit your ability to bond to another partner (hence the object lesson in which tape loses its stickiness).

Shelly Donahue's national abstinence curriculum capitalized on this concept of soul ties, teaching high school students that "your kissing locks her heart to yours. Kisses are powerful. . . . Guard your kisses."[17] Further, Donahue warns that if you do have sex and then break up, you won't be able to have a healthy relationship in the future because "soul ties don't care . . . you [will be] having sex with everybody else who's having sex."[18]

As Christians, the questions this brings up are clear: Don't our souls belong to God? Isn't God bigger than any wound left over from a previous relationship or any mistake we've made? Aren't we limiting God's power when we claim he can't break supposed soul ties?

Yes, sex can create an attachment through the release of oxy-tocin.[19] Sex is intended to be a bonding, one-flesh union. It can have physical, emotional, and spiritual consequences. And yes, breakups can create emotional pain and a broken heart; I know this too well. But we are erasing the power of God to forgive and restore us to wholeness when we use fear and shame tactics that tell us what's done is permanent—that God cannot and will not restore our minds, hearts, bodies, and souls to him.

> REFLECT: Do you experience shame from past sexual abuse, loss of virginity, "soul ties," or something else?

Recovering the Truth

The truth is that no matter what you've done or what's been done to you, you are not damaged goods. You are a precious child of God, made in his image, and nothing can take away or add to your intrinsic value and worth. Only Jesus makes us whole.

Saying that Jesus makes us whole does not mean that we are little more than worms,[20] rendered pitiful and disgusting because of our sin. I believe we have both the capacity and propensity to sin *and* immeasurable worth in Christ. In a relationship with Jesus, we accept his gifts of forgiveness and restoration. No longer wounded by our past, we can choose to live integrated lives, with our body, mind, soul, and heart in alignment with God's will for us.

Being a virgin on your wedding day is not the greatest gift you can give your spouse, and it does not guarantee a successful, happy marriage or a satisfying sex life. In the same way, not being a virgin does not mean you are "less than" and unworthy of a loving, godly spouse and a blessed marriage or sex life. No matter your sins, sexual or otherwise, you are a human—one in need of forgiveness and grace.[21] Thankfully, we serve a God who offers both. And if God can forgive our sins, we can (and must) forgive others and ourselves in the same way.

If you have made sexual choices that don't align with God's truth, you may choose to ask him for forgiveness or for help forgiving yourself. Perhaps, like me, you need to repent and forgive yourself for judging others. Or you may want to forgive yourself for teaching purity culture to your own kids. You may have others in your life you want to forgive—your spouse, past partners, your parents and pastors who taught you purity culture, or even an abuse perpetrator.

If this feels complicated or difficult to you, please know you're not alone. In Christian settings, forgiveness has often been used to manipulate victims. But that isn't the way it should be used in your life. True forgiveness cannot be coerced or forced by anyone else. It does *not* have to mean reconciliation or giving up pursuing justice.[22] You make the decision if or when you are ready to forgive. And when you do, let it help you walk forward toward your own healing.

The REACH model of forgiveness,[23] developed by psychology professor Dr. Everett Worthington, is meaningful to me in my personal life and professional work. Perhaps it may help you as you work toward forgiveness in your own way. The steps to REACH are *recall* the hurt, have *empathy* for yourself or others, offer the *altruistic* gift of forgiveness, *commit* to the forgiveness process, and *hold* on to forgiveness. Walk through these steps at your own pace in your own timing. Allow God to work in your heart to move you toward forgiveness for yourself or for others. And remember, ultimately, forgiveness is a gift you give yourself—a decision to set yourself free from shame and blame you were never meant to carry.

You are more than your sexual past—your experience or inexperience. Your identity is not in your virginity or loss of virginity. Your worthiness is not determined by what you wear. Your value is not diminished by what you have done. Your wholeness is not broken by what's been done to you. Jesus says you are worthy; the fact that you are made in his image gives you value. And your salvation through Christ is what makes you whole—that and that alone.

The Damaged Goods Myth is the toxic mold of purity culture, contaminating the beauty of God's heart for sex and feeding our shame. But Jesus's offer of forgiveness, wholeness, and restoration is available to all of us.

Take Elizabeth Smart for example. She is now a speaker, writer, and advocate for child safety. She continues to practice her religion and professes a strong faith in God. And she is a proponent of sex education, giving youth "choices, skills, and permission to fight back, to know that you are of value. . . . You always have value and nothing can change that."[24]

Tools for the Journey

Nonjudgment

As Christians we are commanded not to judge.[25] In DBT, we also practice the skill of nonjudgment:[26] to avoid labeling something as bad or good, wrong or right. You'll notice you're judging when, instead of the facts, you move into ranking, name-calling, or labeling. Judgments add fuel to the fire of our emotions, leading to more intense emotional pain and shame.

Instead, the practice of nonjudgment teaches us to notice but not evaluate; acknowledge differences but not judge them. We describe our feelings as just feelings, recognizing that they are not facts. We observe and acknowledge the facts (the who, what, where, when), separating them from judgments.

Change the following judgments into nonjudgments. I've done the first one for you.

- I was pure when I got married, but my husband wasn't. → I had never had sexual intercourse before we got married. My husband had.
- I'm a failure. → _____
  _____
- I'm a bad Christian for not forgiving. → _____
  _____
- We have "soul ties" to our past partners. → _____
  _____
- I am worthless and used up. → _____
  _____
- No one is going to want me. → _____
  _____

Thought Record, Part 4

In past exercises, you described your beliefs from purity culture, analyzed the truth, and observed how these beliefs affect your emotions and body.

Now it's time for the final thought record. In part 4, you will put everything together, copying down the old beliefs, emotions, and behaviors as well as the new beliefs you've already listed, then discovering how those new beliefs create new emotions and behavior. We are integrating your mind, body, and heart so you not only *think* this new belief but also *feel* it.

Complete the thought record, then end in prayer if you are comfortable. Ask God to help you fight against the myths of purity culture that have kept you captive. Ask him to reveal his truth and make it real to you in your whole being.

Example

Old Belief	Old Emotions and Behavior	New Belief	New Emotions	Behavior (Body Sensations + Actions)
I am damaged goods because I did not save myself for marriage.	Shame, hopeless Keep my past a secret, blame my current struggles on my past	I am forgiven and restored by God.	Relief, hopeful	Relaxed shoulders, deeper breathing I want to share openly with people I trust.

Reconstructing Faith and Sexuality

8

Healing Your Faith

Blessed are we, receiving the gift of doubt, for we trust that it is a doorway, freeing us to become all that we could not otherwise have known.

  Kate Bowler and Jessica Richie, *The Lives We Actually Have*[1]

In summer 2019, Joshua Harris announced his divorce from his wife of nineteen years. In the next breath, he announced his deconversion from the Christian faith. In an Instagram post, Harris shared that he had "undergone a massive shift in regard to my faith in Jesus. The popular phrase for this is 'deconstruction,' the biblical phrase is 'falling away.' By all the measurements that I have for defining a Christian, I am not a Christian."[2] No one who grew up in purity culture could forget Harris's name. His book *I Kissed Dating Goodbye* became *the* Christian cult classic that defined courtship culture and furthered extreme purity ideals. His second release, *Boy Meets Girl*, described his courtship process with his wife[3] and promised that following this method of biblical courtship—including avoiding dating, being alone with the opposite sex, or any physical contact before marriage—would lead to a satisfying Christian marriage.

I want to call Harris the "father" of the evangelical purity movement, but at only twenty-three at the time his book was published, he was hardly old or wise enough to earn that title. He was both a victim and a perpetrator of the shaming and legalistic ideals of purity culture. In 2018, he repented of his role as perpetrator, releasing a statement that denounced the principles in his book and pleaded with his publisher to take the book out of print.[4] He later participated in the 2019 documentary *I Survived I Kissed Dating Goodbye* with filmmaker Jessica Van Der Wyngaard in an "apologies tour" of interviews with pastors, authors, and readers of his book.[5]

Deconstruction.

Disentangling.

Dismantling.

Renegotiating your faith.

Regardless of what you call it, rethinking your beliefs can be a disconcerting and uncomfortable experience. And it almost always goes hand in hand with recovering from purity culture.

Harris's deconversion story remains one of the most popular in evangelical news. It sent ripples through Christian media, but it also deeply affected survivors of purity culture. To see the poster boy of the movement that caused us years of shame, confusion, and agony publicly denounce his former beliefs and his faith was a jarring experience. It once again caused us to question the credibility of purity culture—if one of the "fathers" of the movement is getting divorced and walking away from his faith, where does that leave us? Even in his exit, Harris's influence on evangelical culture continues. His deconstruction played a major role in the subsequent wave of deconstruction and deconversion stories we have seen over the last few years.

But not everyone's deconstruction has to look like this. Yes, some people may deconstruct "all the way into atheism,"[6] and I understand the fear of the slippery slope of rethinking one's beliefs. But many of us who grew up in purity culture deconstruct because we want to hold on to our faith. We want to come to a place of peace and acceptance in our beliefs and identity as Christians. Fortunately, I believe we can heal from purity culture while maintaining our faith. We can dismantle the myths and replace them with truth that is grounded in theology and reason. And we can come out with a stronger, deeper, and more nuanced faith in the end.

Approaches to Deconstruction

As an infant, my friend's son began experiencing severe health and developmental problems. What started as chronic poor sleeping, then food allergies, and then sensory processing difficulties spiraled into more health challenges and treatments with expensive specialists. My friend and her husband were at a loss to what was going on with their son and how to help him.

Eventually they discovered they had a proliferation of black mold in their home. Hidden behind the walls that held framed photos of their wedding and their son lay toxic, carcinogenic mold. They immediately vacated their house, disposed of 80 percent of their possessions, and wore hazmat suits to reenter the house. They hired an expert team to remediate the house and remove the mold, taking it down to the studs and floorboards to clear it of the fungus.

The process of deconstructing our faith is much like this. For some, their faith is like a moldy house, and deconstruction is remediating that house. In order to heal, you have to take your faith all the way down to the studs—all the way to its foundation—to remediate and extract the toxic mold. Then, you bring in new building materials to replace the damaged ones. You rebuild the home so you can reinhabit it.

For some, purity culture took up a large room in their house and this means the entire footprint of the house needs to change. For others, it might be a less invasive remodel, maintaining the home's basic footprint and continuing to live in certain rooms while you renovate other ones.

Or your deconstruction might be like a complete restoration of an old historic home built in your childhood. You have to add in new technology, new plumbing or electrical wiring, and make it function the way you need it to in your adulthood.

And still for others, that old home proves to be uninhabitable, leading to the complete razing of the structure itself with a wrecking ball. You may walk away from your house and choose to start over again from the ground up somewhere else.

The "wrecking ball" approach is what I think many Christians fear will be the result of any deconstruction. It's the approach they warn us away from and judge others in taking. But remember, this is only one approach to deconstruction. Many other Christians choose to keep the foundation of their faith or the basic blueprint of their house but remediate, restore, or remodel the parts they've discovered to be toxic.

My friend Tim Whitaker of The New Evangelicals online community[7] describes deconstruction as exiting the basement of a home (fundamentalism) to explore the other rooms in the house (other Christian traditions and denominations). He acknowledges that some people may find it necessary to leave the house altogether—to leave Christianity or religion behind. But for others, there are still many more floors and rooms to explore than the religious tradition of their youth.

Personally, I define deconstruction as the process by which we examine our previously assumed beliefs to discern which ones are truth and which ones are lies. It's been helpful for me to think of deconstruction as falling along the continuum of home repairs: from a basic remodel, to a modern restoration, to a complete remediation, to a total razing of the house. And because purity culture becomes so entangled with our faith, I think it's impossible to heal from it without going through some type of faith deconstruction—which, contrary to what some may say, is actually a good thing.

> REFLECT: What does deconstruction mean to you? Where do you think you are in your own faith deconstruction?

Faith Development

Several authors and theologians have examined how our faith develops over time and how a crisis of faith can be a good thing.[8] I've found psychologist James Fowler's theory of spiritual development to be helpful in explaining the stages we experience as our faith matures.[9]

For our purposes, we'll dive in at stage 3, the Synthetic-Conventional Stage, where most people tend to remain. They adopt an all-encompassing belief system and have a hard time seeing outside of it. People give authority to individuals or groups that represent their beliefs and look to an institution (such as the church) or leaders (such as parents and pastors) to tell them what to believe. It is common for people in stage 3 to feel deeply threatened when others question their beliefs. They feel most comfortable with concrete thinking. Because our brains don't develop abstract thinking until adolescence or later, they tend to prefer black-and-white answers.

Stage 4, the Individuative-Reflective Stage, often begins in young adulthood. Here, people start to see outside their box and realize there are other belief systems. According to Fowler, they begin to critically examine their beliefs and may become disillusioned with their former faith. There is a greater awareness of the complexities of faith and inconsistencies in doctrine in this stage. To those in stage 3, this exploration can look like those in stage 4 have "backslid" when in reality they have actually moved forward.[10]

Read that again aloud.

Did you experience the big aha moment that I did? As I revisit this theory now, I can see how stage 4 represents the deconstruction process.

Integrating Fowler's theory of spiritual development with other theories of development from psychology,[11] I can also see that each stage of faith involves a developmental task or "crisis" that we must resolve to progress to the next stage. For example, one crisis of adolescence and young adulthood is to decide who we are and what we believe. These crises serve as catalysts to move us along to greater maturity. They also cause internal conflict and emotional distress, which can force us to reevaluate our beliefs and choices, explore our values, and commit to our goals.

The problem with a legalistic faith system such as purity culture is that there is little room to explore our beliefs in such a "crisis." The emphasis is on conformity to right thinking and right behavior, not on fostering a personal faith. But when we are not allowed or encouraged to challenge our beliefs or deconstruct our faith, there is no "crisis" that pushes us onto the next stage. We remain stagnant at earlier stages of development.[12] When we don't explore or question the values and beliefs we've been taught or consider any alternatives, we experience what one theory calls "identity foreclosure." This is when our commitment to an identity or belief system is predetermined by religion, family, culture, or community.[13] We passively accept the script handed to us by others.

It takes both a crisis and what psychology calls a "commitment" to a set of beliefs or values in order to achieve a solid identity or a solid faith. *Deconstruction is the crisis, and reconstruction is the commitment.* Author Sarah Bessey says, "We have to deconstruct in order to reconstruct something worth living for in the next stages of our spiritual development."[14]

Deconstruction is therefore a developmentally normal, even healthy process in which we explore, critically evaluate, and analyze the beliefs we have been taught. We can try out new beliefs or faith practices that we may not have been exposed to, and we can examine the consequences of our beliefs to see if they bear good fruit.[15]

We must not be afraid of this process of crisis and commitment. Deconstruction doesn't have to mean the end of one's faith (although for some people, it might). Like a refining fire with gold, it can ultimately render a faith that is more solid and strong but also malleable.

> **REFLECT**: Do you agree that deconstruction is a normal and healthy process in faith development? How does knowing stages 3 and 4 of faith development help you understand yourself and others better?

Religious Trauma

According to Dr. Laura Anderson, therapist and author of *When Religion Hurts You*, religious trauma is a legitimate form of trauma caused by abuse that occurs under the guise of religion.[16] The Religious Trauma Institute defines religious trauma as "the physical, emotional, or psychological response to religious beliefs, practices, or structures that is experienced by an individual as overwhelming or disruptive and has lasting adverse effects on a person's physical, mental, social, emotional, or spiritual well-being."[17] Religious trauma can occur when we struggle to leave behind a set of high-control beliefs, such as purity culture, and its symptoms are similar to that of complex PTSD.

The research by the Religious Trauma Institute expands the broader research on Adverse Childhood Experiences (ACEs)[18] to define Adverse Religious Experiences (AREs). AREs are "any experience of a religious belief, practice, or structure that undermines an individual's sense of safety or autonomy and/or negatively impacts their physical, social, emotional, relational, or psychological well-being."[19]

Anderson is quick to note that "neither religion nor its practices and beliefs are inherently traumatic; rather, the effect of an experience, belief, or practice on an individual is specific to that person."[20] Remember, trauma is not the event itself but our physiological and emotional reaction to the event. Trauma is subjective, meaning that two people can experience the same stressor but have different reactions to it. One may integrate the experience into their life or belief system in a fairly straightforward way while the other may feel overwhelmed and get "stuck" processing the experience.

The nuance of religious trauma is evident in purity culture: some people develop a trauma response in their bodies, and some don't. And as I learned when I started providing coaching for purity culture recovery, it is a painful road to walk. It's not enough to cognitively leave the myths of purity culture behind. The messages still live in our bodies, hearts, and souls. We need holistic, integrated healing to move forward.

Anderson, a religious and sexual trauma survivor herself, redefines healing as an ongoing process ("I am living in a healing body") rather than an endpoint ("I am healed").[21] Healing religious trauma is just like this. It's a complex process that may involve professional help, a supportive community to journey with, and safe people and places to process your faith experiences.

For some of my clients with religious trauma, leaving their church and taking a step back from all spiritual practices have been necessary to their healing. Many of them reach the point where they are ready to reengage practices that feel comforting and life-giving to them. Many also take the brave step to return to a church or find healthier spiritual communities to be a part of.

If you have religious trauma, I don't know what your healing process will look like or where you will end up. But I hope you find the support from and connection to others, yourself, and God that you need to heal.

> REFLECT: Do you have religious trauma from purity culture or another adverse religious experience? What support or resources do you need to begin healing?

Finding Peace in Deconstruction

With so many opinions about what deconstruction is and how Christians should do it "right," I hesitate to offer a step-by-step process. Deconstruction is not linear, and healing your faith does not look the same for everyone. As someone who finds goodness, truth, and beauty in the Christian story and a life lived in relationship with Jesus, I hope your story ends with reconstructing your faith.

But I can't predict or promise that.

When I work with clients walking through deconstruction, I find it helpful to focus less on an end goal—a clear goalpost of "what my faith will look like in the end"—and more on what is in our control. What can we do to move through this process without fixating on an end result or destination? There are four elements that have been valuable to me and my clients as we navigate the uncertain terrain of deconstruction and reconstruction together. I hope they serve you in the same way.

Examining Your Beliefs

This is the work of deconstruction: examining your previously held beliefs to discern what can be discarded and what can be retained. What is still there as you remodel or remediate your house?

To avoid overwhelming yourself in this process, think about examining one room at a time. You're not tearing the house down; you're leaving the foundation of the house intact. After all, you can't remodel the bathroom layout if there is no flooring or walls! Consider this an invitation to explore what is still there—a positive attribute of God or a belief that still makes sense.[22] For example, holding on to my belief that God is loving and cares for his children provided me a secure base to explore my questions about why this loving God would allow suffering.

There may also be rooms you "close off" and choose not to inhabit while you work on the rest of your house. The theology of creationism vs. science, for example, may feel like too much right now as you try to make sense of other things. Know that it's okay to choose not to enter a room but to leave it in a state of disarray as you live in other parts of the house for a while.

Examining your beliefs allows you the chance to get down to the details in each room. It gives you an opportunity to explore and discern what was biblical and what was cultural, what was wrongly interpreted, or what other sources of knowledge you can integrate. So instead of demolishing the entire structure, consider taking apart one room at a time in an effort to examine your beliefs.

Accepting Doubts

The bad news: deconstruction does not provide all the answers.

The good news: the healing is found in accepting the "not knowing."

Asking questions with curiosity, not being afraid to challenge your beliefs, and making space for new answers are part of deconstruction. But so is accepting that you will always live with doubts, ambiguity, and not knowing. Along the way, we may have to grieve. One of my clients said, "I miss the ignorance I used to have." For me, I grieve the loss of certainty.

Conservative Christianity often goes too far when it says "This is *the* truth. This is the one truth for everyone, and everyone who does not believe this is out!" But progressive Christianity often goes too far when it says, "This is *my* truth. This is one of many truths, and everyone can believe what they want!" Yes, there are absolute truths in Christianity; it's hard to see how we could disagree on the essentials but all claim a common identity. But there are a lot more gray areas than purity culture and fundamentalism led us to believe.

I strive to make peace with the fact that though I may disagree with my sister or brother in Christ on nonessentials, we can both be faithful Christians trying our best to love and follow Jesus. Dialectical thinking (both/and) helps foster this attitude, as does a radical acceptance that on this Earth, I will never have all the answers to my questions or arrive at a place of full understanding. So yes, ask the questions, do the exploring, keep examining and testing your beliefs. *And also*, find a way to accept that in some areas you will not find the certainty or absolutism you thought you would. Make peace with your evolving faith.

Finding Safe Community

Deconstruction is a disorienting and lonely experience. Because our religious beliefs can form our identity, rethinking our beliefs often means a total identity shift. And along with losing our identity comes a loss of community.

Because we need relationships and connection to survive as humans, the threat of losing that is a threat to our very survival. Anderson helpfully points out that ostracism from religious community is one of the reasons people don't "just leave" a toxic belief system.[23]

In 2021, my husband and I made the decision to leave the church we were members of. Since attending that church, we had gotten married, had our first child, and dedicated her in the church. Many of our friends and our biggest support system came from that church. We met with our pastor, and he was gracious and understanding of our reasons for leaving. Although we had overall positive experiences there for many years, we could no longer tolerate the cognitive dissonance of being egalitarians in a complementarian environment.

We have been blessed to transition to a mainline Protestant church that supports women pastors and gender equality. But the loss of our first church community was painful. We felt like we had no community to help us welcome our second child. There were no "new baby casseroles" like there were for our first. As I write this, two years after we made the decision to leave, the sting of lack of belonging still sits in my throat.

The decision to leave or find a spiritual community is a personal one, and my experience is not prescriptive. Some people choose to lean into their church, even if they don't agree with all the church's beliefs or practices. There can be value in committing to a church community and working through or allowing for differences. Some might stay in their church to try to make changes internally. Others may find it necessary to step away from or take a break from organized religion for a time. Some people decide not to return; they find community in other ways. But many Christians find flourishing in safe faith-based spaces. A change of denomination or type of church can be a cleansing breath to the Christian who is suffocating in high-control religion.

As you walk this road yourself, look for a safe community to walk with you.

Being with God

Faith is a relationship with God, not just a set of rules to live by or beliefs to subscribe to. Growing up, I heard that "it's a relationship, not religion," but I rarely saw this practically lived out. The focus was always on legalism—right beliefs and right behavior—not a genuine, personal relationship with Jesus.

Legalism is an attempt to control the behavior of others by restricting their choices or causing them to live in fear.[24] We also use legalism to attempt to control God through our choices, creating an obligation for God to reward us (the if-then formula of purity culture). But when any relationship is characterized by fear and control, it is not a relationship centered on love.[25]

The solution to this fixation on doing the right things and knowing the right things is *being* with God. Podcaster and author Skye Jethani differentiates between life *over* God, in which we're trying to control outcomes, and life *with* God, a communion with him.

Cultivating a life with God allows us to experience his goodness and character so that we begin to trust him regardless of our circumstances. "That's what the Christian life is," says Jethani, "it's not controlling the world or God to get the outcome I want but trusting in the goodness of God because we know who he is. Rather than trying to control God even through righteous obedience to biblical commands, [we] cultivate a life *with* God."[26]

As we find peace in our faith journey, may we rest in being with God.

When I asked my online community what helped them get through their deconstruction, they echoed these themes in their answers:

- "Honesty with myself and others. Being vulnerable with the right people."
- "Seeing in Scripture how God honors those who wrestle with their faith."
- "Knowing that my deconstruction is an attempt to know God better."
- "Trusting myself and God enough to ask questions and know I am able to embrace the answers."
- "Knowing that God doesn't expect us to get everything right."

Still, I recognize that for many in this Christian space, there is much fear surrounding the deconstruction of any part of our faith. One writer warns against faith deconstruction, stating that "the type of faith [you] end up embracing almost never resembles the Christianity [you] formerly knew."[27] To that, I say: *good*. Because

I don't want the Christianity I formerly knew—the one that relied on spiritual platitudes, empty promises of sexual prosperity, black-and-white beliefs, and fear, judgment, and condemnation of anyone who looks or thinks differently. And I don't want that for you either!

I am still a Christian. You may still identify as one too. But I have not finished deconstructing and reconstructing my faith. I have not "arrived." Instead, if my faith looks different than it used to and my beliefs have evolved from the legalism of my childhood, if I still maintain love for God and love for my neighbors, and if I am living in relationship with God, then I find peace in my faith journey. Perhaps instead of saying we have "healed our faith," we can say we are "living with a healing faith."

Tools for the Journey

Acceptance and Change

In chapter 1, I introduced you to dialectical thinking. In DBT, the main dialectic is a balance of acceptance and change. These seem like opposites. But we have to first accept and admit our reality before we can change it. Acceptance in this context does not mean approval or giving up. It is simply an acknowledgment of what is and accepting help to change it.

When it comes to your faith journey, what do you need to accept? What needs to change? How can you strive to maintain a healthy balance of both?

Read through some of these examples of acceptance and change. Then journal about your own faith journey and how you can apply this dialectic.

- I accept my past, *and* I can critically examine what beliefs I want to carry into my future.
- I make peace with my doubts, *and* I continue to ask questions.
- I grieve that my faith doesn't look the same, *and* I commit to continue reconstructing it.
- I accept that I will always have questions, *and* I search for sources of truth.
- I can speak up about my new beliefs, *and* I accept that people have a right to choose how they believe.
- I can advocate for change in the Church, *and* I acknowledge that the system and leaders may not change.

9

Reconstructing Your Sexual Ethic

Instead of feeling like a victim to Christianity or purity culture, I feel complete freedom. I have ownership over my sexual desire and feel empowered that the God of the universe cares about me as a whole person and is an advocate for my personal agency. I am shame free, knowing my sexual desire belongs to me. . . . I feel connected to a deeper story woven throughout the pages of Scripture.

Kat Harris, *Sexless in the City*[1]

In 2008, a young and squeaky-clean Hannah Montana–era Miley Cyrus confessed she wore a purity ring. "Even at my age, a lot of girls are starting to fall [in love], and I think if [staying a virgin] is a commitment girls make, that's great."[2]

Seven years later, in a 2015 interview after her now infamous "twerking" MTV Video Music Awards performance, Cyrus stated, "I am literally open to every single thing that is consenting and doesn't involve an animal and everyone is of age. Everything that's legal, I'm down with."[3]

Cyrus's transformation sums up the massive pendulum swing in American culture's sexual ethic. An ethic is a philosophy that guides your life choices and may stretch to accommodate new experiences or knowledge in your life. It is more encompassing than a belief, value, or moral, although it contains all those elements. A sexual ethic comprises your moral principles about sexuality and sexual behavior, what you consider to be appropriate.

So if I asked you to explain your sexual ethic, what would you say? Like most people coming out of purity culture, you may be confused about your sexual ethic beyond "because the Bible says so." You may question what the Bible says (or doesn't say) about sex. You know purity culture didn't work, but hook-up culture may not feel right to you either. You wonder if there's a middle path—one in which you can explore different beliefs, examine sources of truth, and arrive at your own sexual ethic with clarity, confidence, and integrity to your faith.

Reconstructing your sexual ethic is difficult work, but it's a necessary part of healing from purity culture. Still, some of my coaching clients are reluctant to engage this process. After all, if they are married and only having sex with their spouse, what does it matter?

I would argue it matters a great deal. It's important to be able to articulate what we believe and why. First of all, if you have children or plan to, you will need to know your own beliefs and values to guide what and how you teach your children. Second, overcoming shame requires us to make choices in alignment with our values—and we must know what those values are in order to align our behavior with them. And third, reconstructing your ethic is empowering. It is a journey of critical thinking and self-discovery to formulate a *deeper why* for your beliefs.

My hope is that you'll let this chapter be your guide for *how* to figure out your beliefs without prescribing *what* to believe. That way, you are not just taking what I or any other author or expert say is true and adopting our sexual ethic. You are doing the work of thinking through *your* personal sexual ethic, one that is truly authentic and meaningful for you and that you can defend with more than a trite "because the Bible says so." You *can* do this work. And you don't have to do it alone. Let's walk through it together.

Approaches to Sexual Ethics

As we've seen, a belief in premarital sexual abstinence has been widely preached for most of history (especially for women) and is present in other ethnic cultures and religious traditions.

While many still uphold this ethic today, culturally we're experiencing shifts. Today's dominant sexual ethic—what I call an *ethic of consent*—is relatively new, as recent as the twenty-first century.

An Ethic of Consent

Especially after the #MeToo movement, consent became a hot topic of conversation—and for good reasons. Consent is a necessary ingredient to a healthy sexual ethic. Yet both the dominant culture and evangelicalism have often been guilty of ignoring it. Patriarchy considers women property, the Gatekeepers Myth makes women responsible for men's sexuality, and the Bible tells spouses not to deprive each other, so why is consent even needed?

I applaud the increased attention to consent and consent-based sexual education, and I want to state this clearly here: sex without consent is rape. Despite the promises of purity culture, sex in marriage can be impure if it does not include consent and mutual respect. Those of us disentangling our sexual ethic from purity culture need to know this is true for us—married or single.

Some Christian scholars have argued that consent is a natural outflow of human dignity based on the belief that we are created in the image of God. Beth Felker Jones contends that Christianity "invented consensual sex when it developed a sexual ethics that assumed that God empowers individuals with freedom."[4] Indeed, enthusiastic, uncoerced consent, freely given out of each partner's agency and autonomy, is the foundation of a healthy sexual ethic.

But it is not enough.

The ethic of consent says that any sexual activity—as long as it is legal and agreed upon—is ethical. Many critics of the purity movement now tout the ethic of consent as an alternative to a traditional sexual ethic. Along with consent, they also espouse the values of authenticity, personal expression, freedom, and lack of self-restraint. This attitude toward sexuality has been branded "sex positivity." It's not necessarily wrong.

But still, it is not enough.

Rethinking Sex by journalist Christine Emba analyzes how an ethic solely based on consent falls short, even from a secular perspective. Without invoking theology, Emba dismantles an ethic of consent, demonstrating that consensual sex can still be damaging to an individual, to their partner, and to society.[5] "Even consensual encounters can fail to respect the profundity that we sense sex holds," Emba explains. "Consent doesn't address the gravity of what sex is or how it affects us."[6]

Consent reduces the most intimate act imaginable into little more than a legal agreement. What this ethic fails to consider is that you can objectify a person and use them for your own sexual gratification even with their consent. As Zachary Wagner bluntly states, "Just because it isn't rape doesn't mean it isn't dehumanizing."[7] Examples abound of high-profile men—both in Christian culture and in Hollywood—whose actions may have been legal but nonetheless failed to respect the feelings and dignity of their partners.[8]

In other words, consent makes sex legal, but it doesn't make it ethical.[9] Consent is a floor, not a ceiling.[10] And for Christians, consent alone fails to meet God's heart for sex to be holy, sacred, and covenantal.

We can indeed consent to something that is not in our best interests. It is possible we don't realize what could harm ourselves or others. Or maybe we knowingly participate in the harm (I am thinking of every time I eat fried food, knowing my stomach will not like it hours later). Many of the women I interviewed for this book mentioned how self-destructive casual sex was to them; they knew it was dehumanizing, but they plunged forward anyway.

One of my most illuminating coaching sessions was with Naomi, who described herself as an atheist. Naomi told me that she left the purity culture and legalistic faith of her youth for modern hook-up culture. Naomi admitted, "Hook-up culture felt just as disembodied and incongruent from my values as purity culture."

She explained that the fatalistic "you only live once, so you might as well have fun" mindset of hook-up culture did not lead to "sexual liberation" and fulfillment. "Believing that everything is meaningless kept me just as disconnected from my body and from relationships as purity culture did. I had to turn off the meaning of sex to avoid being devastated in hook-up culture. In sex, I had to keep my mind and body separate and keep my emotions at arms' length."

Now, there is a difference between casual hook-ups and loving, committed sexual relationships that can and do happen outside of marriage. Certainly, there is a spectrum when it comes to sexual ethics. But my critique here is of the ethic of consent—the dominant approach in both secular culture and progressive Christianity—that deems any sexual behavior acceptable as long as it is legal and doesn't appear to hurt others.

An Ethic of Shame

Purity culture is an ethic of shame. And while purity culture as we knew it seems to have faded into the background, a version of it is still alive today in more subtle forms. "Purity culture 2.0"[11] is a repackaging of the original purity culture of the 1990s to 2000s, but this time, it comes with a twist. Now, abstinence until marriage isn't just biblical; it's reframed as self-respect and female empowerment.[12] A woman choosing abstinence under this new version isn't being controlled; she's making a countercultural choice because she knows what she deserves.

But even in this, the very myths we're trying to dismantle are still just below the surface. For example, purity culture 2.0 includes:

- Christian influencers bragging about their wedding night (the Flipped Switch Myth) and tattooing "waiting for marriage" on their body (the Spiritual Barometer Myth)[13]

- Language such as "generosity and hospitality"—give and take—and an emphasis on the male "sacrifice" during orgasm[14] (the Gatekeepers Myth)
- Stating that the sole purpose of dating is marriage, and that dating is practice for divorce[15] (courtship culture and the Damaged Goods Myth)
- Implying that if two people are Jesus followers, the marriage is guaranteed to work out[16] (the Fairy-Tale Myth)
- An influencer embroidering the phrase "Worth the Wait" into her wedding veil and cheering, "I'm having sex for the first time tonight!" at her wedding reception[17] (the Fairy-Tale and Flipped Switch Myths)

As I've made clear, I respect the choice to wait until marriage to have sex. I believe this choice honors God's heart for sex. I don't agree with the repackaging of the myths of purity culture that idolize virginity, promise blessings of a happy marriage and pleasurable sex if you abstain, and make sex largely about men's sexual needs. This still feels like virtue signaling that elevates the worth and identity of those waiting for marriage above those who do not.

What's interesting is that some critics of purity culture may say that my own beliefs represent purity culture 2.0 since I still hold to an ethic of premarital sexual abstinence. But the belief itself is not what makes something purity culture. It is the myths, the false promises, and the if-then formulas that coerce abstinence out of shame and fear. When an ethic of abstinence is born out of your own values with careful consideration of theology, then it is not purity culture.

It is the sexual ethic you have reconstructed for yourself.

REFLECT: What is appealing about an ethic of consent? What about an ethic of shame? Where do each of these ethics fall short?

A Values-Congruent Ethic

There is an alternative to the ethic of consent and the ethic of shame, and it can be found in the middle path: a values-congruent sexual ethic. A common misconception is that the only alternative to purity culture is an ethic of consent, but that's not accurate. And as we continue to unpack shame in the pages ahead, shame is not resolved by discarding your beliefs as if you're throwing off a heavy winter coat for the liberation of spring. Shame is resolved by living from a values-congruent ethic—by having alignment between your beliefs, values, and behavior. And reconstructing your sexual ethic involves determining those values and making choices aligned with them.

Many critics who reject a traditional Christian sexual ethic also preach an ethic based on critical reflection of one's values.[18] Where we may differ is in what those values are grounded. For many Christians, like myself, a values-congruent ethic may continue to be an ethic of premarital sexual abstinence and sexual faithfulness in marriage. My theological belief is that sex is an expression of the covenant of marriage. I continue to be captivated by God's pursuit of his people, his unconditional love, and his covenant with us—traits that can be symbolized and celebrated in healthy marital sexual intimacy. My values are birthed out of my relationship with God; I cannot separate my values from my theology.

We don't have to continue to perpetuate purity culture 2.0. But we also don't have to discard deeply held values if we still believe them to be true and good. As you reconstruct your sexual ethic, my hope is that you will critically examine your beliefs to discern the will of God,[19] and that you'll let that inform the values you hold and the ethic you choose.

Here's the truth: the middle path is the harder way. It's much easier to have a fixed prescription of what's right or wrong, good or bad.[20] It's the difference between following a step-by-step recipe in a cookbook versus experimenting in the kitchen to come up with a dish that is uniquely yours. Neither side of the pendulum—an ethic of consent or an ethic of shame—is liberating. Both are following a set of rules prescribed by someone else. And neither prioritizes the critical thinking and personal evaluation needed for a robust sexual ethic.

Reconstructing Your Sexual Ethic

When content creator and podcaster Kat Harris found herself twenty-seven and living alone in New York City, she realized that after years of "being on [her] virgin high horse," her virginity was now "hanging on by a lacy thread."[21] Harris recognized that her high school commitment to virginity couldn't sustain her, so she began a multiyear search for answers about sexual desire, singleness, and the way of Jesus.

In sum, she set out to do the painstaking work of reconstructing her sexual ethic.

I hope we can do the same together here. Whether you have never rethought your morals about sex or you feel confident in your carefully reconstructed sexual ethic, I invite you to consider the following steps on your path of healing from purity culture.

Find Sources of Truth

When my Purity Culture Recovery Coaching clients are confused about their sexual ethic, instead of giving them answers or prescribing my own, I encourage them to search for sources of truth.

Wesley's Quadrilateral[22] is a helpful concept to identify and search for sources of truth. According to this method, there are four sources of truth and authority when we are trying to make sense of how to live as Christians: Scripture, Christian tradition, reason, and experience. Let's look briefly at each and consider how it may guide you in reconstructing your own sexual ethic.

Scripture. The historic Christian understanding of Scripture is that it is infallible (trustworthy and won't let us down) and authoritative (providing guidance and correction). "All Scripture is inspired by God and is useful to teach us what is true and to make us realize what is wrong in our lives. It corrects us when we are wrong and teaches us to do what is right."[23] In Wesley's

Quadrilateral, Scripture is the highest and final source of truth, the one on which the other three pieces stand.

For those reconstructing their sexual ethic, it can be helpful to look at the whole story of Scripture—the creation, fall, redemption, and restoration story that unfolds over both the Old and New Testaments. This helps us avoid "proof texting," pulling individual verses out of context. Because (spoiler alert!) there is no single verse that says, "Thou shall not have premarital sex." If we are looking for such a verse to blatantly tell us what is and isn't wrong when it comes to sex and our sexual ethic, we will miss the larger biblical vision for sex.

We have all seen examples of Scripture being misinterpreted or misapplied when the original language, purpose, audience, culture, and genre of the book are ignored. In addition, the Bible is not a textbook, sex manual, or relationship self-help book. Therefore, while Scripture is an undeniable source of truth for Christians, we must consider the context and integrate it with other sources to craft a strong sexual ethic.

Christian tradition. Christian tradition looks at the history of our faith, doctrine, and early church fathers and mothers. The classical statements of the Christian faith, such as the Apostles' Creed, can illuminate the work of interpreting Scripture.

Christian tradition is not foolproof though. Early church leaders were fallible humans too. Many sins, such as slavery, were committed in the name of Christian tradition because "that's how it's always been." In humility, we must be attentive to the ways we have misinterpreted or misapplied Scripture and hurt fellow image bearers. We can consider the accepted beliefs of thousands of years of Christian tradition while also applying them in light of the way the Holy Spirit is working in the global church today.

Reason. Our intellect, rational and logical thinking, and critical analysis are gifts from God. He gave us minds to ponder, to analyze, and to come to conclusions. We can use scientific research to see, for example, that there is a correlation between the myths of purity culture, lower marital satisfaction, and higher rates of sexual pain.[24] We can examine the outcomes of abstinence-only education and virginity pledges to prove that they were unsuccessful (see chap. 2). We can also see that early or unsafe sexual activity leads to undesirable outcomes.

The Bible cautions us to "lean not on [our] own understanding" but "in all [our] ways [to] submit to him, and he will make [our] paths straight."[25] But the passage does not say to *ignore* our own reason and understanding. "It merely indicates that we should ask God for help as we seek to use our brains and not to overestimate our ability to comprehend truth or reality fully or perfectly."[26]

Yes, our wisdom is finite. Our minds can tell us thoughts that are untrue. But we can still value the role of intellect and approach it with humility when it comes to reconstructing our sexual ethic.

Experience. Personal, lived experience and observations of others in our daily life are also valuable sources of information. We can ask questions such as, "What does my life tell me about sexual morals?" or "What do I see around me?"

For example, my personal experience showed me that the Fairy-Tale Myth was untrue. Your experience may be different. You may observe or be in loving, committed sexual relationships outside of marriage and wonder how that influences your sexual ethic.

Yes, experience is a valuable teacher, but we have to be careful not to apply our own experience to everyone. Many of my online community members have been hurt by well-meaning friends saying, "Purity culture didn't harm me! How could it be bad?" This invalidates and dismisses the lived experiences of some purity culture survivors.

Our experience can give us both valuable insights *and* biases. It can be a great teacher *and* leave us with blind spots to the truth. We must find the balance of both as we incorporate it into our personal sexual ethic.

> REFLECT: What sources of truth do you tend to prioritize? Which do you overlook or place lesser importance on? Are there any you want to grow in, and if so, what avenues could you pursue for growth?

Explore Your Theology

Like many parents, I have a certain set of parenting practices I favor. Many of my friends have different parenting styles. Some tend to favor the "I'm just trying to survive" philosophy! (Haven't we all been there?)

Underneath our different parenting practices lie distinct assumptions about concepts like sin, authority, and discipline. It's not enough to simply adopt a parenting style; we have to examine the philosophies undergirding these practices.

Similarly, as you reconstruct your sexual ethic, there are some theologies you will have to rethink. The presuppositions underlying your sexual choices will provide the *deeper why* for your sexual ethic and allow you to make values-congruent choices that eliminate guilt and shame.

In keeping with my aim to provoke critical thinking and help you explore the both/and, I offer several theological categories with suggested questions to ponder. Do not look at this list and feel as though you must have it all figured out. These are questions to explore and provoke thought, but they are not exhaustive; feel free to take them at your own pace or explore other areas. I offer no answers or solutions here. Fundamentalism trained us to look outside ourselves for answers and to take what "experts" said as fact. In searching for truth and reconsidering these theologies for yourself, your sexual ethic will be grounded in more than just what any expert, author, or pastor said.

Creation. What is your theology of creation? Did God make the body, and is it good? Did God create sex? What are his purposes for our bodies and sex? Is it sacred and holy, set apart for a divine purpose? Is it just for procreation? Or is it merely recreational and for our enjoyment and pleasure?

Sin and grace. What is sin? What sexual behavior does God consider sin and why? When the Bible says to "flee from sexual immorality,"[27] what does that mean? How can you embody both the second commandment—to love your neighbor as yourself—and the first—to love the Lord God above all else—in your sexual ethic? How do we receive grace and forgiveness for our sins?

Theology of suffering. Why does God allow hardship and suffering? How could a God who is all good and all powerful allow pain like sexual trauma, abuse, and addiction? Is suffering for the glory of God? Or is personal happiness God's greatest goal for us? Does "everything happen for a reason," even states like unwanted singleness, infertility, and unhappy marriages?

Marriage. Is marriage merely a contract in which we each fulfill our end of the bargain, or is it a covenant made between two people and God? Is the purpose of marriage to make us happy, or is it to make us holy—and does that mean we stay married "no matter what"? Is divorce ever an option or is it a sin? Where do you stand on the permanence and purpose of marriage?

Gender and gender roles. Are men and women different? If so, in what ways and why? Are there prescribed biblical gender roles? What are they? How are men and women called to live in relationship with one another in the church, the home, and community?

Sexual and gender identity. Are we born with our sexual identity or is it a choice? What or who determines our gender? Are same-sex attraction and gender dysphoria results of the fall or diverse identities to celebrate? Does God affirm same-sex marriage and the full inclusion of queer Christians in church leadership? If not, why? How does Jesus want us to treat our LGBTQ+ friends?

Power and authority. Who do we submit to? Who is our authority? Is the Bible authoritative? The local church and clergy? How should those in power use it in a godly way? Do we have personal agency and autonomy over our bodies, our sexuality, and our choices—or does something or Someone else have authority?

> REFLECT: Pick one category in this section to explore, and reflect on the questions in that category. Journal your answers, then consider, Where did that answer come from? Do I still believe this is true? Why or why not? If there are some you are unsure about, make a list and begin to explore sources of truth for the answers.

Identify Your Values

Next, we want to explore your personal values to help formulate a values-congruent sexual ethic. Values are characteristics, traits, or qualities that you believe are important. Often, these can be rooted in our religious beliefs and theology, but sometimes they are products of our personalities, temperament, and upbringing.

In therapy, the Personal Values Card Sort exercise can help someone clarify their central values, consider how to reflect those values in daily life, and make decisions aligned with those values.[28] You'll be completing the Sexual Values Card Sort at the end of this chapter. By identifying your top values, you can assess if your current sexual choices and practices reflect those values or if you want to make changes.

Know Your Deeper Why

After reflecting on the sources of truth you've gathered, rethinking foundational theologies, and exploring your values, it's now time to solidify what you believe and why. Reconstructing your sexual ethic means you can explain it and defend it and, at the same time, hold space for and respect those who believe differently. You understand the evidence for and against your beliefs, and you can clearly articulate other positions and the why behind those too. "Knowing the *why* behind your beliefs and decisions connects you to a greater sense of purpose and vision for your life."[29]

Once you know your deeper why, it's time to live it out. Making choices aligned with your sexual ethic means that what you *say* you believe and what you *do* match up. This allows the greatest sense of authenticity and integration: I know who I am, I know what I believe, I live that out in the world, and I am confident in my choices.

━━━

Some of you may be disappointed that I didn't make it easy for you by giving you the "right answers." I promised that this is not a theology book. I have my own journey of examining sources of truth and reconstructing my ethic, just as you will have your own. Look within yourself, integrating Scripture, church history, rational understanding, and personal experience—all within the context of community—to rebuild a values-congruent sexual ethic.

To give you examples, here's what this process looked like for me and two other people. I found freedom from the legalism of purity culture through a relationship with God and living in alignment with his truth. Through my reconstruction, I believe the biblical vision for sex is a holistic mind, body, heart, and soul experience in which we are joined together as one with our spouse after marriage. The Bible supports integration rather than the disconnect of body and heart of both purity culture and hook-up culture. When the covenant of marriage, coupled with consent, precedes the physical act of sex, I see a foundation of trust and security that can allow true freedom, self-expression, and pleasure to bloom.

Journalist Christine Emba's reconstruction process led her to conclude that "total openness wasn't actually more freeing than the cramped confines of purity culture."[30] Emba ultimately settled on an ethic that involves "willing the good of the other"—caring enough about another person to consider how your actions affect them and not just yourself.[31] Emba concludes, "That decision is made not out of repression or fear: it's because I think that sex is meaningful, and I want to treat it as such—to live in alignment with what I believe."[32]

After a years-long search into her beliefs and sexual ethic, Kat Harris concludes her own journey:

> I can now confidently say I am choosing to abstain from sex until marriage. Notice I said *choosing to* instead of *have to*. . . . Shifting my language from *have to* to *choose to* moves me from being a victim to external expectations to being empowered and taking ownership for how I'm showing up in the world. . . . As a follower of Jesus, I am choosing to walk in alignment with the biblical invitation to experience sex inside marriage.[33]

In reconstructing your sexual ethic, perhaps you will agree with Kat Harris and me that "the Bible does indeed offer an invitation to withhold from sex outside of marriage."[34] Or perhaps you will arrive at an ethic resembling Emba's "willing the good of the other." Wherever you land, my hope is that you can use the strategies in this chapter to consider your values and ultimately make decisions aligned with those values, letting this verse guide you: "Finally, brothers and sisters, whatever is true, whatever is noble, whatever is right, whatever is pure, whatever is lovely, whatever is admirable—if anything is excellent or praiseworthy—think about such things."[35]

Tools for the Journey

Sexual Values Card Sort

Step 1: Read through this list of sexual values. Consider what is most important to you. Divide them into three categories: very important, somewhat important, and not as important. From your "very important" pile, keep sorting until you can pick your top three to five values. Remember, there are no right or wrong answers, and your answers may change over time.

Adventure	Assertiveness	Belonging	Boundaries	Closeness
Comfort	Commitment	Confidence	Connection	Consent
Creativity	Curiosity	Desire	Empowerment	Excitement
Faithfulness	Freedom	Fun	Generosity	God's will
Health	Holiness	Humor	Intimacy	Love
Loyalty	Monogamy	Mutuality	Novelty	Nurture
Openness	Passion	Playfulness	Pleasure	Purpose
Respect	Romance	Sacredness	Safety	Self-control
Self-sharing	Shame-free	Spirituality	Spontaneity	Stability
Other: _____	Other: _____	Other: _____	Other: _____	Other: _____

Step 2: Now consider the following questions and reflect on your top three to five values. You may want to journal your responses and share them with your partner, therapist, or a close friend.

- What does this value mean to you?
- What makes this an important value for you?
- How do you display this core value in your sexuality? In what ways are you out of alignment with this value?
- How could you be even more true to this value?

Wise Mind

The concept of *wise mind* can ground us when we are emotionally dysregulated and help us make decisions and act from a place of centeredness and wisdom. Fundamentalism squashes our ability to listen and look inside ourselves; this exercise allows us to grow self-trust.

States of Mind

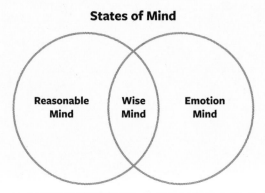

Marsha M. Linehan, *DBT Skills Training Handouts and Worksheets*, 2nd ed. (New York: Guilford Press, 2014).

Emotion mind is the part of our mind that is "hot," when we are ruled by our moods, feelings, urges, impulses, and desires.

Reasonable mind (sometimes called rational mind) is "cool," when we are ruled by facts, logic, rational thinking, and analysis.

The goal is not to swing from the extreme of emotion mind to the extreme of reasonable mind. It is not effective to be either/or. Instead, we seek the dialectic or integration of the two. This is wise mind: the wisdom deep within each person, our intuition and gut, a felt sense of knowing that brings together both emotions and logic.[36] Some Christians might say this is the Holy Spirit within us, providing us with ultimate wisdom and guidance in our thoughts while also ministering to us and comforting our emotions.

Exercise: Breathe in and silently ask your wise mind a question. Breathe out and listen for the answer. Don't force an answer but sit with the sensations and see what comes up for you. If you find yourself rationalizing (a clear sign of reasonable mind) or getting flooded (a sign of emotion mind), see if you can bring yourself back to your center. Continue asking your question with patience and curiosity. If no answer comes, don't judge yourself. Come back to it another time.

If it feels comforting, you might see if you can access wise mind in the form of prayer. What do you know in your soul to be true? What discernment is the Holy Spirit giving you?

10

Singleness and Sexuality

Sexuality is part and parcel of our whole selves; it is not just one part of us. We are ensouled bodies and embodied souls, and our sexuality matters.

Dr. Kim Gaines Eckert, *Things Your Mother Never Told You*[1]

I was giving a podcast interview when I mentioned the ways that purity culture affects single people. As I began to explain more, the podcast host, a pastor and a nice guy in his midthirties, remarked, "Oh, that's interesting! I knew married people were hurt by purity culture, but how does it affect single people?"

I smiled and replied, "You must've gotten married young."

Turns out, he was twenty-one and his wife was twenty when they married.

Those who get married to their first love at a young age are understandably ignorant of the ways purity culture harms single Christians. Often they don't see it because they didn't live it. As someone who married later than purity culture promised, I have some personal experience with the effects on both singleness and marriage. And as a therapist, I walk through purity culture recovery with both married and single clients.

So I can say this with full confidence: single people are not immune from purity culture. In fact, they are often made to feel like second-class citizens. At best, they are left out of the Church's discussion about sexuality. At worst, they are judged, pitied, or ridiculed for their relationship status. Being ignored in these conversations can make single people think they are not sexual beings. They may feel disconnected from their bodies and their sexuality. And they may be confused about how to navigate dating and sexual boundaries as an older single or someone who is single again after divorce or the death of their spouse.

The truth is we are all sexual beings, from womb to tomb, whether married or single. We can be single and still honor both our sexuality and our values. And being comfortable with our bodies, embodiment, and confidently claiming our sexuality is a part of healing from purity culture that is beneficial for us all.

What Is Sexuality?

In a classic experiment in psychology, Henry Harlow took infant rhesus monkeys from their biological mothers and gave them either a surrogate mother constructed of wire or one made of soft cloth. Even when the wire mother provided food, the infant monkeys still preferred the cloth mother and would frequently return to it for comfort. Harlow's findings demonstrated the importance of the parent-child attachment and the primacy of touch in that attachment.[2]

What does this have to do with sexuality? It depends on how you define the term. Sexuality is an inherent part of our humanity. We crave connection, affection, and intimacy. We would literally not survive without human bonds. We were made for attachment, and sexuality is a part of that.

Of course, there is little consensus, in Christian writings and in psychological research, of what constitutes "sex" and "sexuality." Previously, sex has been narrowly defined as just the act of vaginal intercourse. Sexuality, therefore, was something we only expressed or possessed if we had sex, which could only happen once you're married.

Many sex educators have taken to using the term "sexual debut" as a replacement for "losing your virginity." While perhaps a better option, this term implies that our sexuality was "in rehearsal" before "opening night." But as therapist Jay Stringer says, "Sexuality is much more comprehensive than what we choose to do with our genitals or wedding rings." To Stringer, "our sexuality is about how we express our desire to know and be known in all the fear and beauty of what it means to be human."[3] Therefore, sexuality is not something that magically appears on the wedding night, even if we wait until then to have intercourse.

In her helpful guide to female sexuality, *Things Your Mother Never Told You*, psychologist (and my college professor) Dr. Kim Gaines Eckert defines sexuality in four parts: psychological, biological, sociological, and behavioral. "Those four circles are built on the core personhood that God created us with to reflect God in ourselves and in our relationships."[4]

Other definitions of sexuality focus more on the relational dimension. In *Redeeming Sex*, Debra Hirsh defines sexuality as "the deep desire and longing that drives us beyond ourselves in an attempt to connect with, to understand, that which is other than ourselves."[5] In *Practices for Embodied Living*, Dr. Hillary McBride's definition of sexuality is "the ineffable quality of wanting that drives us toward closeness, fulfillment, self-expression, and pleasure in all forms."[6] Eckert acknowledges the unifying nature of sexuality, stating that "sexuality is the drive within us that makes us long for relationship and connection with another human and ultimately, for union with Christ."[7] Others have distinguished between spirituality, our longing for connection with God, and sexuality, our longing for connection with other humans.

We do not "debut" as sexual beings on our wedding day. You are a sexual being, single or married. If our definition of sexuality encompasses our full longings for connection and intimacy with others and with God, then sexuality is present even at birth. Like the rhesus monkeys that preferred a cloth mother or a newborn infant crawling to their mother's breast, we search for closeness, affection, and warmth from another. Since God created all of us with this desire to be known and loved and the capacity for relationship, even my toddler is a sexual being.[8] My abstinent, single adult friend is a sexual being. And my widowed ninety-five-year-old grandmother is a sexual being.

Sexuality isn't defined by relationship status or experience. Sexuality is inherent in all of us as we reflect and embody the imago Dei—the image of God.

Sexual Embodiment

According to McBride, "Embodiment is the conscious knowing of and living as a body, not as a thing distinct from the self or the mind."[9] The body is not something we *have* but something we *are*.

My friend Shari confessed to me, "Purity culture caused me a lot of body shame and disconnection from my body and God. In purity culture, there was always a sense that my body was never mine. It belonged to my future husband, some man I'd never met. It's hard to feel connected to your own body if it's not really your own."[10] The truth is your body belongs to you and God only, not to any human.

Disembodiment is this experience of disconnection from our body. Purity culture teaches that our bodies are sinful, inherently bad, and cause others to stumble. Society teaches that our bodies are projects to improve ("10 steps to your best beach body!") or enemies to subdue. Thus, disembodiment occurs. But practicing embodiment is a way to heal the mind-body divide caused by purity culture and society in order to feel a sense of positive connection and be at home in our bodies.

I have found one of the greatest tools for change is embodied experience—living out in our body the truth that we know in our mind, heart, and soul. Restoring safety to the body is key to enjoying sensual pleasure. Checking in with our body, listening to and respecting her,[11] and valuing our body and emotions are powerful ways to heal our relationship with our body and develop comfort with our sexuality. By appreciating our body as God created her, we are now partners, not enemies.

We are not just minds and souls existing in bodies. We are hearts, minds, and souls *embodied*. And our sexuality is "part and parcel" of our selves.

Embodiment includes acknowledging, appreciating, and expressing our sexuality in ways that are congruent with our values. Even if we are abstinent or committed to celibacy, we can still honor our sexuality. Remember, God made us sexual beings and said that it was good. We can feel connected to our bodies, revel in touch and sensuality, and confidently claim our identity as sexual beings before and after marriage.

Following are some ways to help you become more comfortable with your sexuality:

- Enjoy sensuality, the experience of being connected to your five senses. Experience comforting touch, pleasant smells, soothing sounds, beautiful sights, and delicious tastes.

- Be mindful of pleasure. Smell your favorite candle and allow it to light up your face. Enjoy beautiful sights in nature. Pet your dog and revel in their softness and warmth. Pleasure does not have to be sexual to be enjoyed.[12]

- Make peace with your body. Appreciate your body for what she does for you rather than how she looks to others.

- Acknowledge your desires rather than suppress them. Notice without judgment that they come and go.

- Express gratitude for pleasure. Thank God for your body and sexuality. Take a moment to experience gratitude for beauty and sensuality.

- Ask for and enjoy physical touch. Sometimes this is challenging in our disconnected world, especially if you are single. Ask a friend for a hug, pay for a professional massage or manicure, or get a pet if you feel touch starved.

- Educate yourself about sex and sexuality. Get comfortable with your genitals and use the sex education in this book and others to learn about sex.

- Own your sexuality. It is a part of your personhood, made in the image of God. Using positive affirmations will help you embody your sexuality. (See "Tools for the Journey" at the end of this chapter.)

> **REFLECT:** How comfortable are you with your sexuality? What could you do to become more confident with owning your identity as a sexual being?

Navigating Singleness

Many Christians have no idea how to date after purity culture. The lines were drawn so clearly in purity and courtship practices—lines that provided perceived safety but which proved to be unrealistic or ineffective. Purity culture offered no blueprint for dating after your early twenties. It assumed everyone would marry their first love and have a fairy-tale ending. For Christian singles in their late twenties, thirties, forties, and beyond, how do you navigate singleness and dating?

Redefining Dating

For single people who want a relationship, dating feels daunting. Do you date to marry? Date for fun? Or something in between?

Purity and courtship culture made dating too serious. When "every date is a potential mate," you can't help but envision your future with someone from the moment you meet. I have seen this work out badly in two ways. You might stay in a bad or incompatible relationship too long because you expect to marry the first person you love (the Fairy-Tale Myth). Or you might not give a good person a chance because they don't appear "on paper" to have long-term potential.

I encourage my single clients to think through their purpose of dating before they rewrite their blueprint for dating. Instead of "we have to meet at church," consider giving online dating[13] a try. Instead of demanding that the man make the first move, perhaps the woman can initiate. Emily, a forty-year-old widow, told me, "Learning how to flirt and date again is very different. I dated one person [my late husband] and married him after meeting at church! There are not a lot of single men in my demographic at church, so online dating it is! It's a paradigm shift from the dating scripts of purity culture, but it's okay to be out there and look."

Throw away that "shopping list for him" that purity culture promised you would check off as long as you remained pure. Instead, create a list of your nonnegotiables. Traits like honesty, emotional health, safety, and integrity might be on your list. You might have other nonnegotiables related to career, education, relationship history, faith, and family. What are your red flags? And pay attention to yellow flags too—traits you need to keep your eye on and get outside perspective as you get to know someone.

I think it's unrealistic to expect 100 percent compatibility. I tell my clients to aim for 80 percent—as long as those nonnegotiables are present and there are no red flags. The other 20 percent can be more flexible. My husband knows I didn't expect to marry someone just like him. But God showed me that even though my husband didn't have 100 percent of my shopping list, he had a lot of other strengths and qualities—such as being gentle, giving, and calm—that I didn't even know I needed. If I had not rewritten my dating blueprint and rethought my nonnegotiables, I might have declined a second date with him and missed out on our life together.

The topic of dating is extensive, but healthy Christian dating resources that don't perpetuate courtship and purity culture are scarce. To help fill that gap, let me share some advice from several of the people I interviewed for this book:

- Emily, forty, widowed: "Get to know someone on the first date instead of thinking of marriage. There's no need to have that kind of pressure right away. Do I want to see him again? That's all that should matter."
- Sarah, thirty-eight, single: "Just do what you genuinely enjoy doing. I meet the most people by getting involved in activities or going to events that I want to do. Then I meet friends with similar interests."
- Anonymous: "It's okay not to date. Don't let people pressure you into a relationship you're not ready for or might not want."

- Anonymous: "Adjust your expectations on a regular basis based on what you're learning. Don't hide your own limitations, but if it doesn't feel safe to be vulnerable after three to four dates, reconsider."

- Kristyn,[14] twenty-eight, engaged: "Throw out the curated list and look for two things: genuine kindness and humility—and work to embody them yourself. You likely won't find someone who checks every box, but you may just find a partner you can grow alongside."

- Anonymous: "Go on dates and date for fun. Go on first dates solely to see if you want to go on a second date. Swipe right on anyone who piques your curiosity."

- Amanda, thirty-nine, single: "Dating should also be to learn about yourself. How do you respond to this other person? What does this person bring up in you?"

- MaryB,[15] thirty-three, single: "I used to go into every dating scenario self-conscious and embarrassed because I felt like everyone had more experience than I did. One day I realized that pretty much no one knows what they're doing. When I was able to lower the stakes and embrace what I bring to the table, dating became a lot more fun. I've developed trust and love myself through the process, and it's changed the game for me."

> REFLECT: Have you thought through your purpose for dating? What about your nonnegotiables? How do your current dating practices align with those standards?

Honoring Your Boundaries

When I say the word "boundaries," you may think of rigid rules about what's allowed. Phrases like "guarding your heart," and "how far is too far?" may come to mind. That's because sexual boundaries are often the only type of boundary that purity culture acknowledges. For Christians who were taught to "wait until you get married," it can be heartbreaking when that "until" never comes. It's also confusing when you're no longer a virgin—whether by choice or by sexual trauma—to decide what your sexual boundaries are.

Think about your own boundaries, how you want to communicate them to others and how you will reinforce them in a relationship. Remember, boundaries go far beyond physical. They should also include the type of emotional relationship you want to have with another person. What kind of treatment do you expect or allow from others? How do you treat the person you're in a relationship with? Consider more than the physical when making this list for yourself.

If this is challenging at first, that's okay. It may take some trial and error to figure out what your boundaries are. Purity culture set up a fixed list of don'ts, so we didn't have to think for ourselves. Growing up, you might have heard "don't pray together"—too much spiritual intimacy leads to a desire for greater sexual intimacy. "Don't be alone"—you're just inviting the temptation to have sex. "Don't do more than hold hands"—you'll awaken desires in your body that will make you want to go further. The popular youth group question, "How far is too far?" reflects the legalistic nature of purity culture. There was no nuance; the answer was the same whether you were an engaged couple in your thirties or a teenager going on your first date.

As we know now, the rigid boundaries of purity culture are not only unrealistic; they're too legalistic. Because we are all sexual beings, it is natural that as we spend time with someone we are attracted to and show affection and care for this person, sexual feelings will arise. And those sexual desires are good. Remember, if we shame and suppress sexual desires before marriage, they are likely to still generate shame after marriage.

Instead, acknowledge and accept your sexual feelings rather than stifle your sexuality. Then you can choose how to act in response to those desires in alignment with your values and sexual ethic.

Masturbation

Since it is not directly addressed in the Bible, beliefs about masturbation can vary widely among Christians.[16] Many Christians state that masturbation with the use of pornography or lusting is wrong, but they do not have a clear position on masturbation in and of itself. Others believe masturbation violates the unifying, one-flesh purpose of sexuality. If you have a personal conviction about masturbation, please honor that. Otherwise, you can use the metanarrative of Scripture, Christian tradition, rational thinking, and personal experience (the four sources of truth) in order to form your beliefs.

Certainly masturbation can be a problem, just like any behavior—shopping, social media, alcohol, food—that we use to cope with uncomfortable or unpleasant feelings. But Christians, in particular, overidentify themselves with "sex addiction" even when the frequency of problematic sexual behaviors is lower than the general population.[17] If you have noticed masturbation has become a problem for you—if it is interfering with your daily life, is causing distress, is impairing your functioning, or has become compulsive (meaning you cannot stop even when you want to)—I encourage you to seek a licensed therapist for guidance on a better boundary.

Otherwise, you might consider that masturbation is not always harmful:

> For single women [and men], it can provide a substitute (albeit, ultimately an unfulfilling one) for sexual behavior outside of marriage. . . . Masturbation can sometimes be helpful in coping with sexual feelings . . . [and] can be a way of being sexual in one's body as a single person, confirming the reality that all of us are sexual beings.[18]

Use Wesley's Quadrilateral to search for sources of truth for yourself. And remember, ultimately, "masturbation may not be the black-and-white evil that many of us learned."[19]

REFLECT: What are your beliefs about masturbation? About sexual boundaries? How does your current behavior align with your beliefs?

Single . . . Again

What if you're single again after a divorce or the death of your spouse? Purity culture denied the reality of older singles and those who were married but are single again. As many of the divorced women I interviewed stated, purity culture can contribute to divorce when you are young, unprepared, and marrying for the wrong reasons. The reality is even those who identify as Christian can be emotionally unhealthy, controlling, or potentially abusive.[20] Elizabeth, who divorced at age twenty-five after five years of marriage, said, "[My first husband and I] weren't compatible. We didn't want the same things. But I was told to look for a Christian who saved themselves. We were taught that if you both love Jesus, that was enough. But frankly that's not enough."

When it comes to sexuality, divorced or widowed Christians may question their sexual ethic, as Emily did after becoming a widow in her thirties. "It feels very strange deconstructing my beliefs as a widow. Is it still premarital sex if I've already been married?" she wondered. Emily found a deeper why for her sexual ethic, one that was rooted not just in her religious beliefs, but in honoring her needs for physical, mental, and emotional vulnerability and safety. "Sex is not something I can do without the safe context of marriage," she explained. "That's a profound why for me, and it's not just what I believe God asks of us. There's an even more personal piece for me. The difference is this isn't something other people are putting on me; this is something I am choosing."

Friendship

Having social support is invaluable in any season of life, but at no time in my life were friendships so essential as when I was single. And for Christians who choose to remain celibate, close and meaningful relationships are key to meeting emotional intimacy needs. While friendships aren't the same as a romantic partnership, they can provide community and support.

I encourage you to surround yourself with safe and trustworthy friends—people with whom you can share your life, celebrate, grieve, and cheer each other on. Finding friends like these is not easy, especially because single people are more likely to be transient. Look for friendships where there is mutual respect and trust—where you allow each other to be who you are. To dig deeper, consider Brené Brown's BRAVING Inventory, which breaks down trust into seven traits: boundaries, reliability, accountability, vault (keeping confidences), integrity, nonjudgment, and generosity.[21]

Don't discount married friends either. Yes, they may be less available (especially if they have to plan around childcare and kids' bedtimes). You may have to plan a month in advance! But married people need friends too. I've made a point to continue to nurture friendships with my single friends by trying to take an active interest in their lives. It means a lot when they do the same for me. Ask your married friends to invite you to kids' birthday parties, baptisms, and Labor Day cookouts if you would like to be included. Married friends can make an effort by celebrating their single friend's life and asking about dating, work, and spiritual growth. Be intentional in nurturing and maintaining friendships with both single and married people.

———

Being single as a Christian is not easy—especially past the early twenties. Many single Christians feel they have no place in the church. Like the podcast host I spoke to, many married Christians have no idea how purity culture harms singles. It taught us that you don't need to think or talk about your sexuality until you get married—as if it is something that doesn't exist until you say "I do."

That's why it's important to remember this truth for both single and married people: we are sexual beings who deserve to reclaim that identity, make peace with our bodies, and express our sexuality in values-congruent ways.

As Emily concluded, sexuality matters. "Whether there's a relationship in my future or not, I can heal my sexuality, this part of myself that needs recognition and needs to be seen and heard for what she went through. I am worth the healing."

Tools for the Journey

Sensual Mindfulness, Part 1

Mindfulness is the state of being in the present moment with full awareness and nonjudgment. Numerous studies have found that mindfulness meditation lessens anxiety and depression, lowers stress, increases focus, and helps with sleep.

Mindfulness can also help you become more connected to your body and affirm your sexuality. Practice these skills[22] in everyday life, then begin to incorporate sensuality (mindfulness of your five senses) and pleasure into the skills.

- *Observe*: Just notice your thoughts, body sensations, and emotions. Don't push them away and don't cling to them. For example, you might observe the sensations of a warm bath, notice a thought that arises in your mind, or eat a meal mindfully.
- *Describe*: Put words to your experience. When a feeling or thought arises, acknowledge it nonjudgmentally. You might say, "A feeling of relaxation and pleasure has come over me," or "When I hear this song, I feel an urge to dance."
- *Participate "onemindfully"*: Enter into the experience, becoming one with whatever you're doing. Let go of distractions, just doing one thing at a time. Immerse yourself in the moment. Do yoga, take a run, sing karaoke, get a massage, or play with a pet or a child. With sensual experiences, enter into pleasure, letting go of shame or inhibitions.

Positive Affirmations

Positive affirmations, or mantras, are validating statements to recite and reflect on in moments when you need confidence. To integrate with the spiritual formation practice of breath prayers, you can inhale on the first half of the phrase and exhale on the second half of the phrase, making the mantra a conversation with God.

I've included some of the positive affirmations that my clients find helpful for acknowledging their sexuality. Write down which ones resonate with you and meditate on them.

- My body is good.
- My body and I are one.
- I am known and loved.
- I acknowledge my sexual desires.
- I enjoy touch and sensuality without shame.
- I can be single and still honor my sexuality.
- I can date with intention and have fun.
- *Inhale:* God, you created me / *Exhale:* as a sexual being.
- *Inhale:* I am made / *Exhale:* in God's image.
- *Inhale:* My sexuality / *Exhale:* is a gift from God.

11

After the Wedding Night

Purity culture is like learning how to cook by only learning about food poisoning.

Jay Stringer[1]

Miranda had never had an orgasm.

A fifty-five-year-old woman married thirty years with grown children, Miranda had waited until marriage to have sex. In high school, she heard messages about sex from her mother and her church youth group that set the blueprint for sex. And for three decades, Miranda had been having consistent—sometimes obligation, sometimes mutual—sex with her husband, but no orgasms. Her husband was caring and attentive but neither of them understood why Miranda could never orgasm.

Because of the lack of comprehensive sex education in purity culture, we are set up for disappointment rather than mind-blowing, hot sex. Researcher Sheila Wray Gregoire and her team found that almost 23 percent of Christian women have vaginismus—2.5 times the rate of the general population. They also found that 95 percent of men versus just 48 percent of women frequently or always orgasm during sex, a forty-seven-point discrepancy that

Gregoire calls "the orgasm gap." And they found that certain teachings—like the obligation sex message—can lower women's libidos.[2]

Remember, their research was conducted with a sample of nearly twenty thousand mostly evangelical women. So what the results show us is clear. Purity culture promised a blissful wedding night and endless fulfilling sex in marriage. But for many couples who experience problems like low sex drive, pain during intercourse, and difficulty orgasming, purity culture is the culprit of bad sex.

The good news is there is hope. With education, coaching, and open communication, you and your spouse can enjoy the sex life God intended you to have. And for those who are single and abstinent, arming yourself with the sex education you never received is a vital part of healing from purity culture and reclaiming your sexuality.

Faithful Sexuality

As we've discussed, all of us are sexual beings, and our sexuality encompasses more than our behavior. It also includes our bodies, minds, and social identities. But what is the purpose of sex? What makes sex holy and sacred? How can we live out a faithful sexuality in our marriages?

I turn to the Bible and to God as the Creator to give us the purpose of sex. When we look at God's words to his first human creations, we get a glimpse of his heart for marriage and sex. And, as others[3] have found, the Bible is surprisingly sex-positive.

To demonstrate this, let's look at five characteristics of faithful sexuality in a healthy marriage.[4]

Sex is intimate. It is a "profound knowing"[5] of each other—mind, body, heart, and soul. Our sexuality reflects our need for connection and honors the imago Dei in us. "Then the LORD God said, 'It is not good that the man should be alone; I will make him a helper as his partner.'"[6] Dr. Kim Gaines Eckert writes that "sexual union functions to bond or unite two people into a one-flesh relationship, wherein each partner is called to fully share him- or herself with the other. . . . Sexuality draws us into self-giving relationships with others."[7]

"Therefore a man leaves his father and his mother and clings to his wife, and they become one flesh."[8] This "embodied one-flesh union becomes a testimony to the faithful relationship between Christ and the church"[9] and is a "profound mystery," as Scripture says.[10] Sex has the capacity to draw us closer to the one person we have made a covenant to share our lives with and to deepen our intimacy.

Sex is fruitful. "God blessed them, and God said to them, 'Be fruitful and multiply.'"[11] One definition of "fruitful" is procreation; this is an undeniable purpose of sex. But sex can be fruitful even if it does not lead to procreation. "Our sexuality is that which draws us to give, create, share and care for others,"[12] which can be accomplished without conceiving or bearing children.[13] Fruitfulness also means producing good results, beneficial, and profitable. Sex has positive benefits to individual health and to marital satisfaction; it can lower stress levels, improve sleep, and boost immunity. It can increase trust and bonding to your spouse through the release of oxytocin, endorphins, and other brain chemicals.[14]

Sex is pleasurable. The entire book of Song of Songs[15] is a dedication to the playful, shared delights of married sex. God could have created another way for humans to reproduce, but he chose to use sex and the "one flesh" union to bring about new life. He could have created another purpose for the female clitoris other than pleasure, but alas there is not. He could have eliminated humans' ability to have an orgasm, but instead he gifted us with this pleasure. This doesn't mean that every sexual encounter must be the heights of ecstasy or that we have to orgasm every time. But there should be attention to both partners' physical experience, comfort, and satisfaction each time they come together. When we accept that God created our bodies with the capacity for pleasure, we can enjoy this gift the way he intended.

Sex is mutual. Perhaps this is the most important aspect of sex. "The marriage bed must be a place of mutuality—the husband seeking to satisfy his wife, the wife seeking to satisfy her husband. Marriage is not a place to 'stand up for your rights.' Marriage is a decision to serve the other, whether in bed or out."[16] While other translations of this passage have been used incorrectly to demand "duty sex" from wives (or even to support marital rape), Paul was taking a surprisingly feminist perspective in a time when women were literally considered property. In a Christian marriage, we are supposed to treat each other's bodies as our own. Her feelings matter. So do his. Her body is shared with her husband. His body is shared with her as well. There is no double standard; both sexes are given exactly the same command.[17]

Great sex requires a balance—a dialectic, if you will—of selflessness and selfishness.[18] It is selfless in that we consider our spouse's comfort, needs, and feelings above our own. This *occasionally* means prioritizing our spouse's desires or pleasure in sex (but never in a way that demeans, disrespects, or objectifies our personhood). It is selfish in that we take personal responsibility for our own bodies, sexuality, and experience, and we assertively communicate those with our spouse and advocate for our own pleasure. In my sex therapy practice, I want my clients to move from sex as "give and take" to sex as "sharing." You're not *giving* her an orgasm; he's not *taking* from your body. You are *sharing* an experience—sharing pleasure, time, and your bodies together. It is mutual.

Sex is shameless. "And the man and his wife were both naked and were not ashamed."[19] When I hear my clients say they won't let their husbands see them naked or they still feel like sex is dirty and wrong, I know that reflects the shame Adam and Eve felt after the fall. Insecurities and inhibitions don't make for great sex. But this is not what God intended! God wants us to be able to experience freedom and shamelessness in a healthy, mutually respectful marriage.

Purity culture is an ethic of shame. We know that those who hear negative religiously based messages about sex have more shame and guilt, and this can lead to greater sexual pain and lower levels of desire.[20] But believing in the sanctification of sex in marriage—that sex is sacred and spiritual—and living that out in our bodies can serve as a protective factor to sexual shame and may help buffer against the effects of purity culture.[21] Yes, sacred sex is shameless sex.

If sex reflects God's heart for us—if it is intimate in that it draws our marriage into deeper "one flesh" union; fruitful, in that it benefits each spouse and our marriage; pleasurable, in that both spouses' physical experience matters; mutual, in that we are treating each other's bodies as our own; and shameless, in that we share ourselves without insecurity—then we can be confident that we are living in faithful sexuality.

> **REFLECT:** How would you and your spouse rate your sex life in these five areas? Which areas are strong, and which could use improvement?

Sex Therapy

If you came to my office right now, I'd welcome you in and offer you some water or coffee. You'd feel the couch beneath you and the comfy pillows and nubby throw blanket on it. You'd smell a candle burning—likely Volcano scent, a favorite of mine. The whirring of the sound machines outside my office door would provide a soothing background. A box of tissues would be conveniently within reach whenever you need them. And you'd see me sitting across from you and your spouse, notepad and pen in hand, ready to dive into your sex life with you.

Consider the remainder of this chapter like a sex therapy lesson from me.

In sex therapy, we follow the DEC-R model,[22] which stands for dialogue, education, coaching, and referral. Let's open the dialogue between you and your spouse about how your sex life is going and how you want it to be. I'll give you some education about sexual functioning so you can learn what's normal. Then I'll coach you through some common sexual problems using basic self-help. Lastly, I'll identify when you need a referral for professional treatment.

Dialogue

Let's talk about sex, baby.

For many, this is easier said than done. How comfortable are you talking about sex? How effectively do you and your spouse communicate about how things are going sexually between you?

In purity culture, we were discouraged and condemned for talking about sex before marriage. Having a discussion with our boyfriend or girlfriend about our sexual desires, our bodies, and our expectations was completely off-limits. It could invite lust and open the door for temptation. But that taboo against talking about sex can carry over into marriage.

One of my clients was engaged but hadn't shared her sexual history with her fiancé. She barely had the vocabulary to describe her own body and sexual arousal, much less prepare for marriage. This could have set her up for a disappointing honeymoon and a frustrating start to marriage.

So talk about sex with your spouse. If there are sexual problems, it's not a *me* or *you* problem; it's an *us* problem. Become a team in enhancing your sex life together. Revisit the sexual communications questions in "Tools for the Journey" in chapter 5 to guide your dialogue about your sexual likes and dislikes, your level of satisfaction, and sexual positions or activities you want to try. You may discover that you and your spouse are more on the same page than you expected.

> REFLECT: How comfortable are you talking about sex with your spouse on a scale from 1 to 10?

Education

Sex education is lifelong. We are always learning and discovering new things about ourself and our spouse that affect our love lives. As we saw, education is vital to healing from purity culture. Take the time to clarify incorrect assumptions or myths as you gain more information. Address false expectations you may have of yourself or each other and discuss misinterpretations together.

Learning about the sexual response cycle has been eye-opening for many of my clients. Originally developed by sex researchers Masters and Johnson,[23] these four stages describe the physical changes in men's and women's bodies during sex. What's most interesting for the couples I work with is learning the typical differences between the sexes, not only in their bodies but also in timing.

- The first stage of the sexual response cycle, called *desire* or excitement, lasts minutes to hours. Sexual interest from stimulation, either physical, mental, or both, develops and increases.[24] Physical changes, including a penile erection in men and vaginal lubrication in women, can occur. Heart rate and blood pressure increase for both sexes.

- In the second stage, called *arousal*, sexual excitement continues to build and intensify into a *plateau*, potentially leading to orgasm. This can be the longest and most enjoyable stage. Research has found that during intercourse, a man may reach orgasm after two minutes or less of active thrusting.[25] Meanwhile, it can take up to twenty minutes for a woman's mind to enter the bedroom and then another twenty minutes of active foreplay and clitoral stimulation for a woman to orgasm.[26] So take as much time as you want before moving into intercourse if and when both partners desire it.

- The third stage is *orgasm*. An orgasm is an involuntary reflex in which both men and women experience muscle contractions in their genitals as well as the muscles of the arms, legs, pelvis, and back. Men ejaculate during this stage and women may "squirt" vaginal fluids as well. After orgasm, men experience a refractory period lasting from a few minutes to a few hours or days, depending on their age, during which another erection is not possible. Women, on the other hand, are capable of multiple orgasms minutes apart if both partners want to pursue this. Varying the type of clitoral stimulation (oral or manual) or sexual positions that stimulate the clitoris may help achieve this.

- Lastly, the *resolution* stage is when the body releases tension and returns to its normal state. A feeling of peace and relaxation often follows. This stage can be a good time to cuddle and share verbal affirmation with each other as you express your love.

Sexual Response Cycle

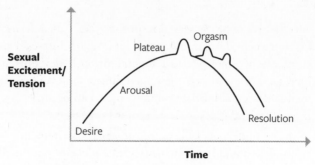

William Masters and Virginia Johnson, *Human Sexual Response* (New York: Bantam Books, 1966).

Coaching for Common Sexual Problems

Now, let's equip you with some skills and techniques to overcome common sexual problems within each stage of the sexual response cycle.

Problems of desire. Low desire is the number one complaint I hear from my female clients. Because desire is so multifaceted and complex, especially for women, it can be difficult to pinpoint the cause and therefore the solution to low desire. (And men are not immune from low desire either!) To help us all, here are some common causes and treatments when it comes to desire:

- *Physical causes*: Talk to your medical provider to see if a physical condition, mental illness, or medication side effects (birth control, antidepressants, blood pressure medications, etc.) might be impacting your libido. For women, this is especially important after pregnancy and childbirth and during menopause.

- *General life stress*: Fatigue, problems at work, kids, household responsibilities, and life stressors in general can affect all of us from time to time. Take steps to improve your basic self-care (move your body, nourish it, and rest), and work with your spouse for a more equal division of childcare, household labor, and other responsibilities. Talk to a therapist if the stress has become unmanageable.

174

- *Unrealistic expectations*: Allison told me her husband wasn't happy with their frequency of sex. She assured me she enjoyed sex when they had it, she orgasmed as often as she would like, and her husband was attentive to her pleasure; she just didn't want sex as much as he did. When I asked how often they were having sex, Allison said it was every other day. And this was a couple with two young children! Allison didn't have low libido; she had a husband with unrealistic expectations for sex, given their context and season of life. Norms for frequency ebb and flow and each couple is different, so work with your spouse to set realistic expectations and to enhance other forms of intimacy.

- *Relationship problems*: You can't create physical intimacy if there is no emotional intimacy. If you're in an unhealthy marriage with blame, disrespect, manipulation, and re-sentment, you likely won't have much sexual desire—nor should you be expected to! You need to restore trust in the marriage before you can work on your sex life; if that is not possible, you need to find safety on your own. Or you might be in an overall healthy marriage, but you and your spouse feel like roommates. Read a healthy marriage book together, schedule date nights and quality time alone, and see a marriage therapist if you need help getting your marriage back on track.[27]

- *Anxiety and negative beliefs about sex*: Megan was a twenty-seven-year-old married client of mine who had anxiety about sex, shame about her body, and embar-rassment about her sexuality. She didn't feel comfortable "being sexy" for her husband and "letting go of control" in bed. Using tools to reframe her thinking and creating experiments to live out her new beliefs allowed Megan to be more confident in her sexuality, let go of body shame, and truly believe that sex was a good gift in her marriage—not just for her husband but for her as well.

> REFLECT: Are you aware of any barriers to desire in your marriage? How could you address these?

Problems of arousal. For women, difficulty building and sustaining arousal is a common occurrence in the arousal stage and can lead to orgasm difficulties. For men, the most obvious sexual problem at this stage is erectile dysfunction (ED). ED is common and expected; in fact, 90 percent of men will experience erectile difficulties at least once by the time they reach age forty.[28] ED can have physical causes, so again, it's important to see your medical provider to check out your general health and medications. If ED is persistent and has psychological causes too, a qualified sex therapist can help.

For both men and women, problems of arousal often result from performance anxiety, also called "spectatoring." Spectatoring is the common experience of feeling like you are watching yourself perform sexually, as if you are outside of your body instead of fully present. Guilt or shame from purity culture and negative teachings about sex can keep you from being in the moment. A practice of sexual mindfulness can be a game changer for women and men who have difficulty staying in their bodies during sex. You can work to develop a mindfulness practice using the tools at the end of this chapter and apply it to your sexual intimacy.

Problems of orgasm. An orgasm is a reflexive release of sexual pressure or tension, a letting go of control. Women who never or rarely orgasm often have difficulty focusing on their body sensations, enjoying and allowing themselves to feel pleasure, and releasing control. Other times, lack of sexual pleasure is caused by a lack of education and communication—either partner not understanding or not communicating about their anatomy and desires.

For Miranda, who struggled to orgasm, increasing her sexual education through reading books written by qualified sex educators was a great starting place.[29] Then she and her husband scheduled time to talk about their sex life, which increased their comfort level and lowered inhibitions. Miranda used thought reframing to challenge and replace negative and false beliefs about sex, such as that sex was dirty and shameful. Instead of seeing herself as defective or broken for not having orgasms, she became an active learner—and teacher to her husband—about her body. Miranda used mindfulness skills to increase her sensual awareness of what brought her body pleasure. She practiced self-stimulation,[30] by herself and eventually with her husband, to help her learn about her body's arousal and release. And she and her husband used sensate focus and other skills to build sexual tension and reduce spectatoring. In all this, Miranda was taking charge of her body and her pleasure so she could surrender to her sexual experience and eventually reach orgasm with her husband.

Problems of pain. The only advice purity culture ever gave when it came to sexual pain was simple: go slow and use lube. And while that suggestion may be true, it's not the whole picture.

Sexual pain is common, but it does not have to be tolerated. In their lifetime, three out of four women will experience sexual pain. It is especially common after childbirth and during menopause. If intercourse is painful or even impossible, here is your permission: *Don't play through the pain.* This can lead to a conditioned pain-and-fear response. Stop and make an appointment with your gynecologist.

As we've learned, a restrictive religious upbringing, poor sexual education, and negative prior experiences (including sexual trauma) can increase the chances of vaginismus. Treatment of sexual pain often involves a physiological and psychological approach. The physiological treatment includes pelvic floor physical therapy, relaxation of the pelvic floor muscles, and the use of vaginal dilators. The psychological treatment includes mental health and/or sex therapy to assess negative beliefs and attitudes about sex or to resolve the effects of past sexual abuse. The good news is sexual pain is treatable—and curable—with the right treatment.

Referral

Some couples will need more help than what reading a book can provide. Referral to a medical provider, licensed mental health professional, marriage therapist, or sex therapist may be necessary, depending on your area of concern. You'll find resources for seeking professional help in appendix 1.

So, how do you feel after our sex therapy lesson? Pause and take a deep breath before diving into "Tools for the Journey." Remember, working on your sex life is a marathon, not a sprint. It took years of programming from purity culture to get your heart, mind, body, and soul to this place. Of course, it will take time to undo that harm. But the beauty of the marriage covenant is that you have your whole lives to figure it out together. Like Miranda learning to orgasm after thirty years of marriage, you *can* fully realize and experience the sex life God intended for your marriage.

Tools for the Journey

Sensual Mindfulness, Part 2

Being fully present—body, heart, mind, and soul—during sex will enhance sexual pleasure and oneness. Set aside time to practice these mindfulness skills during your day. As you build your "mindfulness muscle," you can use these skills during sex to stay present.[31]

1. *Deep breathing*: Sit on a chair or couch in a "mindful posture"—legs uncrossed, feet on the floor, back and neck straight but not rigid. Allow your body to settle into the chair and relax. Close your eyes or look down with a soft gaze. Place one hand on your stomach below your belly button and one hand on your chest. Breathe in deeply through your nose, expanding your diaphragm, so that your hand below your belly button moves out, rather than breathing from your chest. The hand on your chest should stay relatively still until the end of the breath. Then exhale slowly through your mouth or nose. Continue breathing this way for five to ten minutes. It's normal for the mind to wander, so if you find yourself distracted, you're not doing it wrong. Simply congratulate yourself on noticing and then gently bring your attention back to your breath.

2. *Grounding*: Beginning in your mindful posture, notice your immediate surroundings. Tune into your five senses. Name five things in the room that you see, four things you touch, three things you hear, two things you smell, and one thing you taste. The act of noticing and naming sensory details helps ground you in the moment and brings your focus back to the present.

3. *Body scan*: After deep breathing and with your eyes still closed, notice the feeling and position of your body on the chair. Starting with your feet and working your way up, bring complete awareness to each part of your body at one time. Notice your feet in your socks or shoes, the feeling of the ground beneath them, each individual toe. Notice your ankles, calves, and knees. Notice your bottom, pelvic area, hips. Notice your torso, your stomach and abs, your lower back. Move on to your upper back and chest. Notice

your arms, forearms, hands, and fingers. Bring attention to your shoulders and neck. Lastly, notice your facial muscles, jaw, mouth, and tongue. You don't have to change or fix anything; you don't have to analyze or question why you feel what you do. The goal is just to notice any sensations both internal, such as a pit in your stomach or heaviness in your chest, and external, such as an itch on your leg. Continue for about ten minutes.

Sensate Focus

Sensate focus is a widely used technique in sex therapy for a variety of sexual problems.[32] Sensate focus allows you to center nondemand sensual pleasuring with no expectation of orgasm, thus eliminating performance anxiety. It also enhances mutuality, bonding, and connecting and is beneficial for stress and body confidence, making it ideally suited to the five purposes of sex we covered in this chapter.

In this exercise, the couple focuses on sensual massage of each other's nude bodies,[33] taking turns being the active toucher and the touch receiver. The active toucher focuses on touching their partner's body in a way that feels good to both of you. The touch receiver focuses on self-awareness by using their mindfulness skills to notice and enhance sensual pleasure.

Both of you should mutually agree on a time, place (bed, floor, couch), and ambiance (music, lights, temperature) for the exercise. Decide who will take each role first. You might schedule thirty minutes with fifteen minutes in each role or two fifteen-minute sessions in a week.

Sensate focus has three parts:

- In part 1, do not touch breasts and genitals or engage in genital stimulation or sexual intercourse during or after the exercise. Just focus on sensual pleasure. Also, do not provide direct instruction or feedback to your partner during this phase of the exercise. You may use nonverbal cues (sighs, moans, mmms), but if something is painful or uncomfortable for you, please speak up. Otherwise, just revel in the physical sensations.
- In part 2, the couple continues the sensual massage as before but may add touching the breasts and genitals, as desired. Do not have

sexual intercourse or attempt to orgasm. You may add in more direct feedback and affirmation to your partner. The toucher may ask, "Does this feel good? How is this pressure?" The touch receiver may say something like, "I like the way you're massaging my neck" or "It feels good when you do it a little slower."

- In part 3, the couple may add sexual intercourse during or after the sensate focus exercise, if desired. Do not pressure yourself or your partner to engage in more intimacy than they have energy for or want. Allow arousal to build from the first two stages so that when you get to this stage, your body may be ready for intercourse. Continue to give each other verbal and nonverbal affirmation and feedback.

Space out each phase of the exercise by at least a week, practicing it at least once and taking more time to build your comfort if needed.

After each sensate focus session, debrief with each other for ten minutes. You may want to spend a few minutes processing individually in a journal or reflecting before discussing with each other. How did the exercise feel in your body? What thoughts came up for you? What emotions did you notice? How connected did you feel to each other, to yourself, and to God during the exercise? Take time to reaffirm your love and connection with your spouse.

If it feels congruent for you, you may want to pray with your spouse, thanking God for the gifts of intimacy, your bodies, and pleasure.

12

Overcoming Shame

> Only in those instances when our shamed parts are known do they stand a chance to be redeemed. We can love God, love ourselves or love others only to the degree that we are known by God and known by others.
>
> Dr. Curt Thompson, *The Soul of Shame*[1]

Shame is the universal experience of purity culture. No purity culture survivor—male or female, single or married, virgin or not—can escape shame. It is powerful, insidious, and destructive. Shame is the underlying emotion in depression, anxiety, perfectionism, trauma, eating disorders, sexual dysfunctions, and addictions of all kinds. And it contaminates our relationships with ourselves, with others, and with God, as many women have shared.

"Even though we're married now, I can't get comfortable having sex with my husband. The idea of him seeing me feel pleasure feels so embarrassing. I just cringe and want to hide," said Sabrina, my twenty-five-year-old coaching client.

My friend Carrie told me, "It's humiliating to be a thirty-eight-year-old virgin. And I know people think, 'What's the problem? What's wrong with her?' That's the part I'm ashamed of. I feel like I failed because I'm still single."

"I feel like I'm not enough for my husband because I rarely desire sex or any physical touch," explained my client Lenora. "I know God wants it to be a beautiful thing, but I can't live up to the expectations of 'a good wife.' Even though I love him, I find myself withdrawing from my husband."

Perhaps you can relate. Maybe you have shame about your body, sexuality, relationships, and faith. Maybe God has brought to mind areas of shame that need healing in your life even just as you've read these pages.

If that's you, trust me, you're in the right place. Because although shame is toxic and gripping, it can be overcome. Through the healing power of self-compassion, vulnerability with others, and connection with God, you can walk forward without the weight of shame on your back.

What Is Shame?

Researcher Brené Brown has made shame a regular part of our vernacular. She defines shame as

> the intensely painful feeling or experience of believing that we are flawed and therefore unworthy of love, belonging, and connection. . . . Shame is the fear of disconnection—it's the fear that something we've done or failed to do, an ideal that we've not lived up to, or a goal that we've not accomplished makes us unworthy of connection. I'm unlovable. I don't belong.[2]

The emotion of shame evolved to serve a protective function. Shame is ultimately the fear of being rejected or abandoned by our attachment figures or groups. Because group belonging is necessary for survival, shame is culturally useful to keep people in line so that we don't lose the security and protection of a group. Attachment theory suggests that shame is associated with the parts of ourselves that were not embraced by our parents or caregivers, our first sources of survival.[3]

While Brown's work has been revolutionary in popular culture, Dr. Curt Thompson, a psychiatrist who specializes in interpersonal neurobiology, brings a spiritual understanding of shame. His book *The Soul of Shame* defines shame as an "emotional weapon" that "corrupts our relationships with God and each other" and "prevent[s] us from using the gifts we have been given."[4]

Certified sex therapist Dr. Tina Schermer Sellers and licensed counselor Matthias Roberts have made significant contributions to our understanding of religiously based sexual shame. In *Sex, God, and the Conservative Church*, Sellers defines religious sexual shame as shame "prompted by particular religious messages about the sexual self, innate sexual desire, natural sexual curiosity, natural sexual thoughts, and sexual actions."[5] In his book *Beyond Shame*, Roberts explains that because of how closely tied our sexuality is to our personhood, sexuality is a place where we feel shame most acutely.[6]

Since shame likes to hide, we first have to identify it and differentiate it from other emotions. Once you learn shame, you can't unsee it. Like when you get a new car and suddenly see that model everywhere, you'll see the telltale signs of shame in yourself and others once you know how to spot it.

Shame vs. Guilt

Shame is often confused with emotions such as guilt, embarrassment, and humiliation, which are collectively labeled self-conscious emotions. Unlike happiness, sadness, anger, and fear, which are neurologically hardwired in us and present from birth, self-conscious emotions don't develop until later in life. They require a "theory of self," meaning that I understand I am a separate being from you. I can put myself in your shoes and imagine what you feel and think and how that is different from what I feel and think.

Guilt is a focus on behavior: "I made a mistake" or "I did something wrong." The behavior is specific and changeable.

We experience guilt when our actions aren't aligned with our values—when we fall short of our own standards or expectations.[7] The antidote to guilt is to make amends, apologize, and repair the behavior; we make changes going forward. Healthy guilt leads us to set things right, or as Scripture says, leads us to repentance: "Godly sorrow [guilt or conviction] brings repentance that leads to salvation and leaves no regret, but worldly sorrow [shame] brings death."[8]

Shame, on the other hand, is an attack on the self. It is deeply isolating because shame tells us we are the only one. Shame says, "I am a mistake" or "I am bad." Shame dressed up in its Sunday best is perfectionism—"I'm not good enough." When what we are ashamed of is not a specific action that we can change but rather our very selves, our core identity, then shame is felt even more intensely. Research has found that people prone to depression tend to view negative life events as being internal ("This is my fault"), global ("This affects everything in my life"), and stable ("This is always going to happen").[9] People prone to shame make similar attributions.

Shame has sociocultural roots; there is a risk of rejection or isolation from community. This leads us to want to hide, isolate, stay silent, and judge ourselves. Shame affects our limbic system, particularly the amygdala, which is responsible for processing emotions like fear and is a part of our fight, flight, freeze, or fawn response.[10] Shame tends to affect us most when it's about something salient to our identity. This is why, for example, I may experience more shame in my identity as a mother or a Christian but not in my cooking abilities.

While guilt can be healthy and adaptive, shame never is. We can change what we do, but we feel hopeless to change who we are. Guilt tends to draw our attention to another person to fix the hurt we caused. Shame, on the other hand, separates us from others, leading us to hide and cover up what we are ashamed of.[11]

To heal shame, we have to start with recognizing it in ourselves, slowing down to notice the physiological sensations and urges we feel, and differentiate it from guilt.

Shame and Guilt[12]

	Shame	Guilt
Prompting Event *What happened to set off the emotion*	Being rejected, betrayed, or criticized; doing something that others believe is wrong or immoral; comparing yourself to a standard and feeling you fall short; being reminded of something wrong, immoral, or "shameful" that you did in the past; having emotions or experiences invalidated	Doing something that violates your own personal values; causing harm to another person or yourself
Physical Sensations *Nervous system changes, feelings in the body*	Pit in your stomach, dread, wanting to disappear, shutting down or blocking emotions, feeling isolated or alienated	Hot, red face; nervousness
Action Urge *What you want to do with the emotion*	Hide from others, avoid, withdraw, cover up, shrink down	Cover up and hide *or* apologize and make amends, fix the damage
Aftereffects *What you may continue to feel and do even after the emotion passes*	Isolate, disconnect, judge yourself, block emotions, avoid or ruminate, dissociate, increased shame	Increased guilt and shame if you continue to ruminate; relief and increased connection if repair is made
Antidote *Healthy, adaptive response to regulate the emotion*	Be vulnerable with people who won't reject you, expose the feeling, validate yourself, reach out for connection, receive empathy	Make changes in your behavior to align with your values; apologize and forgive yourself

Shame and Sexuality

Shame and sexuality have existed together since the fall when Adam and Eve went from being naked and unashamed to hiding from God and covering themselves. Shame targets the core of our identity, and our sexuality exists at that very core. This is why sexual shame can be so far-reaching and long-lasting. The shame that suppressed our sexuality in purity culture lives not only in our minds but also in our bodies. Even when you cognitively leave behind the myths of purity culture, the shame is embedded in your nervous system.[13]

Author Bridget Eileen Rivera spoke to me about the unique ways shame affects queer Christians: "An LGBTQ person experiences shame just by virtue of existing, by inhabiting their bodies. Same-sex attraction, this experience you can't control, is often seen as inherently sinful. When your very existence is sinful and there is no escape, you fall into shame and despair." Instead, Rivera believes "LGBTQ people need to know that God loves them regardless of who they are attracted to."[14]

Roberts explains in his book that shame hijacks a sense of safety for us all. Sexual intimacy depends on feeling safe and free from messages of shame.[15] Because it urges us to hide, cover up, and withdraw out of fear of abandonment, shame is the antithesis to sexual vulnerability, arousal, and pleasure.[16] Therefore, we have to overcome shame if we want to heal our sexuality from the lies of purity culture.

> **REFLECT:** In what ways do you experience shame in your sexuality?

Does Shame Fit the Facts?

A helpful skill from dialectical behavior therapy to identify and deconstruct shame is called "check the facts."[17] When you experience an emotion, ask yourself, "Does this emotion or its intensity fit the facts of the situation?" In DBT, we use the terms "justified" to describe emotions that do fit the facts and "unjustified" when emotions don't fit the facts. This helps us avoid judgments like saying an emotion is stupid, wrong, or you shouldn't feel that way.

When an emotion is justified, the solution is to act on the emotion's action urge or problem solve the situation in some way. When the emotion is unjustified, we act opposite to that urge and seek out the antidote.

For example, guilt is justified when our behavior violates our *own* values or moral code.[18] If I make a comment that hurts my friend's feelings (even if unintentionally), I would feel healthy guilt because my values are to treat others with kindness and mutual respect. But guilt is unjustified if my actions align with my own values but not someone else's. I highly value boundaries and self-respect, so when I say no to a request for help, the other person may not like it. But I have not violated my own values, so any guilt I feel would be unjustified.

To apply this to shame, my client Sabrina felt discomfort with her sexuality and shame about experiencing sexual pleasure. She had an urge to withdraw sexually, cringe, and cover up in front of her husband. Sabrina knew her shame did not fit the facts; she was in a healthy marriage and her values aligned with expressing herself sexually within her marriage. Her shame was unjustified.

Earlier I said that shame is never healthy, but unfortunately, it can be justified. When you will be rejected by a person or group if they know what you are ashamed of, then shame does fit the facts. If Carrie told a friend that she was a virgin and that friend mocked or judged her for it, then her worst fear becomes realized. Carrie's shame is justified. To avoid feeling the shame of exposure, she could keep her values a secret. Or she could find nonjudgmental friends who will accept and embrace her—offering shame's antidote of empathy and connection.

How to Heal Shame: Looking Inward

The process of healing shame is both intrapersonal and interpersonal; it happens both within us and with others. Ultimately, if shame is about fear of disconnection, then the antidote is connection. To start, we must connect with ourselves. "When we connect and integrate those parts of ourselves that we feel shame around, we build resilience."[19]

Mindfulness

A crucial aspect of overcoming shame is using mindfulness to recognize it. If we are not attending to our feelings, it will be easy to go on autopilot and let shame take over.[20] Begin to notice the physiological signs of shame, name it, and figure out what triggered it. The mindfulness skills you've learned in this book are helpful for this purpose.[21]

In mindfulness, we want to have a "Teflon mind," meaning that we observe thoughts, feelings, and sensations without automatically taking them as truth.[22] The skills of nonjudgment and validation[23] will also help you be mindful of shame without acting on it.

Brown encourages us to practice critical awareness of shame.[24] Reality check the messages and expectations that are driving your shame. Where did they come from? Your family? Church? Purity culture? Or perhaps you are from a cultural background that looks down on bringing shame to the family. Take time to be aware of and process cultural contributions to shame.

The thought records[25] you did will also enhance this critical awareness. Using her thought records, Lenora analyzed her beliefs about how a "good wife" should be and the expectations from purity culture (especially the Gatekeepers Myth). In analyzing the evidence for and against these beliefs, she was able to arrive at a new truth that she was indeed a sexual person and sex was about *sharing*, not giving and taking. Based on this new truth, Lenora could seek out a new experience of mutual, pleasurable sex with her husband.

Self-Compassion

The practice of self-compassion, pioneered by the research of Dr. Kristin Neff,[26] is the psychological sibling to the Christian virtue of agape love. But the recipient of this unconditional love, kindness, and acceptance is us. Because shame cannot survive empathy, self-compassion is a way to offer empathy to ourselves. Self-compassion has three main components:

- *Self-kindness vs. self-judgment* includes offering ourselves understanding and warmth instead of criticism.[27] Inflicting shame on others or ourselves never leads to meaningful and sustained change. Instead, we offer lovingkindness.

- *Common humanity vs. isolation* recognizes that many of the reasons we feel shame are universal. You are not alone in your shame as a purity culture survivor. As Sabrina told me, "I realized I must not be 'weird' because you have made a whole career out of helping people with these same problems."

- *Mindfulness vs. overidentification* reaches back to our mindfulness skills to get unstuck from painful emotions like shame. We can externalize our shame, observing it as something outside of ourselves ("I experience shame"), instead of overidentifying with it ("I am shame").

Cognitive Dissonance

Avery's boyfriend was moving in with her after his lease ended. Previously, Avery had been taught that living together before marriage was a sin. When I asked her how she was feeling about him moving in, her response was, "I just try not to think about it." She admitted that she felt guilty and uncomfortable but that she was unlikely to make a different decision.

The guilt she was feeling is an example of cognitive dissonance, the psychological discomfort we feel when our beliefs and our choices do not line up. Brown says, "[Guilt] is a psychologically uncomfortable feeling, but one that's helpful. The discomfort of cognitive dissonance is what drives meaningful change."[28] For example, if your beliefs are that recycling is good for the environment and an important part of caring for our Earth but you do not recycle, you will likely experience healthy, justified guilt.

In order to resolve this discrepancy between your espoused beliefs and your actions, you can either change your beliefs ("Recycling isn't that important. One person doesn't make a big difference.") or change your behavior (start recycling).

Likewise, when it comes to her sexual or lifestyle choices, Avery can either change her beliefs ("Living together is a healthy and normal choice to make for us. It is not a sin.") or change her behavior (choose not to cohabitate). Avoidance, the "just try not to think about it" method, maintains the dissonance and guilt and can start to affect your relationship, self-esteem, and even your sexual functioning.

It's tempting to want to change our beliefs in order to resolve the discomfort of guilt. And when guilt is unjustified, that may be the appropriate choice. But a more powerful agent of change is to evaluate if our actions are aligned with our values and then make changes if they are not. This embodied action, though challenging at times, is the best antidote to healthy, justified guilt.

> **REFLECT**: In what areas do you experience cognitive dissonance? Take account of your current habits and practices in areas like health, finances, spiritual disciplines, and sexual behavior and see if they align with your beliefs. If not, how will you resolve this cognitive dissonance?

How to Heal Shame: Looking Outward

With a sturdy grasp of our values and a felt sense of safety within us, we can then venture outward. "Shame is not something we 'fix' in the privacy of our mental processes," Thompson says.[29] "It is in the *movement toward another*, toward connection with someone who is safe, that we come to know life and freedom from this prison."[30] Remember, it is not enough to *think* differently. We also have to *do* differently.

Opposite Action

We have talked about the importance of new, embodied experiences to internalize new beliefs. This is congruent with the research from *The Body Keeps the Score*;[31] meaningful change comes not just from top-down processing (learning that goes from mind to body), but also from bottom-up processing (learning that goes from body to mind). Because shame is an embodied emotion, we will need more than facts or new beliefs to change it. Thompson reminds us that "we are dust and breath, and healing shame will necessarily mean we act differently with our bodies."[32]

This is where the DBT skill called "opposite action"[33] provides a new, corrective experience. In opposite action, if our emotion is unjustified, we act opposite to its urge. Research demonstrates that the neural networks in our brains change when we inhibit old behaviors coupled with intentional repetition of new, healthier behaviors.[34] By acting contrary to our unjustified emotion,[35] we create a shift in our bodies and brains, and we begin to *embody* our new truth.

Lenora's shame came from the belief that she should never say no to her husband's request for sex. When she ignored her body and gave in to obligation sex, this reinforced her low sexual desire and pleasure. But if she said no, she experienced guilt and shame because "a good wife" must always meet her husband's needs.

Because Lenora's husband, Jay, was a healthy, loving man who wanted a mutual sex life, he told Lenora that he did not want to have sex if she did not desire it. He gave her space to say no, and he was understanding and patient when this inevitably led to a decrease in sexual frequency. Yet Lenora couldn't shake the pervasive shame. Even though Jay (and myself as their therapist) told her she was allowed to say no, she continued to wonder, *Was it really okay?*

After helping Lenora discern that her shame was unjustified— she would not be rejected or abandoned by Jay for saying no—I encouraged her to use opposite action. I challenged her to say no or abstain from sex as much as she needed and only have sex when she truly wanted it. Every time Lenora said no or did not "give" Jay sex out of duty, she was practicing opposite action. She was giving herself a *disconfirming experience*—training her body that her old belief ("I must always give him sex") was faulty and her shame from that belief was unjustified. This provided a *corrective experience* in that it strengthened her new belief ("I am allowed to say no") and feelings of confidence. Now when Jay and Lenora have sex, it is truly intimate, pleasurable, and shameless for them both.[36]

Empathy

According to Brown, shame thrives on secrecy, silence, and judgment. But the one thing it cannot survive? Empathy. That's why hearing "Me too" or "I feel the same way" is so powerful.

Developing and healing shame is a two-person process. It can't be done in isolation. Brown says, "Shame happens between people and it heals between people."[37] Likewise, Thompson teaches that "healing shame requires our being vulnerable with other people in embodied actions. There is no other way, but shame will . . . attempt to convince us otherwise."[38]

If shame is the fear of disconnection, the way to work through shame is by embracing connection.[39] Reaching out for connection, being vulnerable, and receiving empathy dissolve shame. Instead of hiding and isolating out of fear of rejection, we use opposite action to reach out to others and find belonging.[40]

If this sounds scary to you, it's because it is! Elizabeth was terrified of her community's reactions when she divorced her unfaithful husband. And she did encounter judgment—like from her sister who said sarcastically, "Wow, how does it feel to be twenty-five and divorced?"

But she also experienced empathy from friends. She found accepting friends who walked with her through her divorce, drove her to therapy, encouraged her to start dating when she was ready, and helped her process her grief.

So, like Elizabeth, find safe and trustworthy people to share your story. It can be challenging to find "your people" if you have left a former faith community. But take a risk. Many other Christians are working to deconstruct the toxic parts of our childhood religion.

In other words, you are in good company.

We need a community to realize the fullness of healing, to remind us of the truth. And we need connection that reminds us of the story God writes in us, not the story shame tells us.

> **REFLECT**: What makes it hard for you to be vulnerable? Who in your life can you be vulnerable with?

Connection to God

Shame is also healed through our connection to God. Seeing ourselves as God sees us obliterates shame. When God looks at us, "there is no hint of shame in his gaze or voice."[41] There is only love, acceptance, and a passionate yearning to be in an intimate relationship with us. Many Christians coming out of legalistic religion do not view God in this way. You may picture a wrathful God waiting to throw thunderbolts down from heaven. But Scripture reassures us, "There is now no condemnation for those who are in Christ Jesus."[42]

According to Thompson, we must direct our attention to Jesus as the healer of our shame. "We must literally look to Jesus in embodied ways in order to know how being loved in community brings shame to its knees and lifts us up and into acts of goodness and beauty."[43] When we see ourselves through God's eyes, "we lose all awareness of the shame that has for so long kept parts of us hiding in the dark."[44]

If you have guilt that is keeping you from an authentic connection with God, you may want to confess and repent of it in prayer so you can receive the soothing balm of his forgiveness. Then, remove the fig leaves of shame. Shame is not from God. And he does not leave you. He will not reject you. Our heavenly parent is safe to be vulnerable with and will comfort us as a mother comforts her child.[45]

We cannot immunize ourselves against shame. The paradox is, as we embrace our shame, it begins to lose its power.[46] Embracing our shame can be empowering if we allow it to connect us to other people and to God. Through this, we develop shame resilience,[47] a way to cultivate courage, compassion, and creativity in the face of shame—a way to overcome the shame of purity culture once and for all.

Tools for the Journey

Opposite Action

Pick a situation related to purity culture that causes you shame. It could be something related to your sexuality, doubts in your faith, or disconnection in your relationships.

1. Using mindfulness, identify your emotions and body sensations. Do you feel shame, guilt, or something else?

2. Once you have identified your feeling as shame, clarify if it is justified or unjustified. Remember, this requires a sturdy understanding of your values. Does your shame fit the facts?

3. Apply opposite action. How can you act opposite to the urge to hide or cover up? In your mind, body, and heart, how can you provide a healing experience?

4. Reach out for empathy. Call a safe and trusted friend and tell them about the situation. Share it with a counselor or mentor. Consider revealing your feelings to God too. What might he say to you? What is his heart toward you?

13

Parenting after Purity Culture

May my daughter possess an integrated sexuality that brings her back to herself; a sexuality that makes her feel fully alive and inspired; a sexuality that supports her voice, agency, and well-being. May she be like Eve: naked and unashamed.

Shannon K. Evans, *Feminist Prayers for My Daughter*[1]

Liberate us, Lord, from the binds of toxic masculinity. . . . We pray for our son, that he would be empowered while divesting his power. . . . Our culture has not modeled well . . . what it is to raise a son, what it is to be a man. But we have hope . . .

Kayla Craig, *To Light Their Way*[2]

I cried during both ultrasounds when I found out the sex of my children. The first time, I assumed I was having a boy. My husband comes from an extended family full of boys. Although in the secret corners of my heart I had always longed for a girl, I still prepared myself for my first to be a boy.

"It's a girl!" the technician said as she pointed out the three little lines that depicted my daughter's genitals.

I immediately dissolved into tears—ugly crying, snorting, snotting tears. My daughter was our gift of grace, and I knew having her first would force me to confront some of my own issues as a woman, with body image, having a strong voice, and mother-daughter relationships.

My second pregnancy, I knew before the technician announced it. "It's a boy, isn't it?" I asked when I saw him on the screen.

She confirmed that what I saw was indeed my son's penis, and once again, I broke down in sobs. Blessed with a healthy baby and our family complete with children of both sexes, I felt relieved. But I also knew having a son would challenge me to face some of my own issues with men, with power and inequality, stereotypes, and distrust of men.

As it turns out, so much of the work of parenting has been reparenting myself. Parenting has smacked me in the face with my own attachment wounds from childhood and sent me back to therapy with my still unresolved issues.

And this can show up in no place more than in teaching our kids about sex. One of the most common questions I get asked is this: "What do we teach our kids now?" For parents who were raised in purity culture and have since rejected it, knowing what sexual guidance to give our kids can feel daunting. We know purity culture didn't work, and now we want to spare our children the sexual shame, religious trauma, and broken relationships that we ourselves have suffered as a result.

Yet the world's offer of an ethic of consent doesn't feel right either. Most Christian parents, even those who had premarital sex themselves or no longer hold a traditional sexual ethic, want more for our kids than "as long as it's legal, go for it!" We know the power and beauty that sex can hold, and we believe there's more to sexual ethics than just not breaking the law.

If we don't want to control our kids through the shame and fear tactics that were used with us or offer enticing guarantees that turn into empty promises, what do we do?

My client Heather felt like this. Growing up in a high-control religious group, Heather didn't want her kids to inherit the problems she experienced in her intimacy and faith. But she also didn't want to swing in the opposite direction and give in to hook-up culture.

"I don't want my daughter to think her vagina or vulva are dirty," she said, "but I also don't want her to feel like she has to be a porn star. I want my kids to save sex for marriage—or ideally for a committed relationship—but I don't want them to believe that sex is shameful and just a duty or obligation for the wife, like I have struggled with. It feels like the pendulum swings too far."

I am not a parenting expert. I won't tell you whether you should sleep train your baby or give your tween a phone. My kids are still young, and I am firmly on this parenting—and reparenting—journey as a fellow traveler and not an authority. But here's what I know is true: You *can* raise kids with shame-free, values-congruent, and God-honoring sexual ethics even if you didn't have that yourself. You can teach your kids to feel safe in their bodies, view sex as a gift, and set them up for sacred, mutually pleasurable sex in marriage.

But first, let's examine what *not* to do and why it doesn't work.

Why Purity Culture Failed for So Many

What was your sexual education like growing up? How did you first learn about sex and who taught you? What do you like and not like about how you were taught about sex?

I call this your *sexual story*—the story of how you came to learn about sex. What emotions and feelings in your body do you remember about this time? Did you feel shame? Disgust? Arousal? Curiosity? Interest? All of the above are normal!

As we learned from the research on the purity movement, purity culture wasn't successful in keeping young adults abstinent before marriage. And as we've seen throughout this book, it also had unintended consequences. I believe the main reason purity culture failed us was because it didn't foster the emotional skills, critical thinking, and self-efficacy that are needed to make morally complex decisions.

Allow me to slip on my psychology professor hat for a moment and explain how we develop our moral reasoning. Lawrence

Kohlberg's theory of moral development[3] is widely taught in psychology classes to explain how humans think about moral dilemmas throughout their lifespan.

In Level I (stages 1–2), which occurs during young childhood, morals are based on avoiding punishment and obtaining rewards. Children are motivated by what benefits them, and they focus on the consequences of actions rather than intentions. We see this when a child doesn't touch a breakable vase "because I'll get in trouble if I do" or gives parents peace and quiet in the grocery store for the reward of candy at the checkout counter.

In Level II (stages 3–4), during the school years, children make moral decisions based on a desire to belong and be accepted, to be seen as a "good girl" or "good boy," and a drive to obey external rules and regulations to conform to social order. Children are focused on gaining approval, fitting social roles, and obeying authority. A child may decide not to cheat on a test because his parents will be disappointed in him, or a girl may make fun of another student at school to fit in with her friends.

In Level III (stages 5–6), during adulthood, we base our moral reasoning on our own values and ethics. These stages are rarely seen before college age, and Kohlberg found that the final stage, stage 6, is rarely reached at all. There is an emphasis on a balance of social order and individual rights as adults develop universal ethics driven by internal moral principles. Here we see people who fight for inclusion and equality of a marginalized group, not out of personal benefit but because of their own principles of justice and diversity.

Moral Development Stages

Level/Stage	Age Range	Description	Purity Culture Example[4]
I/1: Obedience/ Punishment	Infancy	Avoid punishment	Damaged Goods Myth, Gatekeepers Myth
I/2: Self-Interest	Preschool	Obtain rewards, self-benefit	Fairy-Tale Myth, Flipped Switch Myth

Level/Stage	Age Range	Description	Purity Culture Example
II/3: Conformity	School age	"Good boy/good girl," secure approval and maintain friendly relations	Spiritual Barometer Myth
II/4: Authority	School age	Fixed rules, social order, please authority	
III/5: Social Contract	Adolescence to adult	Mutual benefit, reciprocity, utilitarian rules that make life better for everyone	
III/6: Universal Principles	Adult	Morality transcends personal benefit	

Purity culture's myths are aimed at the first four stages—you abstain from sex to avoid pregnancy and STIs (punishment) or because "you won't be respected if you give in to sex" (self-interest). You should remain a virgin because of the status it gives you as a "better Christian" ("good girl/good boy") and because your parents, your church, and the Bible want you to (social approval, obeying authority). For example, abstinence speaker Shelly Donahue instructed parents, "The number one reason our kids delay sex is because you asked them to. . . . The best birth control we have is dad."[5] These statements encapsulate less mature moral reasoning.

Purity culture rarely offered a reason for abstinence beyond Levels I and II.[6] It did not encourage the development of one's own sexual ethic based on internal values and beliefs. Adults are left without a solid, personal sexual ethic on which to base their decisions. Moreover, it doesn't take long for the myths to fall apart and to see that reality is very different from what purity culture promised. Thus, past the teen years, the purity message is no longer compelling and loses steam.

This is why purity culture didn't work: we never developed a deeper why. In fact, when people have a deeper, moral reason for abstinence—such as wanting to honor God—instead of a practical one like avoiding pregnancy, they are more likely to remain virgins in their midtwenties.[7] It takes a deeper, more nuanced faith *and* a more robust moral reasoning to make decisions aligned with a Christian sexual ethic.

Before you can teach your kids about sex, you must do the work of healing your own faith and rebuilding your sexual ethic—knowing what you believe and why. I hope the skills and resources I've offered in this book will help you do that. Then, building off a stronger foundation, you can offer your kids Level III moral reasoning and help them discern their own values and ethic.

> **REFLECT**: Can you think of some examples from Levels I and II that purity culture taught you? Were there any Level III reasons?

Goals of Sex Education

Before I began writing this book, I had to think through my goals for the book. Equally important, I had to consider what my goals for this book were *not*. Knowing the goals and the audience helped me decide what content to include and not include. It also helped me frame my approach, determine my tone, choose the stories I use to illustrate my points, and discern what I wanted you to take away from the book.

Likewise, we cannot jump into teaching our kids about sex without thinking through our goals and our audience (our kids). What do we want them to learn about sex and their bodies? What stories or examples do we want to offer? What do we want them to take away from our conversations—not just the content but also how they *feel* about us as their parents and about sexuality as a whole?

OPEN is a helpful acronym for my overarching goals when it comes to teaching kids about sex, backed up by research and evidenced-based practices for parenting.

- *Open and comfortable conversations.* No more awkward sex talks! We want to take the anxiety out of talking about sex. By our getting comfortable speaking matter-of-factly and openly about sex, we can model this for our kids. We want to be approachable so that our kids come to us with questions—before seeking information from their peers, online, or through porn. Whether my three-year-old wants to know how her baby brother was born or my teenage son asks about wet dreams, I want my kids to come to me with any sex-related question or concern.

- *Promote respect for self and others.* Making wise sexual decisions flows out of self-respect and respect for others. I want my daughter and son to respect their bodies and themselves enough that they can say no in any uncomfortable situation. I want both of them to treat others with respect. This starts with me showing respect for my children as people and treating their bodies, emotions, thoughts, and words as worthy of my time and attention.

- *Empower them with age-appropriate information.* Knowledge is power. My children are biologically hardwired to look to me for survival, and that includes knowledge about their bodies. Let's not raise children who are ignorant about the basic functions of their bodies. We want kids to feel confident, not ashamed or fearful. Inspiring confidence in our kids requires us to empower them as the authority over their bodies—with God as the ultimate authority—rather than us being in charge.

- *Nurture critical thinking.* We want to communicate our family's values with critical, nuanced thinking. I want my children to know and understand the deeper why for our family's beliefs about sex. I want them to question and analyze the reasons for premarital abstinence. And ultimately, I respect their right to make their own choice based on this critical examination.

I practice OPEN within a parenting philosophy that centers relationship and connection with my kids instead of control. Dr. Becky Kennedy, clinical psychologist and parenting expert, writes:

> When we sacrifice relationship building in favor of control tactics, our children may age, but in many ways, they developmentally remain toddlers, because they miss out on years of building the

emotion regulation, coping skills, intrinsic motivation, and inhibition of desires that are necessary for life success. When we are busy exerting extrinsic control over our children's external behavior, we sacrifice teaching these critical internal skills.[8]

I'll be clear: my overarching goal for sex education for my kids is *not* that they are virgins on their wedding day. It would be wonderful if they are, but it's not my top priority. It's more important to me that they develop their own values within a context of responsive, supportive relationships with me and their dad, and within a strong, personal relationship with Jesus.

If they have dated and made a commitment to marriage (or singleness) with integrity to their values; if they have made thoughtful decisions from a robust faith and sexual ethic; and if I have maintained a strong connection with them along the way—this will be a success regardless of their virginity.

Guidelines for Talking to Kids

If the goals of sex education are our *what,* these guidelines are our *how*—how to talk to kids about their bodies and sex.

Before the "sex ed" day in my sixth grade health class, my parents figured they'd better teach me about sex first. They gave me a Focus on the Family book[9] and sent me away to read it, telling me to let them know if I had any questions.

Unsurprisingly, I didn't.

This "one and done" sex talk was a popular practice in purity culture. Like most parents, mine were doing the best they could with what they knew. I guess it may be better than the alternative! When I polled my social media audience on how their parents talked to them about sex, the most popular answer was "They didn't."

Well, like Maya Angelou says, when you know better, do better.[10] Following are some guidelines for having healthy, shame-free sex education in your home:

- *Make it an ongoing conversation.* We need to change our mindset from "the sex talk"—a onetime, usually awkward lecture between the child and their same-sex parent—to sex education as an ongoing conversation. We don't have one big "money talk" before kids go off to college or one "faith talk" about our beliefs in God. As Dr. Tina Schermer Sellers says, it's "one hundred one-minute conversations"[11] that add up to sex education for our kids.

- *Make the most of natural opportunities.* We get to the one hundred one-minute conversations by infusing sex ed into everyday moments. Rituals like baths, a new baby, birthdays, themes on TV or in books, and situations with friends and family all present opportunities to talk to our kids about their bodies and sex. Jump on these moments when it's natural, and then, when it's time to teach them about intercourse, you've laid the foundation.

- *Don't shy away from questions.* I heard the phrase "we'll tell you that when you're older" so often as a child that I started writing down all my questions (except we never got back to them). Instead, validate kids for their natural curiosity. If a question comes at an inopportune time, you might say, "That's a good question. Let's talk about it when we get home. I want to make sure I can focus and pay attention when we talk." If you don't know how to answer their question, be honest and say, "I'm so glad you asked me that. I'm not sure how to answer you right now. Let me think about it and I'll get back to you." Then be sure you do it!

- *Use the correct terms.* Whenever possible, use correct anatomical terms. Using nicknames like "coochie" or "wee-wee" conveys discomfort and insecurity to our kids, which can lead to shame about their bodies. Using correct terms is also part of responsible sexual abuse prevention. If a child can accurately label their genitals, they may be less likely to be abused, or if they are, more likely to report the abuse quickly.[12]

- *Incorporate your family's values and beliefs.* As you infuse everyday moments with sex ed, include your family's values into your answers. I often tell my children that they are gifts from God to me. We acknowledge and respect differences, but we often talk about marriage and children in the order we believe is God's best. We typically say things like, "After you're married, you can share a house with your husband/wife and then you might have a baby."

REFLECT: What are some healthy, values-congruent resources, such as books, podcasts, social media accounts, and role models, that you can share with your children?

Let's Talk about Sex

Now, let's get into the content of what to teach kids. Remember, conversations about sex need to be couched into larger conversations about values in general. With that in mind, here are a few things to consider as you talk to your kids about sex.

Bodies

Emphasize the beauty and goodness of bodies. We teach our kids that they were made in God's image and all of their body is good—even their genitals. You might say, "God made your arms, your legs, your hair, your vulva/penis, and it is all good and beautiful!"

We meet their questions where they're at. For example, like many mothers of young kids, I rarely go to the bathroom by myself at home. One time my daughter followed me in the bathroom and saw blood in my underwear.

"What's that?" she asked simply.

"Sometimes I bleed from my vagina, and this pad catches the blood. I'm not hurt or sick; this is normal for most women," I replied.

She was perfectly content with this answer and walked off. I didn't need to explain the menstrual cycle to her or the details of internal female anatomy. This answer satisfied her, and she won't be shocked and disturbed when it comes time to give her more details about starting her period.

To foster a positive body image, I emphasize the function of bodies over their appearance. We can celebrate our whole bodies when we pay attention to what they do for us, not just how they look. My toddler's belly is not just adorable; it also tells him when he is hungry so he can fill it with good food. Similarly, in marriage, breasts are not just for sexual pleasure; they may also nourish a baby.

Modesty

Dressing appropriately is a life skill, just like learning to load the dishwasher, write a résumé, and schedule an appointment. When it comes to modesty, we focus on practical considerations rather than what other people think. We ask our kids to choose clothing that is appropriate to the occasion, setting, and weather. Are your clothes comfortable, functionable, and reflect your character? What you wear is also about respect—self-respect and respect for others and other cultures. I want my children to dress in a way that respects their bodies as a gift from God. They can also respect that the way we dress at grandma's church may be different from the way we dress at our church.

Yes, modesty is a biblical virtue. But it is about more than how clothing covers your body. A modest spirit that respects self and others is the goal to strive for.

Consent

Consent is modeled with actions—caught, not taught. Respectful parenting educator Janet Lansbury[13] advocates asking for permission to touch your child, even with infants. We can say, "I'm going to change your diaper now," and explain what we are doing. Babies may not understand our language, but they will feel our respectful tone. We are modeling respect for their bodily autonomy—their right to make decisions about what is best for their bodies.

In my family, we don't force hugs and kisses on our children. An empowering moment for me came when my dad was tickling my daughter and continued even after she said stop.

"Dad, in our house we stop when she says stop," I said.

My dad respected this and did stop. It was healing to model consent like this for my daughter, to use my voice with my father, and to reparent myself. Saying "stop" to tickling or hugs was not respected when I was a child, but I can make sure it is now for my children.

To be sure, there are exceptions to bodily consent. When it comes to health and safety, my children don't get to choose to get their runny noses wiped, be buckled into their car seats, or get checkups at the pediatrician. But as much as possible, we offer them autonomy, even saying, "You know your body best. We trust you."

Abuse Prevention

It's an unfortunate reality that, no matter what we do, abuse can happen to children. As a therapist who hears stories of child sexual abuse (and an Enneagram 6 who fears for my children's safety), I've had to lean on the skill of acceptance and change[14] to help me focus on what I can change or control and accept the inherent risk in situations out of my control.

As best as we can, we want to empower our kids and protect them. So talk to your kids about safe touch and bad touch. For my young children, I tell them that no one should touch their private parts except for health (the pediatrician when mom or dad is present) or hygiene (such as diaper changes, baths, and potty assistance). For older children, talk about how to ask for and give ongoing consent to any touch as they discern their boundaries.

Talk about the difference between secrets and surprises. Surprises are fun news that we will reveal at a later time to make the other person happy—like a birthday gift for Daddy! Secrets are scary or mean, never shared, and will make the other person sad.

I also can't overstate the importance of monitoring adults in your children's lives. A shocking 93 percent of sexual abuse perpetrators are someone the child and their family know.[15] This might mean limiting or eliminating unsupervised playdates or sleepovers.

I've heard too many stories to take the risk of my children being around unknown adults or even older children unsupervised.

Porn and Masturbation

As we dive into this topic, a caveat: a thorough examination of porn and masturbation is beyond the scope of this book. I encourage you to seek out healthy resources to dig deeper into these topics. That being said, let's talk about what we have space for here.

The average age a child is exposed to pornography is twelve.[16] Clearly, we need to address hot topics like this early and often. Again, remember it is an ongoing conversation that builds on each previous conversation and starts with natural opportunities. When my toddler son touches his penis, I say, "I see you're touching your penis. But that is not polite to do in public, just like picking your nose. Let's find something else to do with your hands." This builds a shame-free foundation to talk about masturbation at a later age.

If your children are at the age of tablets, laptops, or smart-phones, talk to them ahead of time about what to do if they come across sexually explicit material. Don't be shy about having child protection software and monitoring their usage.[17] Take phones away at bedtime and set limits on screen time. But also talk about the *why* behind your family's beliefs about porn and masturbation. Remember, it's not enough to set up external consequences and rewards—that's Level I moral reasoning. We also have to help kids critically think through and internalize a deeper why.

Sexual Values

When it comes to teaching kids about sex, start with a straight-forward answer that provides basic information. You could say something like, "Sex is sometimes called making love; it's one way adults can show they love each other. It is when a husband and wife are kissing and touching each other's bodies and being very close—so close that they put the husband's penis inside the wife's vagina. This feels good to both of them and makes them feel warm and loving."

A script to help communicate sexual values could also help. Try something like this: "In our family, we believe sex is ___. Our religion (or faith tradition) teaches ___. We believe this is important because of ___. We want you to make choices that respect yourself and others. What do you think of this? What questions do you have?"

Through these examples, you *can* talk to your kids about your family's values, including your religious beliefs, without the myths of purity culture. There's no reward and punishment language. We're not using "good girl/boy" and "bad girl/boy" language. We can avoid the extremes of demonizing sex ("Sex is a sin; don't do it!") or idolizing it ("Sex is the greatest gift you'll give your future spouse!"). And we emphasize moral and personal integrity over false promises.

> **REFLECT**: What have you told your kids so far about sex and sexual values? How can you communicate a deeper why to your kids?

You don't have to swing from the extremes of purity culture to an ethic of consent. You can share your family's values and religious beliefs, which may include premarital abstinence, without shaming your kids or coercing and controlling them.

Talking to your kids about sex starts with your own work first. Identify the purity culture myths in your own beliefs. Pay attention to which myths affect you, and use the tools in this book to heal from these distorted beliefs instead of perpetuating them to your children. Work on reconstructing your own sexual ethic so you have a foundation from which to guide your kids.

Second, infuse conversations about sexual values within the broader values and skills you want to teach your kids—like empowerment, respect for self and others, critical thinking, and intrinsic motivation.

Lastly, instead of false promises and gender stereotypes, you can emphasize the value of honoring God, faithfulness, and integrity.

As part of reparenting myself and my ongoing sex education with my daughter and son, I plan to teach them that chastity is a lifelong spiritual discipline that reflects God's heart for us—not a list of dos and don'ts. I hope to say to them, "You were created in the image of God and your body is good and beautiful. Sexuality is a gift, and we believe God asks us in the Bible to save sex only for your spouse when you are married. We believe this reflects God's love for us and the promise he makes to never stop loving us. We want to honor God, ourselves, and others with our bodies. We hope that as you grow older, you will talk to us, ask questions, read the Bible, and pray and ask Jesus what he wants you to do and what decisions he wants you to make with your body and your sexuality."

Tools for the Journey

Reparenting

Part 1: Write a letter to yourself as a child, telling yourself what you needed to hear about your body and sex. This is the work of reparenting, giving yourself what you didn't get. After you finish writing, pick an age and visualize yourself as a child of that age. What were you wearing? Where were you? Who were you with and what were you doing? What do you hear, smell, or taste?

While picturing your child self in the scene, place your hands over your heart and read your letter aloud, addressing yourself. (For example, mine would be "Dear eleven-year-old Camden . . .") Allow any emotions or body sensations to come up for you and take your time, giving both your adult self and your child self the validation and support you need.

Part 2: Write a letter to your child(ren) as an adult, telling them what you want them to believe and feel about their bodies and sex. After you finish writing, read the letter aloud as a prayer to God. Ask God for guidance and wisdom as you raise your children. Ask God for the courage to parent them without shame and to gift them with a sexual story you wish you had.

Conclusion

The Path Forward

I wish I had one big, pivotal aha moment to wrap up my story of purity culture recovery. But like any trauma, healing has been gradual for me. It's been a combination of learning the truth, feeling acceptance and empathy from my husband and trusted friends, freedom from emotions like shame, and growing an authentic, nuanced faith in God.

And I imagine it will be gradual for you too.

Recovering from purity culture will not mean that you are no longer affected, don't experience triggers, or have forgotten about your past. You are not a failure if you continue to struggle in some way. Eventually, as you continue the work of mind-body integration and embodied experiences, the wounds may turn into scars, reminding you that you are a survivor.

I know because I've experienced it myself and with my clients.

Michelle and Jack, the "poster children" for purity culture whom I introduced in chapter 1, finished their work with me not only with a new understanding of sex, their marriage, and their faith but also with a new experience of sex as mutual, pleasurable for both of them, and shameless. At the end of our meetings, the couple said, "It's been hard work disentangling from wrong beliefs within purity culture that we had built our marriage on. We had to discover new and healthy ways to think, relate, and connect—with ourselves and each other."

By finding congruence between her thoughts, emotions, and actions, Tiffany, who feared any interaction with men, finally felt safe within herself and around healthy men. Through new, embodied experiences, she felt at peace in her male friendships. At the end of our coaching, Tiffany told me, "I've moved from self-doubt and fear toward confidence and security. I *can* have healthy, respectful interactions and relationships with men."

Ruth and Mitchell, the couple who struggled with obligation sex and expanding intimacy, deconstructed the lies that affected their marriage. "We were facing the same recurring fight that never seemed to change," they said. "Our marriage was struggling, and our thinking was flawed, in part because of the purity culture myths."

After doing this recovery work, they shared, "Our eyes were opened to lies we believed, and we began to see each other in a new light. We are seeing the fruit of this now and are finally getting back to a place of shared intimacy with each other."

As you can see, the work of these purity culture survivors is not over. But they have found the path forward and can keep walking in recovery. And I believe you can too.

Embodied Healing

To help you continue your journey, let's revisit some final healing themes. Consider the questions that come with each and be honest with yourself about where you are now and how you hope to continue to grow as you heal from the trauma of purity culture.

Healing Your Relationships

What relationships need further healing? What beliefs are you stuck on? You might revisit the five myths. You can even retake the personal assessments,[1] measuring your belief in each of the statements now as opposed to when you started reading this book. Where are you now with each of these myths? What support do you need to continue to address them?

Healing Your Sexuality

What problems in your sexuality has this book revealed? Where are you in terms of reconstructing your sexual ethic? What resources or professional help will you pursue as you work toward healing?

Healing Your Faith

Remember, deconstruction and reconstruction may be ongoing, lifelong journeys. Where are you in your faith journey? How can you find a supportive community?

It is common to go through the stages of grief[2] as you experience changes in your faith:

- *Denial*: In this stage, you are in denial that you are going through a faith deconstruction. You may minimize, suppress, or deny the harm of purity culture. You refuse to see the problems in your theology or the cultural beliefs that aren't working for you anymore.
- *Anger*: You may feel angry and place blame on the Church, the people who raised you in your faith, and Christianity as a whole. Your anger is justified as you consider what purity culture has stolen from you. This is a valid emotion, and you absolutely have a right to feel angry and hold others accountable, but you don't want to stay here forever.
- *Bargaining*: You start to bargain to avoid the shift in your beliefs and the work of deconstructing purity culture. You may try to make superficial changes or find a quick fix to bypass the discomfort you're feeling.
- *Depression*: You may feel depressed about the state of the Church and hopeless about your faith, sexuality, and relationships. You mourn what purity culture has taken from you and feel a sense of loss. You believe that nothing can get better, and you'll be in a perpetual state of disillusionment indefinitely.
- *Acceptance*: You arrive at a place of peace and acceptance in your faith and purity culture recovery. You are better

able to see both/and instead of either/or. This may result in a faith or sexual ethic that looks different from before. But you feel more meaning and congruence between your beliefs, values, and behavior.

Integration

Check in again with your mind, heart, body, and soul. The Bible encourages us to "love the LORD your God with all your heart, all your soul, all your mind, and all your strength."[3] Where are you now in each of these areas?

For Christians, I believe full and complete healing—an integration of body, mind, heart, and soul—will always involve living in alignment with God's heart for his people. As we restore the goodness, beauty, and truth about sex to what God intended instead of what purity culture warped, we love God. We love him through our *mind*, our beliefs and thoughts that are aligned with his will. We love him through our *heart*, our emotions and affections rightly centered on him and the people he created and loves. We love him through our *soul*, our connection to God and to our faith as sacred, divine mystery. We love him through our strength, our *bodies*, actions, and the embodied choices we make that show our devotion and obedience to him. And as an outflow of his love for us, we love ourselves and our neighbors.[4]

When the compassion of our hearts meets the wisdom of our minds and the strength of our bodies, we can connect to the sacredness of our souls in Christ.

Revisiting Your Story

For our last "Tools for the Journey," I encourage you to revisit the Writing Your Story exercise in chapter 1. Reread your story and note anything new that comes up for you in your head, heart, body, and soul. I hope you notice new beliefs and new understandings of sexuality and faith. Perhaps you feel surprised at what you used to believe, frustrated that you are still struggling in some areas, or proud of how far you've come. You may experience body sensations that point you to unprocessed emotions or unfinished work. And I pray you experience fresh peace in your soul.

Post-Traumatic Growth

A final theme in trauma treatment is the concept of post-traumatic growth, the belief that we can ultimately discover a greater sense of freedom, wisdom, strength, and peace as we heal the shame of trauma.[5] For many survivors, this may include "giving back" or "paying it forward," as a way to make meaning out of their pain.

For me, post-traumatic growth from purity culture has included writing this book and speaking out about the harm of purity culture. It's been empowering for me to speak to fellow Christians as I argue that we can still value a Christian sexual ethic without the myths and control of purity culture. It's been enlightening to connect with Christians who hold different beliefs than me and yet are united in our recovery from purity culture. And it's been healing to share my personal experience with you—my readers, clients, and online community—and bring you tools from my profession to support your own healing.

What does post-traumatic growth look like for you? Could God be calling you to speak out about your purity culture experience? How could you use your story to bring hope and healing to others? Or could this mean parenting in a way that honors what you have now learned and how far you've come in your recovery?

Take this at your own pace. You are not required to open up to everyone. A good adage is to "speak from your scars, not your wounds." Take time to focus on your own healing before you decide if you are ready to publicly share your story with others.

Benediction

Ultimately, our healing is found in Jesus; he is both the source and the destination. He is who we've walked this path with but also who we are walking toward. This passage guided me as I considered purity culture recovery: "Therefore, I urge you, brothers and sisters, in view of God's mercy, to offer your bodies as a living sacrifice, holy and pleasing to God—this is your true and proper worship. Do not conform to the pattern of this world, but be transformed by the renewing of your mind. Then you will be able to test and approve what God's will is—his good, pleasing and perfect will."[6] As we integrate our bodies and minds, heal our faith, and rebuild our sexuality, we offer up this work as an act of worship to God.

Finally, this is my prayer for us as we deconstruct purity culture:

God, so many of us were affected by the lies of purity culture.

So many of us are picking up the pieces of a belief system as we deconstruct, trying to see what can be salvaged and what needs to be thrown away.

It is not always easy to grasp your "overwhelming, never-ending, reckless love"[7] when what we have experienced has been fear, control, and shame.

We want to believe. Help us with our unbelief.[8]

We are clinging to your promise that you never leave us nor forsake us.[9]

We are trusting that you leave the ninety-nine to pursue the one—even me—as I wander and try to find my way back to you.[10]

God, "there's no lie you won't tear down"[11] in your love for me.

Not the lie that my identity, worth, and purpose are tied to my performance and following the rules.

Not the lie that I have to accept black-and-white answers and cannot wrestle with, question, or doubt my faith.

Not the lie that women or men are dangerous, dehumanized, and enemies.

Not the lie that I am damaged goods, a wilting rose, unlovable, unworthy, undeserving, broken.

Jesus, your love is strong enough to break any lie.

Amen.

APPENDIX 1

How to Find Professional Help

After reading this book, you may realize you need more extensive, personalized help. If so, congratulations on taking this brave step.

Here are some considerations for finding professional help for purity culture recovery or faith deconstruction.

Medical professionals. Whenever there is a sexual issue, it's always good to first treat any physical causes with a visit to your primary care provider, gynecologist, or urologist. Issues of sexual pain, low sex drive, or erectile difficulties can have both physiological and psychological causes. Often treating the physical causes is simpler, so talking with your medical provider is the first step. They may refer you to a pelvic floor physical therapist for issues of sexual pain, prescribe or make modifications to your medication, or refer you to a mental health therapist as a next step.

Mental health professionals. When looking for a therapist, I strongly recommend you see a licensed, trauma-informed mental health professional. A licensed mental health professional has at least a master's degree and several years of supervised counseling experience. Find someone trained in couples therapy, trauma, religious issues, or sex therapy depending on your presenting concern. The degree (master's or doctorate) or license type (licensed counselor, social worker, psychologist, etc.) of the professional is often not as important as their specialization. Licensing laws typically only allow clinicians to practice in their home state, so your options may be geographically limited.

I often hear from my therapy clients that seeing a biblical counselor did more harm than good. While these types of counselors may be helpful for some issues, proceed with caution. Pastoral or biblical counselors are rarely trained in treating sexual disorders, sexual or religious trauma, addiction, or complex relationship issues, so find a licensed therapist you trust and feel safe with.

You can find a therapist by asking your medical provider or friends for a referral, seeing if your work has an Employee Assistance Program (EAP), or checking with your insurance if you wish to use this as payment. If you are financially able, you may want to look for a therapist who is out of network or self-pay only. While you may pay more out of pocket, this can be worth it because you can select someone who is highly trained and specialized in your problems and who is not restricted or limited by insurance. If finances are a barrier, consider seeing an intern or a prelicensed mental health professional (someone with a graduate degree who has not yet completed licensure requirements), asking your therapist for a reduced fee, or accessing a community mental health center.

Here are some databases to search for a therapist. Many of these allow you to filter by location, specialty, and insurance.

- PsychologyToday.com
- TherapyDen.com
- OpenPathCollective.org (reduced-fee therapists)
- ReclamationCollective.com (religious trauma–specific)
- EMDRIA.org (trauma and EMDR–specific)
- SexualWholeness.com (American Board of Christian Sex Therapists)
- AASECT.org (American Association of Sexuality Educators, Counselors and Therapists)

- Gottman.com (Gottman Institute–trained marriage therapists)

Coaching. Coaching is a professional relationship that offers the convenience of online help without location restrictions. Coaching is unregulated—meaning anyone can call themselves a "coach"—so you'll want to look for someone with credibility and an established record of speaking to the issues you face. But be aware; coaching is not mental health treatment. Coaching may not be appropriate for those with a complex trauma history, untreated mental illness, or suicidal thoughts, so check with your coach or consider licensed therapy in addition to coaching.

APPENDIX 2

Further Reading

Please note: inclusion on this list does not necessarily mean I agree with the book or the author's body of work. I believe in reading widely, and I regularly read and learn from authors with whom I disagree. Some of these books may belong to more than one category, but I have tried to include it in the category it fits best.

Sexuality and Purity Culture

Eckert, Kim Gaines. *Things Your Mother Never Told You: A Woman's Guide to Sexuality*. Downers Grove, IL: InterVarsity, 2014.

Gardner, Christine J. *Making Chastity Sexy: The Rhetoric of Evangelical Abstinence Campaigns*. Berkeley: University of California Press, 2011.

Gregoire, Sheila Wray. *The Good Girl's Guide to Great Sex: Creating a Marriage That's Both Holy and Hot*. Grand Rapids: Zondervan, 2022.

Gregoire, Sheila Wray, and Keith Gregoire. *The Good Guy's Guide to Great Sex: Because Good Guys Make the Best Lovers*. Grand Rapids: Zondervan, 2022.

Gregoire, Sheila Wray, Rebecca Gregoire Lindenbach, and Joanna Sawatsky. *The Great Sex Rescue: The Lies You've Been Taught and How to Recover What God Intended*. Grand Rapids: Baker Books, 2021.

Hirsch, Debra. *Redeeming Sex: Naked Conversations about Sexuality and Spirituality*. Downers Grove, IL: InterVarsity, 2015.

Penner, Clifford, and Joyce Penner. *The Gift of Sex: A Guide to Sexual Fulfillment*. Nashville: Thomas Nelson, 2003.

Rosenau, Douglas E. *A Celebration of Sex: A Guide to Enjoying God's Gift of Sexual Intimacy*. Nashville: Thomas Nelson, 2002.

Wagner, Zachary. *Non-Toxic Masculinity: Recovering Healthy Male Sexuality*. Downers Grove, IL: InterVarsity, 2023.

Welcher, Rachel Joy. *Talking Back to Purity Culture: Rediscovering Faithful Christian Sexuality*. Downers Grove, IL: InterVarsity, 2020.

Winner, Lauren F. *Real Sex: The Naked Truth about Chastity*. Grand Rapids: Baker Books, 2006.

Sexual Health

Nagoski, Emily. *Come as You Are: The Surprising New Science That Will Transform Your Sex Life*. New York: Simon & Schuster, 2015.

Nagoski, Emily. *Come Together: The Science (and Art!) of Creating Lasting Sexual Connections*. New York: Ballantine Books, 2024.

Theology of Sexuality

Allberry, Sam. *Why Does God Care Who I Sleep With?* Vol. 4 of *Questioning Faith*. Epsom, England: The Good Book Company, 2020.

Jones, Beth Felker. *Faithful: A Theology of Sex*. Grand Rapids: Zondervan, 2015.

Slattery, Juli. *God, Sex, and Your Marriage*. Chicago: Moody, 2022.

Slattery, Juli. *Rethinking Sexuality: God's Design and Why It Matters*. Portland, OR: Multnomah, 2018.

Progressive Sexual Ethics

Allison, Emily Joy. *#ChurchToo: How Purity Culture Upholds Abuse and How to Find Healing*. Minneapolis: Broadleaf Books, 2021.

Anderson, Dianna. *Damaged Goods: New Perspectives on Christian Purity*. Nashville: Jericho Books, 2015.

Bolz-Weber, Nadia. *Shameless: A Case for Not Feeling Bad about Feeling Good (about Sex)*. Rev. ed. Colorado Springs: Convergent Books, 2020.

Klein, Linda Kay. *Pure: Inside the Evangelical Movement That Shamed a Generation of Young Women and How I Broke Free*. New York: Atria Books, 2018.

McCleneghan, Bromleigh. *Good Christian Sex: Why Chastity Isn't the Only Option—and Other Things the Bible Says About Sex*. San Francisco: HarperOne, 2016.

Roberts, Matthias. *Beyond Shame: Creating a Healthy Sex Life on Your Own Terms*. Minneapolis: Fortress Press, 2020.

Historical-Cultural Perspectives on Sexuality and Gender

Barr, Beth Allison. *The Making of Biblical Womanhood: How the Subjugation of Women Became Gospel Truth*. Grand Rapids: Baker Books, 2021.

DeRogatis, Amy. *Saving Sex: Sexuality and Salvation in American Evangelicalism*. Oxford: Oxford University Press, 2014.

Du Mez, Kristin Kobes. *Jesus and John Wayne: How White Evangelicals Corrupted a Faith and Fractured a Nation*. New York: Liveright, 2020.

Emba, Christine. *Rethinking Sex: A Provocation*. New York: Sentinel, 2022.

Freitas, Donna. *Sex and the Soul: Juggling Sexuality, Spirituality, Romance, and Religion on America's College Campuses*. Oxford: Oxford University Press, 2008.

Moslener, Sara. *Virgin Nation: Sexual Purity and American Adolescence*. Oxford: Oxford University Press, 2015.

Valenti, Jessica. *The Purity Myth: How America's Obsession with Virginity Is Hurting Young Women*. New York: Seal Press, 2009.

Trauma and Embodiment

Anderson, Laura E. *When Religion Hurts You: Healing from Religious Trauma and the Impact of High-Control Religion*. Grand Rapids: Brazos, 2023.

Kolber, Aundi. *Strong like Water: Finding the Freedom, Safety, and Compassion to Move through Hard Things—and Experience True Flourishing*. Wheaton: Tyndale Refresh, 2023.

Kolber, Aundi. *Try Softer: A Fresh Approach to Move Us out of Anxiety, Stress, and Survival Mode—and into a Life of Connection and Joy*. Wheaton: Tyndale Refresh, 2020.

McBride, Hillary L. *Practices for Embodied Living: Experiencing the Wisdom of Your Body*. Grand Rapids: Brazos, 2024.

McBride, Hillary L. *The Wisdom of Your Body: Finding Healing, Wholeness, and Connection through Embodied Living*. Grand Rapids: Brazos, 2021.

van der Kolk, Bessel. *The Body Keeps the Score: Brain, Mind, and Body in the Healing of Trauma*. London: Penguin Books, 2014.

Shame

Brown, Brené. *I Thought It Was Just Me (but It Isn't): Making the Journey from "What Will People Think?" to "I Am Enough."* New York: Avery, 2007.

Sellers, Tina Schermer. *Sex, God, and the Conservative Church: Erasing Shame from Sexual Intimacy*. Oxfordshire: Routledge, 2017.

Thompson, Curt. *The Soul of Shame: Retelling the Stories We Believe about Ourselves*. Downers Grove, IL: InterVarsity, 2015.

Dialectical Behavior Therapy

Linehan, Marsha M. *DBT Skills Training Handouts and Worksheets*. 2nd ed. New York: Guilford Press, 2014.

Linehan, Marsha M. *DBT Skills Training Manual*. 2nd ed. New York: Guilford Press, 2014.

Emotional Health

Brown, Brené. *Daring Greatly: How the Courage to Be Vulnerable Transforms the Way We Live, Love, Parent, and Lead*. New York: Avery, 2012.

Brown, Brené. *The Gifts of Imperfection: Let Go of Who You Think You're Supposed to Be and Embrace Who You Are*. Center City, MN: Hazelden, 2010.

Cook, Alison. *The Best of You: Break Free from Painful Patterns, Mend Your Past, and Discover Your True Self in God*. Nashville: Thomas Nelson, 2022.

Neff, Kristin, and Christopher Germer. *The Mindful Self-Compassion Workbook: A Proven Way to Accept Yourself, Build Inner Strength, and Thrive*. New York: Guilford Press, 2018.

Tawwab, Nedra Glover. *Set Boundaries, Find Peace: A Guide to Reclaiming Yourself*. New York: TarcherPerigee, 2021.

Marriage

Gottman, John, and Nan Silver. *The Seven Principles for Making Marriage Work: A Practical Guide from the Country's Foremost Relationship Expert*. Rev. ed. New York: Harmony, 2015.

Hardin, Christa. *The Enneagram in Marriage: Your Guide to Thriving Together in Your Unique Pairing*. Grand Rapids: Baker Books, 2023.

Johnson, Sue. *Hold Me Tight: Seven Conversations for a Lifetime of Love*. Boston: Little, Brown Spark, 2008.

Sexual Addiction, Infidelity, and Abusive Marriages

Hoffman, Natalie. Flying Free, https://www.flyingfreenow.com.

McDugal, Sarah. Wilderness to WILD, https://www.wildernesstowild.com.

Snyder, Douglas K., Donald H. Baucom, and Kristina Coop Gordon. *Getting Past the Affair: A Program to Help You Cope, Heal, and Move On—Together or Apart*. New York: Guilford Press, 2007.

Stringer, Jay. *Unwanted: How Sexual Brokenness Reveals Our Way to Healing*. Colorado Springs: NavPress, 2018.

Singleness

Allberry, Sam. *7 Myths about Singleness*. Wheaton: Crossway, 2019.

Callaway, Kutter. *Breaking the Marriage Idol: Reconstructing Our Cultural and Spiritual Norms*. Downers Grove, IL: InterVarsity, 2018.

Harris, Kat. *Sexless in the City: A Sometimes Sassy, Sometimes Painful, Always Honest Look at Dating, Desire, and Sex*. Grand Rapids: Zondervan, 2021.

Smith, Joy Beth. *Party of One: Truth, Longing, and the Subtle Art of Singleness*. Nashville: Thomas Nelson, 2018.

Parenting

Gregoire, Sheila Wray, Rebecca Gregoire Lindenbach, and Joanna Sawatsky. *She Deserves Better: Raising Girls to Resist Toxic Teachings on Sex, Self, and Speaking Up*. Grand Rapids: Baker Books, 2023.

Kennedy, Becky. *Good Inside: A Guide to Becoming the Parent You Want to Be*. New York: Harper Wave, 2022.

Lansbury, Janet. *No Bad Kids: Toddler Discipline without Shame*. Scotts Valley, CA: CreateSpace, 2014.

Miller, Meredith. *Woven: Nurturing a Faith Your Kid Doesn't Have to Heal From.* Brentwood: Worthy Books, 2023.

Sellers, Tina Schermer. *Shameless Parenting: Everything You Need to Raise Shame-Free, Confident Kids and Heal Your Shame Too!* Self-published, 2021.

Siegel, Daniel J., and Tina Payne Bryson. *The Power of Showing Up: How Parental Presence Shapes Who Our Kids Become and How Their Brains Get Wired.* New York: Ballantine Books, 2020.

Deconstruction

Bessey, Sarah. *Field Notes for the Wilderness: Practices for an Evolving Faith.* Colorado Springs: Convergent, 2024.

Billups, Sara. *Orphaned Believers: How a Generation of Christian Exiles Can Find the Way Home.* Grand Rapids: Baker Books, 2023.

Boyd, Kate. *An Untidy Faith: Journeying Back to the Joy of Following Jesus.* Harrisonburg, VA: Herald Press, 2023.

Herrington, Angela J. *Deconstructing Your Faith without Losing Yourself.* Grand Rapids: Eerdmans, 2024.

McCammon, Sarah. *The Exvangelicals: Loving, Living, and Leaving the White Evangelical Church.* New York: St. Martin's Press, 2024.

LGBTQ+ Perspectives

Rivera, Bridget Eileen. *Heavy Burdens: Seven Ways LGBTQ Christians Experience Harm in the Church.* Grand Rapids: Brazos, 2021.

Acknowledgments

Writing a book has been a lifelong dream of mine and is now one of my proudest accomplishments. This book would not have been possible without my other most valued accomplishments: earning my doctorate and maintaining my faith and values through my deconstruction.

I have many people to thank who have contributed to these endeavors.

As many in the helping professions feel, my clients are my greatest teachers. Writing this book while simultaneously doing coaching and therapy for purity culture recovery made this work embodied. I am grateful for the women and men who shared the tender parts of their stories with me and allowed me to be a part of their healing.

Thanks to my agent Keely Boeving for believing in me and for your patient commitment to this project. Thanks to my editor Stephanie Duncan Smith and the team at Baker Books for helping me bring this book to fruition. I am indebted to my assistant, Bekah Owsley Tatem, for her valuable contributions as a sounding board.

I have made so many wonderful writing friends online, especially through Hope Writers. Thanks to my online community who were my first dialogue partners as I started writing and speaking about purity culture.

I am especially grateful to Sheila Wray Gregoire for writing the foreword to my book. She is a pioneer in exposing harmful teachings about sexuality and has been a mentor to me in many ways. Sheila is generous in sharing her platform to point the spotlight on up-and-coming voices, and her support has had a positive impact on my work. Thanks to the other authors and leaders who shared their enthusiasm for this book as well.

I am thankful to my college and graduate school professors and clinical supervisors for training me to be the psychologist I am today. I especially want to thank my human sexuality professors for teaching me sex education and sex therapy. And I thank my own therapists who have been with me on my healing journey over the years.

Thank you to early readers of my manuscript who provided feedback and additional perspectives from their fields of psychology, theology, trauma, sex therapy, parenting, and/or religious deconstruction: Amy Dilworth, Dr. Emily Oliver, Dr. Elizabeth Paddrick, Matthew Schantz, Shari Smith, Zachary Wagner, and Amanda Waldron.

Thanks to those I interviewed who shared their expertise and diverse stories, including Brittany Broaddus-Smith, Sarah McDugal, Bridget Eileen Rivera, Dr. Rachel Smith, and several anonymous women.

I want to thank my family and friends for their support, especially Sarah Beth, whose early conversations about purity culture ignited my passion to write this book.

"For women to step into their full power in the world, it requires men to step into their full power in the home."[1] My husband exemplifies this quote, supporting me and our family in a hundred unseen ways and giving me the time and space that make my career possible. We had no idea when we married that I would create a public career about sex, and I am thankful for his loyalty and the encouragement to pursue my dreams. He has also been the key to my healing from purity culture because of the security and acceptance he gives me. John, you are a gift of grace to me in every way, and I am grateful to share my life with you and to create our life together.

My children won't read this book for many years (or ever!), but I hope they will be proud that Mommy was scared to write a book—and did it anyway. I pray that I embody every truth in this book to them and that as they grow, they will know a faith based not on rules but on being loved in a relationship with God. Grace Anne, you are God's gift to me and to the world. Samuel, may you hear the voice of God and follow it.

And thanks to you—my fellow purity culture survivors—for giving me a deeper why to write this book.

Notes

Introduction

1. Africa Without Borders, "Desiring God Conference Pastor Chandler," June 29, 2011, https://www.youtube.com/watch?v=xM7nHMOvKpg. In 2022, Matt Chandler was placed on a paid leave from his role as a pastor of The Village church due to "inappropriate coarse joking" between himself and a female church attendee on social media. After three months, Chandler was reinstated to his position, with elders comparing his return to a football player returning to the field after a knee injury. Details about Chandler's alleged indiscretions and the restoration process were never made public, leading to wide criticism of The Village church for their lack of transparency. See Bob Smietana, "Matt Chandler, Megachurch Pastor and ACTS 29 Leader, Placed on Leave," Religion News Service, August 29, 2022, https://religionnews.com/2022/08/29/matt-chandler-megachurch-pastor-and-acts-29-leader-placed-on-leave-for-unhealth-instagram-messages-woman. See also Daniel Silliman, "Matt Chandler Restored to Ministry after Three Months," *Christianity Today*, December 4, 2022, https://www.christianity today.com/news/2022/december/matt-chandler-returns-pulpit-restored-village-church.html.

2. True Love Waits Organization. True Love Waits was created in 1993 by the Southern Baptist Convention and is sponsored by Lifeway Christian Resources. You can find current True Love Waits Resources on Lifeway's website, https://www.lifeway.com/en/product-family/true-love-waits.

3. Age 30 is not "old," and I have many dear friends and clients who continue to experience unwanted singleness through their thirties, forties, and beyond. However, the average age of marriage for women in America at the time I married was 27, but it was 23.5 for evangelical Protestant women. (See Lyman Stone and Brad Wilcox, "The Religious Marriage Paradox: Younger Marriage, Less Divorce," Institute for Family Studies, December 15, 2021, https://ifstudies.org/blog/the-religious-marriage-paradox-younger-marriage-less-divorce.) I validate

233

the pain I experienced in my singleness and hold space for the pain of those whose unwanted singleness lasts much longer.

4. When I use the term "the Church," I am generally referring to conservative, white American evangelicalism and its churches.

5. You are in charge of the pace. If your emotional or physical arousal becomes overwhelming, don't push through. Stop and process with a safe and trusted friend or a therapist. Use Containment (chap. 2, "Tools for the Journey") and Grounding (chap. 11, "Tools for the Journey") to calm your body and mind. See if you can come back to the exercise later when you feel ready.

6. Cognitive-behavioral therapy is an evidenced-based treatment for a multitude of issues, including depression and anxiety. Dialectical behavior therapy, developed by Dr. Marsha Linehan, was originally intended to treat borderline personality disorder but is also evidenced-based for a variety of other mental health problems. I have drawn from DBT skills in emotion regulation, mindfulness meditation, and somatic therapies to heal the mind-body connection.

7. Thank you to my coaching client A.S. who showed me that the soul had to be integrated with mind, body, and heart to experience holistic healing.

Chapter 1 Surviving Purity Culture

1. Laura E. Anderson, *When Religion Hurts You: Healing from Religious Trauma and the Impact of High-Control Religion* (Grand Rapids: Brazos, 2023), loc. 936 of 4320, Kindle.

2. Standards of purity are not exclusive to the evangelical Christian faith. I have spoken with orthodox Jewish women, Muslim women, and Latter-day Saints women who also relate to the experience of purity culture. Many other faiths preach the same sexual ethic of premarital abstinence as well as many of the harmful messages, such as emphasizing purity for women rather than men, equating virginity with spiritual maturity, and shaming women who are not virgins. While the broader experience of purity culture extends beyond evangelicalism, the sociocultural expressions were largely central to evangelical culture. Because of this emphasis, as well as my own personal background and that of the majority of my audience, this is the faith tradition I will speak from.

3. When I use the term "traditional Christian sexual ethic," I am referring to the belief that God created sexual intimacy to be reserved between two people (historically, a husband and wife) in a lifelong, covenantal marriage. This includes the belief in premarital sexual abstinence and sexual faithfulness in marriage.

4. Emily Joy Allison, *#ChurchToo: How Purity Culture Upholds Abuse and How to Find Healing* (Minneapolis: Broadleaf Books, 2021), 179. While I disagree with Allison's definition of purity culture and her rejection of traditional sexual morals like monogamy, she does raise excellent points about the connection between purity culture and rape culture. Her book is thought-provoking and worth the read even if there are significant areas of disagreement.

5. For a detailed analysis of how patriarchal gender roles infiltrated mainstream theological beliefs, see Beth Allison Barr, *The Making of Biblical Womanhood: How the Subjugation of Women Became Gospel Truth* (Grand Rapids: Brazos, 2021).

6. Parts of this section previously appeared in Camden Morgante, "Is Purity Culture Trauma?," *Bare Marriage*, September 5, 2023, https://baremarriage.com /2023/09/is-purity-culture-trauma.

7. This is a well-established truth in traumatology. I have learned the most about trauma and the body from the works of Dr. Laura Anderson, Aundi Kolber, LPC, Dr. Hillary McBride, and Dr. Arielle Schwartz, as well as from my training in EMDR therapy through EMDR Consulting.

8. A diagnosis of PTSD requires a person be exposed to a life-threatening event, reexperience the event, avoid thinking about it, have negative thoughts and feelings, and have physiological arousal and reactivity. See https://www.ptsd.va .gov/professional/treat/essentials/dsm5_ptsd.asp.

9. This is also sometimes called "complex trauma." See the work of Aundi Kolber and Dr. Arielle Schwartz to learn more.

10. Francine Shapiro, *Eye Movement Desensitization and Reprocessing (EMDR) Therapy*, 3rd ed. (New York: Guilford Press, 2018), 39.

11. Of course, those who grew up in purity culture can experience both "little t" and "big T" traumas. Purity culture is closely connected to other forms of trauma, especially sexual abuse, which will be explored more in chaps. 2 and 7.

12. See Shapiro, *Eye Movement Desensitization and Reprocessing (EMDR) Therapy*.

13. Elyssa Barbash, "Different Types of Trauma: Small 't' versus Large 'T,'" Psychology Today, March 13, 2017, https://www.psychologytoday.com/us/blog /trauma-and-hope/201703/different-types-trauma-small-t-versus-large-t.

14. Bessel van der Kolk, *The Body Keeps the Score: Brain, Mind, and Body in the Healing of Trauma* (London: Penguin Books, 2014).

15. Anderson, *When Religion Hurts You*.

16. Some of my interviewees mentioned that purity culture led them to make more thoughtful dating choices and made sexual boundaries more clear-cut in dating. A dissertation study on purity culture found that some women reported feelings of trust and safety in their marital sex, which they attributed to waiting for sex until marriage with their spouse. See Emily Aikins Oliver, "'Nothing Like We Expected': Examining the Relationship between Purity Culture and Sexual Functioning and Satisfaction in Adulthood" (PhD diss., Lee University, 2023).

17. Zachary Wagner, *Non-Toxic Masculinity: Recovering Healthy Male Sexuality* (Downers Grove, IL: InterVarsity, 2023), 24.

18. Ashley Pikel, "Framed by Sexuality: An Examination of Identity-Messages in 'Purity Culture' Reflections" (master's thesis, South Dakota State University, 2018).

19. Jer. 17:9 NKJV.

20. I am grateful to Aundi Kolber for giving me this language. See Aundi Kolber, *Try Softer: A Fresh Approach to Move Us out of Anxiety, Stress, and Survival Mode—and into a Life of Connection and Joy* (Wheaton: Tyndale Refresh, 2020).

21. *Willy Wonka and the Chocolate Factory*, directed by Mel Stuart (Paramount Pictures, 1971).

22. Ps. 37:4.

23. Katelyn Beaty, "Joshua Harris and the Sexual Prosperity Gospel," Religious News Service, July 26, 2019, https://religionnews.com/2019/07/26/joshua-harris -and-the-sexual-prosperity-gospel.

24. Other common reasons my audience gave are sociopolitical events, such as the evangelical Church's response to the pandemic and to racially motivated murders, the widespread evangelical support for the election of Donald Trump, and the Church's historic treatment of the LGBTQ+ community.

25. "Religion's Relationship to Happiness, Civic Engagement and Health around the World," Pew Research Center, January 31, 2019, https://www.pew research.org/religion/2019/01/31/religions-relationship-to-happiness-civic-engage ment-and-health-around-the-world.

26. American Psychiatric Association, *Diagnostic and Statistical Manual of Mental Disorders, Fifth Edition (DSM-5)* (Arlington, TX: American Psychiatric Association Publishing, 2014), 439. The research on the link between sexual pain disorders with inadequate sexual education and religious orthodoxy is mixed. The *DSM-5* notes that "this perception appears to be confirmed by recent reports from Turkey, a primarily Muslim country. . . . However, most available research, al-though limited in scope, does not support this notion." Recent research on twenty thousand evangelical women, however, found that they are 2.5 times more likely to have vaginismus than the general population. See Sheila Wray Gregoire, Rebecca Gregoire Lindenbach, and Joanna Sawatsky, *The Great Sex Rescue* (Grand Rapids: Baker Books, 2021), chaps. 3 and 10.

27. American Psychiatric Association, *DSM-5*.

28. See Tina Schermer Sellers, *Sex, God, and the Conservative Church: Erasing Shame from Sexual Intimacy* (New York: Routledge, 2017). In addition, Gregoire, Lindenbach, and Sawatsky's research found similar rates of vaginismus between women who were sexually abused and women who believed the messages of purity culture. See *The Great Sex Rescue*, 189.

29. See Gregoire, Lindenbach, and Sawatsky, *The Great Sex Rescue*, chaps. 3, 7, and 10.

30. One dissertation on the effects of purity culture on sexual functioning found that those with negative experiences with purity culture had lower ratings of sexual satisfaction and sexual functioning, including arousal, lubrication, and orgasm. See Oliver, "'Nothing like We Expected.'" A study of postpartum women found that those who identified as Catholic or Protestant were three times more likely to experience sexual dysfunction. See Juliana Bento de Lima Holanda et al., "Sexual Dysfunction and Associated Factors Reported in the Postpartum Period/ *Disfunção Sexual e Fatores Associados Relatados No Período Pós-Parto*," *Acta Paulista De Enfermagem* 27, no. 6 (2014): 573–78.

31. N. D. Leonhardt, D. M. Busby, and B. J. Willoughby, "Sex Guilt or Sanc-tification? The Indirect Role of Religiosity on Sexual Satisfaction," *Psychology of Religion and Spirituality* 12, no. 2 (2016): 213–22. Jane S. T. Woo et al., "Sex Guilt Mediates the Relationship between Religiosity and Sexual Desire in East Asian and Euro-Canadian College-Aged Women," *Archives of Sexual Behavior* 41 (2012): 1485–95.

32. Father Richard Rohr (@RichardRohrOFM), "We do not think ourselves into a new way of living, we live ourselves into a new way of thinking," X (formerly

known as Twitter), January 1, 2014, 1:20 p.m., https://twitter.com/richardrohrofm/status/418446686718296064. Rohr may have been influenced by the developer of dialectical behavior therapy, Marsha Linehan, who says, "You can't think yourself into new ways of acting; you can only act yourself into new ways of thinking." See Marsha M. Linehan, *Building a Life Worth Living: A Memoir* (New York: Random House, 2020), 147.

33. Aundi Kolber, *Strong like Water: Finding the Freedom, Safety, and Compassion to Move through Hard Things—and Experience True Flourishing* (Wheaton: Tyndale Refresh, 2023), 60.

34. The language of "new understanding and new experience" comes from Hanna Levenson, *Time-Limited Dynamic Psychotherapy: A Guide to Clinical Practice* (New York: Basic Books, 1995).

35. Hillary L. McBride, *The Wisdom of Your Body: Finding Healing, Wholeness, and Connection through Embodied Living* (Grand Rapids: Brazos, 2021), loc. 665 of 4399, Kindle.

36. To learn more about DBT or reference a more thorough description of some of the techniques described in this book, see Marsha M. Linehan, *Cognitive-Behavioral Treatment of Borderline Personality Disorder* (New York: Guilford Press, 1993); Marsha M. Linehan, *DBT Skills Training Manual*, 2nd ed. (New York: Guilford Press, 2014); Marsha M. Linehan, *DBT Skills Training Handouts and Worksheets*, 2nd ed. (New York: Guilford Press, 2014).

37. Suggested answers:
   1. Black and white. This statement clearly uses either/or language and sets up a dichotomy with no room for nuance.
   2. Dialectical. This sentence avoids extremes by stating "regardless."
   3. Black and white. The author of this statement presents an either/or binary: if you choose to teach premarital sexual abstinence, you are teaching purity culture.
   4. Dialectical. This may seem like opposing statements, but it allows room for people to *both* heal from what was harmful *and* maintain a Christian sexual ethic.
   5. Black and white. Either you deconstruct or you remain a Christian. There is no room to do both in this statement.
   6. Dialectical. This statement holds space for the possibility of both questioning your beliefs and arriving at a deeper faith.

38. Allison, *#ChurchToo*, 213.

Chapter 2 Toxic "Christian" Cultures

1. Barr, *The Making of Biblical Womanhood*, loc. 492 of 3972, Kindle.
2. *The Virgin Daughters*, directed by Jane Treays (ITV, 2008).
3. *Virgin Nation: Sexual Purity and American Adolescence* by historian Sara Moslener is an academic look at the history of purity ideals. Dianna E. Anderson's *Damaged Goods: New Perspectives on Christian Purity* provides a review of the Christian purity movement. Zachary Wagner's *Non-Toxic Masculinity* helpfully traces the sexual mores of each generation from Baby Boomers to Gen Z. *Jesus and John Wayne: How White Evangelicals Corrupted a Faith and Fractured a Nation* by Kristin Kobes Du Mez details the historical connection between Christian

masculinity and violence. Andrew Whitehead's *American Idolatry: How Christian Nationalism Betrays the Gospel and Threatens the Church* is an accessible read on white Christian nationalism.

4. See Jean M. Twenge, *Generations: The Real Differences between Gen Z, Millennials, Gen X, Boomers, and Silents—and What They Mean for America's Future* (New York: Atria, 2023).

5. *Mean Girls*, directed by Mark Waters (Paramount Pictures, 2004).

6. "A History of Abstinence-Only-Until-Marriage (AOUM) Funding," *SIECUS*, May 2019, https://siecus.org/resources/a-history-of-abstinence-only-federal-funding.

7. John S. Santelli et al., "Abstinence-Only-Until-Marriage: An Updated Review of U.S. Policies and Programs and Their Impact," *Journal of Adolescent Health* 61 (May 2017): 273.

8. One study of a health care facility found a greater lack of sexual health knowledge and education among their religiously affiliated patients than among their nonreligious ones. This lack of knowledge was related to anatomy and physiology as well as overall reproductive and sexual health. See K. Hobern, "Religion in Sexual Health: A Staff Perspective," *Journal of Religion and Health* 53, no. 2 (April 2014): 461–68.

9. Melina M. Bersamin et al., "Promising to Wait: Virginity Pledges and Adolescent Sexual Behavior," *Journal of Adolescent Health* 36, May 2005, https://www.ncbi.nlm.nih.gov/pmc/articles/PMC1949026.

10. Santelli et al., "Abstinence-Only-Until-Marriage," 276.

11. E. Gish, "Are You a 'Trashable' Styrofoam Cup? Harm and Damage Rhetoric in the Contemporary American Sexual Purity Movement," *Journal of Feminist Studies in Religion* 34, no. 2 (2018): 5–22.

12. Antoinette M. Landor and Leslie Gordon Simons, "Why Virginity Pledges Succeed or Fail: The Moderating Effect of Religious Commitment versus Religious Participation," *Journal of Child and Family Studies* 23, no. 3 (August 2014): 1103.

13. Another study found that those who made formal, public pledges were less likely to remain abstinent than those who made informal, personal, and private pledges, suggesting an internalized commitment to abstinence rather than external pressure to conform. See R. Haenfler, "Changing the World One Virgin at a Time: Abstinence Pledgers, Lifestyle Movements, and Social Change," *Social Movement Studies* 18, no. 4 (2019): 425–43.

14. David Ayers, *After the Revolution: Sex and the Single Evangelical* (Bellingham, WA: Lexham Press, 2022). In addition, some research has suggested that youth who were willing to make an abstinence pledge already had protective factors present that could additionally promote abstinence, such as parental monitoring, friends and parents who opposed premarital sex, participation in clubs and community activities, and negative expectations of the consequences of sex. See S. C. Martino et al., "Virginity Pledges among the Willing: Delays in First Intercourse and Consistency of Condom Use," *Journal of Adolescent Health* 43, no. 4 (2008): 7, 341–48.

15. Allison, #*ChurchToo*, 105.

16. See Linda Kay Klein, *Pure: Inside the Evangelical Movement That Shamed a Generation of Young Women and How I Broke Free* (New York: Atria Books, 2018); and Moslener, *Virgin Nation*.

17. When two minority identities (such as Black and female) combine and interact to create greater discrimination, this is called intersectionality.

18. Interview with Brittany Broaddus-Smith, LSW, MEd, on August 8, 2023. Learn more at https://www.theintimacyfirm.com.

19. "The Historical Roots of the Sexualization of Black Women and Girls," *Blackburn Center*, February 20, 2019, https://www.blackburncenter.org/post/2019/02/20/the-historical-roots-of-the-sexualization-of-black-women-and-girls.

20. Interview with Brittany Broaddus-Smith.

21. Interview with Bridget Eileen Rivera on October 6, 2023. Learn more at https://bridgeteileenrivera.com/ or see Bridget Eileen Rivera, *Heavy Burdens: Seven Ways LGBTQ Christians Experience Harm in the Church* (Grand Rapids: Brazos, 2021).

22. Pieter L. Valk, "Recognizing & Responding to Romance Idolatry," *Pieter L Valk*, August 1, 2022, https://www.pieterlvalk.com/blog/recognizing-amp-responding-to-romance-idolatry.

23. Klein, *Pure*, 265.

24. Parts of this section previously appeared in Camden Morgante, "5 Toxic Christian Cultures," *Dr. Camden Morgante*, July 5, 2021, https://drcamden.com/2021/07/05/5-toxic-christian-cultures.

25. Allison, *#ChurchToo*.

26. See K. R. Klement and B. J. Sagarin, "Nobody Wants to Date a Whore: Rape-Supportive Messages in Women-Directed Christian Dating Books," *Sexuality & Culture* 21 (2014): 205–23; and K. R. Klement, B. J. Sagarin, and J. J. Skowronski, "The One Ring Model: Rape Culture Beliefs Are Linked to Purity Culture Beliefs," *Sexuality & Culture* 26 (2002): 2070–106.

27. Wagner, *Non-Toxic Masculinity*, 141.

28. Wagner, *Non-Toxic Masculinity*, 32, 43.

29. Adrian Warnock, "Gender: Complementarian vs Egalitarian Spectrum," *Patheos*, September 24, 2012, https://www.patheos.com/blogs/adrianwarnock/2012/09/gender-roles-a-complementarian-and-egalitarian-spectrum.

30. These positions are commonly labeled complementarianism and egalitarianism, respectively. For my purposes here, I make a distinction between complementarianism and patriarchy; other scholars such as Beth Allison Barr do not. To learn more about complementarianism, see the Council of Biblical Manhood and Womanhood at https://cbmw.org/. To learn more about egalitarianism, see Christians for Biblical Equality at https://www.cbeinternational.org.

31. Interview with Dr. Rachel Smith of Agave Studio on August 29, 2023. Learn more at https://www.agavechicago.com.

32. CBT is a well-respected and popular therapy approach originally developed by Dr. Aaron Beck. Cognitive-behavioral theory proposes that like a triangle, our emotions, thoughts, and behavior are all connected. If we can change one part of the triangle, we can change the whole shape of the triangle, and thus change our experience. See Judith S. Beth, *Cognitive Behavior Therapy: The Basics and Beyond, Third Edition* (New York: Guilford Press, 2020). The thought records in this book are adapted from various techniques I learned in my graduate training, as well as the ones described in Dennis Greenberger and Christine A. Padesky, *Mind Over Mood: Change How You Feel by Changing the Way You Think*, 1st ed.

(New York: Guilford Press, 1995). While CBT and thought records are excellent for identifying and challenging negative thoughts, it is not enough to heal the mind-body disconnection from purity culture. Therefore, CBT will be integrated with other somatic, mindfulness, and emotion regulation skills throughout this book.

33. Arielle Schwartz, *The Complex PTSD Treatment Manual: An Integrative, Mind-Body Approach to Trauma Recovery* (Eau Claire, WI: PESI Publishing, 2021); and Arielle Schwartz, "EMDR, CBT and Somatic Based Interventions to Move Clients from Surviving to Thriving." CE Training offered through PESI, Inc. on July 13–14, 2023.

34. Schwartz, *The Complex PTSD Treatment Manual*.

Chapter 3 Myth #1

1. Mo Isom, *Sex, Jesus, and the Conversations the Church Forgot* (Grand Rapids: Baker Books, 2018), 89.

2. "The Problem with Purity Rings (and Other Bad Symbols & Metaphors)," *Where Do We Go from Here* podcast, episode 132, July 25, 2023, https://where dowegopod.com/132-2/. For more on symbols in evangelicalism, see Karen Swallow Prior, *The Evangelical Imagination: How Stories, Images, and Metaphors Created a Culture in Crisis* (Grand Rapids: Brazos, 2023).

3. Rebecca Lemke, *The Scarlet Virgins: When Sex Replaces Salvation* (Norman, OK: Anatole Publishing, 2017), 93.

4. Wagner, *Non-Toxic Masculinity*, chap. 2.

5. Jon Ward, *Testimony: Inside the Evangelical Movement That Failed a Generation* (Grand Rapids: Brazos, 2023), loc. 1204 of 6521, Kindle.

6. Samuel L. Perry, *Addicted to Lust: Pornography in the Lives of Conservative Protestants* (Oxford: Oxford University Press, 2019).

7. Kat Harris, *Sexless in the City: A Sometimes Sassy, Sometimes Painful, Always Honest Look at Dating, Desire, and Sex* (Grand Rapids: Zondervan, 2021), 147.

8. Rachel Joy Welcher, *Talking Back to Purity Culture: Rediscovering Faithful Christian Sexuality* (Downers Grove, IL: InterVarsity, 2020), loc. 329 of 2548, Kindle.

9. Meredith Miller, *Woven: Nurturing a Faith Your Kid Doesn't Have to Heal From* (New York: Worthy, 2023), 28.

10. Matt. 7:1.

11. A. J. Swoboda, *After Doubt: How to Question Your Faith without Losing It* (Grand Rapids: Brazos, 2021), 141.

12. Matt. 7:17–18 NCV.

13. Gal. 5:22–23 NLT.

14. Rom. 3:23.

15. 1 John 1:7.

16. Jay Stringer, *Unwanted: How Sexual Brokenness Reveals Our Way to Healing* (Colorado Springs: NavPress, 2018), 213.

17. For more on spiritual disciplines broadly, see Richard Foster, *Celebration of Discipline*; Donald S. Whitney, *Spiritual Disciplines for the Christian Life*; and Adle Ahlberg Calhoun, *Spiritual Disciplines Handbook*. For more on the spiritual discipline of chastity, see Lauren Winner, *Real Sex*.

18. Lauren F. Winner, "Sex in the Body of Christ," *Christianity Today*, May 13, 2005, https://www.christianitytoday.com/ct/2005/may/34.28.html. See also Winner, *Real Sex*.

19. Rom. 12:1.

20. Beth Felker Jones, *Faithful: A Theology of Sex* (Grand Rapids: Zondervan, 2015), 20, 68, 85.

Chapter 4 Myth #2

1. Dannah Gresh, *And the Bride Wore White: Seven Secrets to Sexual Purity* (Chicago: Moody, 2012), loc. 140, 155 of 488, PDF.

2. Gresh, *And the Bride Wore White*, loc. 393, 54 of 488, PDF.

3. Christine J. Gardner, *Making Chastity Sexy: The Rhetoric of Evangelical Abstinence Campaigns* (Berkeley: University of California Press, 2011).

4. Welcher, *Talking Back to Purity Culture*.

5. Interview with Bridget Eileen Rivera.

6. Welcher, *Talking Back to Purity Culture*, loc. 873 of 2548, Kindle.

7. Joy Beth Smith, *Party of One: Truth, Longing, and the Subtle Art of Singleness* (Nashville: Thomas Nelson, 2018), 61.

8. My study of grace made such an impact on me that I decided if I ever had a daughter, I would name her Grace. Six years after I published my dissertation, my daughter, Grace Anne, was born.

9. John 16:33.

10. Felker Jones, *Faithful*, 85.

11. Ambiguous grief comes when there is a physical presence but an emotional absence, or an emotional absence with a physical presence. Examples of this include an aging relative with Alzheimer's who is physically present but not emotionally present, or a future spouse who is emotionally present in your hopes and dreams but not physically present. Ambiguous losses like this can also lead to the experience of disenfranchised grief, when our grief is overlooked or unacknowledged by our communities. For more about ambiguous grief and loss, coined by Dr. Pauline Voss, visit https://www.ambiguousloss.com/.

12. Welcher, *Talking Back to Purity Culture*, loc. 974 of 2548, Kindle.

13. Heb. 13:5 NRSVue.

Chapter 5 Myth #3

1. Shannon Ethridge and Stephen Arterburn, *Every Young Woman's Battle: Guarding Your Mind, Heart, and Body in a Sex-Saturated World* (Colorado Springs: WaterBrook, 2009), 21.

2. Gardner, *Making Chastity Sexy*, 51.

3. Debby Jones and Jackie Kendall, *Lady in Waiting: Developing Your Love Relationships* (Shippensburg, PA: Destiny Image Publishers, 1995), 79.

4. Gresh, *And the Bride Wore White*, loc. 391, 393 of 488, PDF.

5. Shelly Donahue, "TALL Truth Student Video Clip #1 Introduction," YouTube video, July 7, 2015, https://www.youtube.com/watch?v=q9GJiNq6qoc. See also Christina Capatides, "A Cup Full of Spit, a Chewed Up Piece of Gum. These Are the Metaphors Used to Teach Kids about Sex," *CBS News*, April 29, 2019,

https://www.cbsnews.com/news/a-cup-full-of-spit-a-chewed-up-piece-of-gum
-these-are-the-metaphors-used-to-teach-kids-about-sex.

6. MrsKevOnStage, "#TheLoveHour | Broken Promises of Purity Culture,"
YouTube video, April 22, 2021, https://www.youtube.com/watch?v=-ryC_Jyix_A.
See also Kevin and Melissa Fredericks, *Marriage Be Hard: 12 Conversations to
Keep You Laughing, Loving, and Learning with Your Partner* (Colorado Springs:
Convergent, 2022).

7. One study of women with vaginismus found that 87.5 percent of their
participants had not received any information related to sexual development in
their formative years and 57.5 percent were exposed to negative religiously based
views of sexuality. See R. Fadul et al., "Psychosocial Correlates of Vaginismus
Diagnosis: A Case-Control Study," *Journal of Sex & Marital Therapy* 45, no. 1
(2010): 73–83. Another study found that religiously induced guilt about sex was
correlated with greater sexual pain. The researchers concluded that an internaliza-
tion of negative religious messages about sex leads to greater likelihood of sexual
pain. See K. A. Azim et al., "Exploring Relationships between Genito-Pelvic Pain/
Penetration Disorder, Sex Guilt, and Religiosity among College Women in the
U.S.," *Journal of Sexual Medicine* 18 (2021): 770–82.

8. See Gregoire, Lindenbach, and Sawatsky, *The Great Sex Rescue*, chap. 10.

9. Interview with Hanna Ward, September 1, 2023. Learn more at https://
saywhatpodcast.co.

10. I also wonder if their depictions of marital sex on YouTube match their
reality of what they are sharing with their marriage therapist, gynecologist, or
best friend.

11. Emily Nagoski, *Come Together: The Science (and Art!) of Creating Lasting
Sexual Connections* (New York: Ballantine Books, 2024), loc. 548 of 5847, Kindle.

12. Emily Nagoski, *Come as You Are: The Surprising New Science That Will
Transform Your Sex Life* (New York: Simon & Schuster, 2015).

13. See chap. 7 for more science and research about the hymen.

Chapter 6 Myth #4

1. Stephen Arterburn and Fred Stoeker, with Mike Yorkey, *Every Man's Battle:
Winning the War on Sexual Temptation One Victory at a Time* (Colorado Springs:
WaterBrook, 2009), 118, 120.

2. "Michelle Duggar's Marriage Advice," *The Hollywood Reporter*, October
12, 2015, https://www.hollywoodreporter.com /lifestyle/lifestyle-news/michelle
-duggar-marriage-advice-sex-831382/.

3. Jill Duggar, Derick Dillard, and Craig Borlase, *Counting the Cost* (New
York: Gallery Books, 2023).

4. Wagner, *Non-Toxic Masculinity*, 48.

5. Libby Anne, "Pastor Mark Driscoll Called Women 'Penis Homes,'" *Patheos*,
September 8, 2014, https://www.patheos.com/blogs/lovejoyfeminism/2014/09
/pastor-mark-driscoll-called-women-penis-homes.html.

6. Wagner, *Non-Toxic Masculinity*, 60.

7. Gregoire, Lindenbach, and Sawatsky, *The Great Sex Rescue*.

8. See Gregoire, Lindenbach, and Sawatsky, *The Great Sex Rescue*, chaps. 9,
5, and 6, respectively.

9. Gregoire, Lindenbach, and Sawatsky, *The Great Sex Rescue*, 161.

10. Nagoski, *Come as You Are*.

11. Nagoski explains that spontaneous desire is like knowing there's cake in your fridge, and you can't stop thinking about and wanting that cake. Responsive desire is like showing up at a party where there's cake, and while you weren't seeking it out, you join in with pleasure. See Nagoski, *Come Together*, loc. 846 of 5847, Kindle.

12. In *Come as You Are*, Nagoski states that 30 percent of women experience responsive desire as their primary form of desire, 15 percent have a spontaneous desire style, and the rest experience a combination of the two. See loc. 521 of 850, Libby.

13. Here I am referring to my work with married, heterosexual women who report lower sex drive than they would like and disconnection from their sexuality. This is distinct from the experience of *asexuality*, which is beyond the scope of this book.

14. See "Sensual Mindfulness: Part 1" in chap. 10 and "Sensual Mindfulness: Part 2" in chap. 11.

15. Stephanie Gauvin and Caroline Pukall, "The SexFlex Scale: A Measure of Sexual Script Flexibility When Approaching Sexual Problems in a Relationship," *Journal of Sex and Marital Therapy* 44, no. 4 (2018): 382–97.

Chapter 7 Myth #5

1. Sarah Mally, *Before You Meet Prince Charming: A Guide to Radiant Purity* (Marion, IA: Tomorrow's Forefathers, 2006), 184–85.

2. Capatides, "A Cup Full of Spit."

3. "Elizabeth Smart Visits Johns Hopkins," YouTube video, posted by David Rosowski, May 30, 2014, https://youtu.be/kzBVzBf-Dn4.

4. Gresh, *And the Bride Wore White*, loc. 177 of 488, PDF.

5. Eric Conn (@EricConn), "Many 'christian' fathers will pay big money to send their girls to college," X, September 20, 2023, 2:43 p.m., https://x.com/Eric _Conn/status/1704566851320299777?s=20.

6. John 8:1–11.

7. American Psychiatric Association, *DSM-5*.

8. Oliver, "'Nothing Like We Expected.'"

9. Hillary McBride, "Episode 1: The House Is Haunted," *Holy/Hurt Podcast*, July 12, 2023, https://holyhurtpodcast.com/ep-01-the-house-is-haunted/.

10. See appendix 1 for resources and suggestions on how to find a therapist.

11. Richard Beck, *Unclean: Meditations on Purity, Hospitality, and Mortality* (Eugene, OR: Cascade Books, 2011).

12. "Hymen," Cleveland Clinic, last reviewed, April 13, 2022, https://my.cleve landclinic.org/health/body/22718-hymen; also see Ranit Mishori et al., "The Little Tissue That Couldn't—Dispelling Myths about the Hymen's Role in Determining Sexual History and Assault," *Reproductive Health* 16 (June 3, 2019).

13. See Madison Griffiths, "Is It Time to Reclaim the Word 'Virgin' to Its Original Meaning?," *SBS*, April 13, 2017, https://www.sbs.com.au/voices/article /is-it-time-to-reclaim-the-word-virgin-to-its-original-meaning/rmzn1aau4; and Kristine Shields, "The Meaning of 'Virgin' Morphed—We Should Reclaim the

Original Intent," *Kristine Shields*, March 13, 2021, https://kristineshieldsauthor
.com/2021/03/13/virgin-didnt-mean-what-we-thought-it-did-the-ancient-interpre
tation-was-better/.

14. Again, the hymen is not a reliable indicator of virginity and can wear
down through nonsexual physical activity. I am referencing it here because of the
overemphasis on virginity and the hymen in purity culture.

15. 1 Sam. 16:7.

16. Brittany Broaddus-Smith informed me that "soul ties" are heavily emphasized in the Black church. According to Broaddus-Smith, a belief in soul ties
is often traced to 1 Corinthians 6:16 and 1 Samuel 18:1. To understand more
about soul ties in evangelicalism, see Sheila Wray Gregoire, "Our Soul Ties Series:
What Are Soul Ties? And Do We Need to Break Soul Ties?," *Bare Marriage*,
November 6, 2019, https://baremarriage.com/2019/11/what-are-soul-ties-how-to
-break-soul-ties/.

17. Donahue, "TALL Truth Student Video Clip."

18. Donahue, "TALL Truth Student Video Clip."

19. Other activities, like childbirth and breastfeeding, also release oxytocin.
Yet interestingly, I have never heard anyone make the argument that giving birth to
and breastfeeding one infant reduces your ability to bond to a subsequent infant.
Read more about oxytocin at "Oxytocin," Cleveland Clinic, last reviewed March
27, 2022, https://my.clevelandclinic.org/health/articles/22618-oxytocin.

20. This idea comes from "worm theology." See Mark Galli, "Asking the Right
Question," *Christianity Today*, April 1, 2010, https://www.christianitytoday.com
/ct/2010/aprilweb-only/23-51.0.html.

21. Ps. 130:3–4.

22. Former gymnast and activist Rachael Denhollander, one of the 150 survivors of sexual abuse from USA Gymnastics team doctor Larry Nassar, has been
an amazing example of both profound forgiveness *and* accountability and justice.
The stunning victim impact statement she read at Nassar's sentencing went viral.
See Morgan Lee, "My Larry Nassar Testimony Went Viral. But There's More
to the Gospel Than Forgiveness," *Christianity Today*, January 31, 2018, https://
www.christianitytoday.com/ct/2018/january-web-only/rachael-denhollander-larry
-nassar-forgiveness-gospel.html. Read her impact statement at https://www.cnn
.com/2018/01/24/us/rachael-denhollander-full-statement/.

23. See "REACH Forgiveness of Others," *Everett Worthington*, http://www
.evworthington-forgiveness.com/reach-forgiveness-of-others; and Everett L.
Worthington Jr. and Nathaniel G. Wade, eds., *Handbook of Forgiveness* (New
York: Routledge, 2019).

24. "Elizabeth Smart Visits Johns Hopkins."

25. Matt. 7:1–5.

26. Linehan, *DBT Skills Training Handouts and Worksheets*.

Chapter 8 Healing Your Faith

1. Kate Bowler and Jessica Richie, *The Lives We Actually Have: 100 Blessings
for Imperfect Days* (New York: Convergent, 2023), 100.

2. Relevant, "'I Kissed Dating Goodbye' Author Josh Harris: 'I Am Not a Christian,'" *Relevant*, July 29, 2019, https://relevantmagazine.com/faith/i-kissed -dating-goodbye-author-josh-harris-i-am-not-a-christian/.

3. In 2023, Harris's ex-wife Shannon Harris published *The Woman They Wanted* (Minneapolis: Broadleaf, 2023), describing her own deconversion from Christianity. See Sarah Stankorb, "I Kissed 'Biblical Womanhood' Goodbye," *Slate*, September 4, 2023, https://slate.com/human-interest/2023/09/joshua-shannon -harris-kissed-dating-goodbye.html.

4. Joshua Harris, "'I Kissed Dating Goodbye' Author: How and Why I've Rethought Dating and Purity Culture," *USA Today*, November 23, 2018, https:// www.usatoday.com/story/opinion/voices/2018/11/23/christianity-kissed-dating -goodbye-relationships-sex-book-column/2071273002.

5. *I Survived I Kissed Dating Goodbye*, documentary, produced by DOCSol-ogy, 2019, https://www.isurvivedikdg.com.

6. Alisa Childers, "Why We Should Not Redeem 'Deconstruction,'" *The Gospel Coalition*, February 18, 2022, https://www.thegospelcoalition.org/article /redeem-reconstruction.

7. The New Evangelicals, https://www.thenewevangelicals.com.

8. See Brian McLaren, *Faith After Doubt: Why Your Beliefs Stopped Working and What to Do About It* (New York: St. Martin's Essentials, 2021).

9. In his book *Stages of Faith* (New York: Harper, 1981), James W. Fowler developed a theory of six stages that people go through as their faith matures. For a description of the stages, see Thomas Armstrong, "The Stages of Faith According to James W. Fowler," *American Institute for Learning and Human Development*, June 12, 2020, https://www.institute4learning.com/2020/06/12/the -stages-of-faith-according-to-james-w-fowler.

10. According to Fowler, it is rare to reach stage 5, conjunctive faith, before midlife. During this stage, people resolve the conflicts of the previous stage by adopting a complex, multifaceted understanding of faith. This stage is when people begin to embrace mystery, paradox, and sacred stories and symbols without being stuck in a theological box. They also accept that some aspects of faith are unknown. There is an integration and acceptance of various dimensions of faith beliefs, with an openness to other religious traditions. Fowler notes that few people reach stage 6, universalizing faith, the final stage. See Fowler, *Stages of Faith*.

11. See also Lawrence Kohlberg's theory of moral development, Jean Piaget's theory of cognitive development, Eric Erickson's theory of psychosocial develop-ment, and James Marcia's theory of adolescent identity development.

12. I have noticed that deconstruction can sometimes become another form of fundamentalism in which those who don't hold the same beliefs are judged as "less evolved." We should be careful not to judge others at earlier stages of faith development and to recognize that people may go through stage 4 and higher but still hold different beliefs than us.

13. See James Marcia's theory of adolescent identity development.

14. Sarah Bessey, "Someone Else's Deconversion," *Sarah Bessey's Field Notes*, August 1, 2023, https://sarahbessey.substack.com/p/someone-elses-deconversion -dbf.

15. Matt. 7:17–20.

16. Anderson, *When Religion Hurts You.*

17. Religious Trauma Institute, accessed March, 20, 2024, https://www.religioustraumainstitute.com.

18. See ACEs Aware, https://www.acesaware.org.

19. Anderson, *When Religion Hurts You,* loc. 895 of 4320, Kindle.

20. Anderson, *When Religion Hurts You,* loc. 1186 of 4320, Kindle.

21. See Anderson, *When Religion Hurts You.*

22. Amanda Waldron, "How to Hold On to Your Faith in Deconstruction," *Dr. Camden Morgante,* August 16, 2021, https://drcamden.com/2021/08/16/how-to-hold-on-to-your-faith-in-deconstruction.

23. See Anderson, *When Religion Hurts You,* chap. 3.

24. Tiffany Yecke Brooks, *Gaslighted by God: Reconstructing a Disillusioned Faith* (Grand Rapids: Eerdmans, 2022).

25. 1 John 4:18.

26. "Shiny Happy Certainty & How Women Led in the Early Church with Nijay Gupta," episode 569, *The Holy Post,* accessed March 20, 2024, https://www.holypost.com/holy-post-podcast/episode/20b7b687/569-shiny-happy-certainty-and-how-women-led-in-the-early-church-with-nijay-gupta. See also Skye Jethani, *With: Reimagining the Way You Relate to God* (Nashville: Thomas Nelson, 2011).

27. Childers, "Why We Should Not Redeem 'Deconstruction.'"

Chapter 9 Reconstructing Your Sexual Ethic

1. Harris, *Sexless in the City,* 136.

2. "Miley Cyrus on God, Remaking 'Sex and the City' and Her Purity Ring," *Huffpost,* July 23, 2008, https://www.huffpost.com/entry/miley-cyrus-on-god-remaki_n_112891.

3. NME News Desk, "Miley Cyrus: 'I Am Open to Every Single Thing That Is Consenting and Doesn't Involve an Animal,'" *NME,* June 10, 2015, https://www.nme.com/news/music/miley-cyrus-33-1209000.

4. Felker Jones, *Faithful,* 80.

5. Christine Emba, *Rethinking Sex: A Provocation* (New York: Sentinel, 2022), 17.

6. Emba, *Rethinking Sex,* 106.

7. Wagner, *Non-Toxic Masculinity,* 51.

8. Two prominent examples are Christian comedian John Crist and actor/comedian Aziz Ansari. In 2019, Crist was accused of sexual misconduct by fans. In 2017, Ansari faced allegations of sexual misconduct from an anonymous woman who accused him of pressuring her into sexual activity on a date, which Ansari asserts was consensual. While these situations were technically consensual and fall short of the legal description of sexual assault, the power dynamics and coercion make them problematic. They also showed a lack of care for the other party. See Emma Stefansky, "Aziz Ansari Accused of Sexual Misconduct," *Vanity Fair,* January 14, 2018, https://www.vanityfair.com/hollywood/2018/01/aziz-ansari-accused-of-sexual-misconduct. See also Lisa Respers France, "Christian Comedian John Crist Apologizes after Sexual Misconduct Allegations," CNN Entertainment, November 7, 2019, https://www.cnn.com/2019/11/07/entertainment/john-crist-sexual-misconduct-trnd/index.html.

9. Emba, *Rethinking Sex*, 17.

10. Emba, *Rethinking Sex*, 169.

11. Devi Abraham, "It's Back: Purity Culture 2.0, Gen Z Style," Religion News Service, December 2, 2021, https://religionnews.com/2021/12/02/its-back -purity-culture-2-0-gen-z-style.

12. See Stephanie McNeal, "Madi Prewett Troutt Is an Influencer for Jesus," *Glamour*, September 19, 2023, https://www.glamour.com/story/madi-prewett -troutt-is-an-influencer-for-jesus.

13. See Paul and Morgan, "What It's Like Being a Virgin on Your Wedding Night," YouTube video, March 2, 2023, https://www.youtube.com/watch?v=5 _ZM1D7mIUg; and Paul and Morgan, "Is Waiting Until Marriage Worth It?— From a Christian Who Didn't Wait," YouTube video, November 19, 2019, https:// www.youtube.com/watch?v=zb5yH6h1j9M&t=439s.

14. Joshua Ryan Butler, *Beautiful Union: How God's Vision for Sex Points Us to the Good, Unlocks the True, and (Sort of) Explains Everything* (Colorado Springs: Multnomah, 2023). Butler proposes a bride "embraces her most intimate guest" and "accepts the sacrificial offering he bestows upon the altar within her Most Holy Place," i.e., his ejaculation into her vagina, loc. 281 of 5427, Kindle.

15. "Mike Todd—The Concept of What We Call Dating, Is Honestly Practicing Divorce," YouTube video, posted by Millionaire Moveclub, June 8, 2022, https://www.youtube.com/watch?v=fcPPpWCiuZk.

16. Cara Hoekstra, "Dated and Overrated: A Review of Jonathan Pokluda's *Outdated*," *Patheos*, August 24, 2022, https://www.patheos.com/blogs/anxious bench/2022/08/dated-and-overrated-a-review-of-jonathan-pokludas-outdated.

17. See Meredith Nardino, "Everything Bachelor's Madison Prewett Has Said about Sex and Saving Herself for Marriage," *US*, October 31, 2022, https://www .usmagazine.com/celebrity-news/pictures/madison-prewetts-quotes-about-sex -saving-herself-for-marriage.

18. Allison, *#ChurchToo*, who rejects a sexual ethic based on monogamy or marriage, states, "Everyone is allowed to find the path that leads to healing for them" (183). "Listening to the body doesn't mean uncritically following all its impulses. It can mean acknowledging and still making a different choice that is rooted in your values" (189).

19. Rom. 12:2.

20. Anderson, *When Religion Hurts You*.

21. Harris, *Sexless in the City*, 4.

22. Chris Bounds, "The Wesleyan Quadrilateral," *The Wesleyan Church*, January 24, 2022, https://www.wesleyan.org/the-wesleyan-quadrilateral.

23. 2 Tim. 3:16 NLT.

24. Gregoire, Lindenbach, and Sawatsky, *The Great Sex Rescue*.

25. Prov. 3:5–6.

26. Ward, *Testimony*, loc. 3504 of 6521, Kindle.

27. 1 Cor. 6:18.

28. The Personal Values Card Sort is in the public domain and many versions are accessible for free online. See William R. Miller, Janet C'de Baca, Daniel B. Matthews, and Paula L. Wilbourne's version at https://www.guilford.com/add /miller11_old/pers_val.pdf?t=1.

29. Harris, *Sexless in the City*, 138.

30. Emba, *Rethinking Sex*, 185.

31. Emba, *Rethinking Sex*, 161.

32. Emba, *Rethinking Sex*, 186.

33. Harris, *Sexless in the City*, 138, emphasis original.

34. Harris, *Sexless in the City*, 135.

35. Phil. 4:8.

36. Linehan, *DBT Skills Training Handouts and Worksheets*.

Chapter 10 Singleness and Sexuality

1. Kim Gaines Eckert, *Things Your Mother Never Told You: A Woman's Guide to Sexuality* (Downers Grove, IL: InterVarsity, 2014), 12.

2. "Harlow's Classic Studies Revealed the Importance of Maternal Contact," Association for Psychological Science, June 20, 2018, https://www.psychologicalscience.org/publications/observer/obsonline/harlows-classic-studies-revealed-the-importance-of-maternal-contact.html.

3. Stringer, *Unwanted*, 20–21.

4. Eckert, *Things Your Mother Never Told You*, 23.

5. Debra Hirsch, *Redeeming Sex: Naked Conversations about Sexuality and Spirituality* (Downers Grove, IL: InterVarsity, 2015), 26.

6. Hillary L. McBride, *Practices for Embodied Living: Experiencing the Wisdom of Your Body* (Grand Rapids: Brazos, 2024), 117.

7. Eckert, *Things Your Mother Never Told You*, 25.

8. Of course, this does not mean toddlers have sexual desires or should be sexualized. They have an inherent need and longing for connection, attachment, and intimacy with others, which is part of the definition of sexuality.

9. McBride, *The Wisdom of Your Body*, loc. 305 of 4399, Kindle.

10. Shari Smith, https://shariasmith.com.

11. McBride encourages us to talk to and about our bodies using our pronouns (she/he/they) rather than "it." Although this still feels awkward at times to me, I am finding it helps me show compassion to my body and think of her as a part of me rather than a project to subdue.

12. See Laura Anderson, *When Religion Hurts You*, for more ideas for experiencing nonsexual pleasure.

13. A 2019 study using 2017 data found that 39 percent of couples met online and only 4 percent met at church. The pandemic has made online dating even more popular. Michael J. Rosenfeld, Reuben J. Thomas, and Sonia Hausen, "Disintermediating Your Friends: How Online Dating in the United States Displaces Other Ways of Meeting," *PNAS* 116, no. 36 (2019), https://www.pnas.org/doi/full/10.1073/pnas.1908630116.

14. Kristyn DeNooyer, https://kristyndenooyer.com.

15. MaryB Safrit, https://www.marybsafrit.com.

16. See Rachel Held Evans, "Christians & Masturbation: Seven Perspectives," *Rachel Held Evans*, June 3, 2013, https://rachelheldevans.com/blog/christians-masturbation.

17. See Perry, *Addicted to Lust*.

18. Eckert, *Things Your Mother Never Told You*, 74, 118.

19. Eckert, *Things Your Mother Never Told You*, 75.

20. A few of the women I interviewed mentioned that even "Christian" men can be manipulative, controlling, and narcissistic, making it difficult to ascertain their suitability as a partner. Someone saying all the right things does not mean they are a safe person. Because patriarchy results in power imbalances, women may be more at risk for getting into emotionally, physically, or sexually abusive relationships. Clearly, this danger exists, but will need more exploration than what I address in this book. See the appendixes for further resources for abusive relationships.

21. Brené Brown, "Dare to Lead: The BRAVING Inventory," accessed March 13, 2024, https://brenebrown.com/resources/the-braving-inventory/.

22. Skills adapted from Linehan, *DBT Skills Training Handouts and Worksheets*.

Chapter 11 After the Wedding Night

1. "Unraveling the Source of Our Sexual Shame: Jay Stringer Deconstructs Purity Culture," *For the Love with Jen Hatmaker*, August 17, 2022, https://podcasts.apple.com/us/podcast/unraveling-the-source-of-our-sexual-shame-jay/id1258388821?i=1000576371625.

2. See Gregoire, Lindenbach, and Sawatsky, *The Great Sex Rescue*, chap. 3.

3. In my description of faithful sexuality, I have built on the work of other authors. In Eckert's *Things Your Mother Never Told You*, she proposes that sex is relational, fruitful, and pleasurable. In *The Good Girl's Guide to Great Sex*, Gregoire argues there are three markers of great sex as God intended it: pleasurable, intimate, and mutual. In *The Great Sex Rescue*, Gregoire, Lindenbach, and Sawatsky write that a healthy sex life should be personal, pleasurable, pure, prioritized, pressure-free, put the other first, and passionate.

4. This advice is intended for those in a healthy marriage, which is characterized by mutual respect, care, and valuing. If you are in an unhealthy marriage that lacks trust, safety, commitment, respect, or value for your personhood, then that needs to be addressed before sexual intimacy. You cannot create sexual safety and intimacy without emotional safety and intimacy. Couples and sex therapy is contraindicated if you are in a physically or emotionally abusive relationship. Please seek individual therapy from a licensed mental health professional and see the appendixes for more resources.

5. In *The Great Sex Rescue*, Gregoire, Lindenbach, and Sawatsky call sex a "deep knowing" (94).

6. Gen. 2:18 NRSVue. According to theologian Marg Mowczko, being a "helper" (the Greek word *ezer*) is not gender-specific to women and reflects God's heart for mutuality in marriage. She says, "Being an ezer is not a gender role—women do not have a special obligation to be helpers. We are all meant to help each other and care for each other depending on the situations we are faced with and depending on our individual abilities." See "Being an Ezer Is Not a Gender Role," *Marg Mowczko*, January 2, 2023, https://margmowczko.com/ezer-gender-role.

7. Eckert, *Things Your Mother Never Told You*, 27.

8. Gen. 2:24 NRSVue.

9. Felker Jones, *Faithful*, 98.

10. Eph. 5:32.

11. Gen. 1:28 NRSVue.

12. Eckert, *Things Your Mother Never Told You*, 28.

13. See Katelyn Beaty, *A Woman's Place: A Christian Vision for Your Calling in the Office, the Home, and the World* (Brentwood: Howard Books, 2017), particularly chap. 7, for more examples of "fruitfulness" apart from procreation.

14. Juli Slattery, *God, Sex, and Your Marriage* (Chicago: Moody, 2022).

15. In *Faithful*, theologian Felker Jones also writes that "the Song highlights egalitarianism, mutuality, and reciprocity between the lovers" (57).

16. 1 Cor. 7:3–5 MSG.

17. Marg Mowczko, "A Wife Has No Authority of Her Own Body? (1 Cor. 7:4)," *Marg Mowczko*, January 7, 2015, https://margmowczko.com/1-corinthians -74-in-a-nutshell. It is also worth mentioning that there are other ways we share our bodies with and serve our spouse and family's needs besides sex. Breastfeeding an infant, caring for children, working to support the family, preparing a meal, and the many tasks required to maintain a home are all embodied ways we share ourselves.

18. Douglas E. Rosenau, *A Celebration of Sex: A Guide to Enjoying God's Gift of Sexual Intimacy* (Nashville: Thomas Nelson, 2002).

19. Gen. 2:25 NRSVue.

20. Woo et al., "Sex Guilt Mediates the Relationship between Religiosity and Sexual Desire in East Asian and Euro-Canadian College-Aged Women"; and Azim et al. "Exploring Relationships between Genito-Pelvic Pain/Penetration Disorder, Sex Guilt, and Religiosity among College Women in the U.S."

21. N. D. Leonhardt et al., "Sex Guilt or Sanctification? The Indirect Role of Religiosity on Sexual Satisfaction," *Psychology of Religion and Spirituality* 12, no. 2 (2019): 213–22.

22. Rosenau, *A Celebration of Sex*.

23. William Masters and Virginia Johnson, *Human Sexual Response* (New York: Bantam Books, 1966).

24. Revisit the differences between spontaneous and responsive desire in the "Desire and Pleasure" section in chap. 6.

25. Rosenau, *A Celebration of Sex*, 38.

26. Laurie Watson, "Sex in the Cycle: Working with Couples' Sexual Cycles Using Emotion Focused Therapy," CE Training, April 24, 2023, Knoxville, TN. Watson stated it can take twenty minutes for a woman's mind to "leave the kitchen"; I have changed the language to be more gender neutral.

27. If you are in an abusive marriage, couples therapy is not recommended. Please seek individual therapy from a licensed mental health professional and see the appendixes for more resources.

28. Rosenau, *A Celebration of Sex*, 273.

29. See appendix 2 for book recommendations.

30. Self-stimulation, with or without the use of a vibrator, is a common intervention in sex therapy to improve partnered sexual intimacy. Always assess your own beliefs and values first to make a values-congruent choice about this or any other therapy intervention. Reading sex-positive Christian books and working

with a Christian sex therapist may help couples who would like to incorporate the use of a vibrator or self-stimulation but are hesitant.

31. A study by Chelom E. Leavitt et al. defines sexual mindfulness as "the state of being present, nonjudgmental, and embodied during sex" and found that couples who utilized sexual mindfulness had greater relational and sexual well-being (Chelom E. Leavitt, Eva S. Lefkowitz, and Emily A. Waterman, "The Role of Sexual Mindfulness in Sexual Wellbeing, Relational Wellbeing, and Self-Esteem," *Journal of Sex and Marital Therapy* 45, no. 6 [March 12, 2019]: 497–509, https://doi.org/10.1080/0092623x.2019.1572680).

32. This exercise is adapted from various sensate focus protocols I learned in my graduate training as well as the one described in Rosenau, *A Celebration of Sex*, chap. 9.

33. Some couples may not be ready for full nudity and may need to start the exercise clothed before working up to this state.

Chapter 12 Overcoming Shame

1. Curt Thompson, *The Soul of Shame: Retelling the Stories We Believe about Ourselves* (Downers Grove, IL: InterVarsity, 2015), 126–27.

2. Brené Brown, *Atlas of the Heart: Mapping Meaningful Connection and the Language of Human Experience* (New York: Random House, 2021), 137.

3. Becky Kennedy, *Good Inside: A Guide to Becoming the Parent You Want to Be* (New York: Harper, 2022), 91. Kennedy says, "For many of us, shame is wired into our bodies. It essentially attached itself to the parts of ourselves that were not embraced by our parents."

4. Thompson, *The Soul of Shame*, 13.

5. Sellers, *Sex, God, and the Conservative Church*, xxiv.

6. Matthias Roberts, *Beyond Shame: Creating a Healthy Sex Life on Your Own Terms* (Minneapolis: Fortress Press, 2020), 169.

7. Brown, *Atlas of the Heart*, 146.

8. 2 Cor. 7:10.

9. Martin E. Seligman, Lyn Y. Abramson, Amy Semmel, and Carl von Baeyer, "Depressive Attributional Style," *Journal of Abnormal Psychology* 88, no. 3 (1979): 242–47, https://doi.org/10.1037/0021-843X.88.3.242.

10. Cynthia Mulder, LCSW, "Listening for Shame in Psychotherapy," *Clearly Clinical* podcast, episode 157, https://clearlyclinical.com/podcast/ceu-shame.

11. Thompson, *The Soul of Shame*.

12. Material adapted from Marsha M. Linehan, *DBT Skills Training Manual*, 2nd ed.

13. McBride, *The Wisdom of Your Body*.

14. Interview with Bridget Eileen Rivera.

15. Roberts, *Beyond Shame*, 138.

16. Thompson, *The Soul of Shame*, 122.

17. Linehan, *DBT Skills Training Handouts and Worksheets*.

18. This is why it is so important to create the groundwork of clarifying your values and sexual ethic. See chap. 9.

19. Roberts, *Beyond Shame*, 173.

20. Thompson, *The Soul of Shame*.

21. See "Sensual Mindfulness: Part 1" in chap. 10 and "Sensual Mindfulness: Part 2" in chap. 11.

22. Linehan, *DBT Skills Training Handouts and Worksheets.*

23. See chap. 7, "Tools for the Journey," and chap. 4, "Tools for the Journey."

24. See Brené Brown, *I Thought It Was Just Me (but It Isn't)* (New York: Gotham Books, 2007), chap. 4.

25. Thought records, parts 1 through 4, can be found in "Tools for the Journey" in chaps. 2, 3, 4, and 7, respectively.

26. Dr. Kristin Neff, Self-Compassion, accessed March 14, 2024, https://self -compassion.org.

27. See Kristin Neff and Christopher Germer, *The Mindful Self-Compassion Workbook: A Proven Way to Accept Yourself, Build Inner Strength, and Thrive* (New York: Guilford Press, 2018).

28. Brown, *Atlas of the Heart,* 147.

29. Thompson, *The Soul of Shame,* loc. 172 of 3325, Kindle.

30. Thompson, *The Soul of Shame,* 27.

31. Van der Kolk, *The Body Keeps the Score.*

32. Thompson, *The Soul of Shame,* 198.

33. Linehan, *DBT Skills Training Manual.*

34. Schwartz, "EMDR, CBT and Somatic Based Interventions."

35. It is very important that you have first clarified if your emotion is justified or unjustified. Opposite action is used only when the emotion (or its intensity) is unjustified. Acting opposite to a justified emotion (e.g., acting on sexual urges that are not in line with your values and therefore bring guilt and shame) can create disastrous consequences and is not recommended.

36. In this case, the skill of opposite action was used in conjunction with other skills to improve the couple's communication, intimacy, and sexual technique, and Lenora's sexual desire. This couple had a healthy, loving marriage with safety, mutual respect, and caring. It could be unsafe to use opposite action (say no to sex) in an abusive or coercive marriage. If you are in a marriage that is unsafe or in which you are not allowed to say no to sex, please seek the help of a licensed individual therapist. Marriage and sex therapy are contraindicated in emotionally, physically, or spiritually abusive marriages.

37. Brown, *Atlas of the Heart,* 138.

38. Thompson, *The Soul of Shame,* loc. 119 of 3225, Kindle.

39. Roberts, *Beyond Shame,* 170.

40. Brené Brown, *Braving the Wilderness: The Quest for True Belonging and the Courage to Stand Alone* (New York: Random House, 2017). Brown also cautions, if you have to change yourself to fit in, it's not belonging. And it actually increases shame.

41. Thompson, *The Soul of Shame,* 242.

42. Rom. 8:1.

43. Thompson, *The Soul of Shame,* 169.

44. Thompson, *The Soul of Shame,* 242.

45. Passages such as Isa. 49:15 and Matt. 23:37 depict God comforting his children with maternal imagery.

46. Roberts, *Beyond Shame*, 173.
47. Brown, *I Thought It Was Just Me*.

Chapter 13 Parenting after Purity Culture

1. Shannon K. Evans, *Feminist Prayers for My Daughter: Powerful Petitions for Every Stage of Her Life* (Grand Rapids: Brazos, 2023), loc. 328 of 1115, Kindle.

2. Kayla Craig, *To Light Their Way: A Collection of Prayers and Liturgies for Parents* (Wheaton: Tyndale Momentum, 2021), 130–32.

3. See Saul McLeod, "Kohlberg's Stages of Moral Development," Simply Psychology, last updated January 17, 2024, https://www.simplypsychology.org/kohlberg.html.

4. Although parts of each myth could fit into Levels I or II, I have organized them in the level they most clearly demonstrate.

5. Shelly Donahue, "TALL Truth Parent Education: Parents Are the Reason Teens Wait," July 2, 2015, https://www.youtube.com/watch?v=va-x2Tc3cBE; Shelly Donahue, "TALL Truth Parent Education: Best Birth Control Is Dad," July 2, 2015, https://www.youtube.com/watch?v=LYA9--cmVmA.

6. Interestingly, levels I and II reasons for sexual purity parallel the prosperity gospel's reasons for becoming a Christian: you'll be a good person, have a better life, avoid hell, gain social approval, and please your parents.

7. See David J. Ayers, "Sex and the Single Evangelical," *Institute for Family Studies*, August 14, 2019, https://ifstudies.org/blog/sex-and-the-single-evangelical.

8. Kennedy, *Good Inside*, 77.

9. James Dobson, *Preparing for Adolescence* (Ventura, CA: Regal Books, 1989).

10. Maya Angelou (@DrMayaAngelou), "Do the best you can until you know better. Then when you know better, do better," X (formerly known as Twitter), August 12, 2018, 11:23 a.m., https://twitter.com/DrMayaAngelou/status/1028663286512930817?lang=en.

11. Sellers, *Sex, God, and the Conservative Church*. See also her book *Shameless Parenting*.

12. Unfortunately, no matter what we do, a child may be abused. If you did not teach your child correct anatomical terms and they were abused, you are not at fault or to blame.

13. I highly recommend Janet Lansbury's book *No Bad Kids*, podcast *Unruffled*, and online parenting course "No Bad Kids."

14. See chap. 8, "Tools for the Journey."

15. "Children and Teens: Statistics," RAINN, accessed March 15, 2024, https://www.rainn.org/statistics/children-and-teens.

16. Paula Tutman and Brandon Carr, "Common Sense Media Survey Finds Average Age Kids Were Exposed to Pornography Was 12 Years Old," *Click On Detroit*, January 10, 2023, https://www.clickondetroit.com/news/local/2023/01/10/common-sense-media-survey-finds-average-age-kids-were-exposed-to-pornography-was-12-years-old.

17. There are other important reasons to monitor kids' online activity, like cyberbullying and the effect social media has on mental health and body image.

Conclusion

1. See "Personal Assessment" in chaps. 3, 4, 5, 6, and 7, or take an electronic version at https://drcamden.com.

2. When originally developed by Dr. Elisabeth Kubler-Ross, her theory was applied to terminally ill patients as they faced their own death. The stages of grief are not linear or step-by-step. They have been widely applied to other losses, and here I make generous accommodations to apply them to grieving faith changes.

3. Mark 12:30 NLT.

4. Mark 12:31.

5. Schwartz, "EMDR, CBT and Somatic Based Interventions."

6. Rom. 12:1–2.

7. "Reckless Love," track 1 on Cory Asbury, *Reckless Love*, Bethel Music, 2018.

8. Mark 9:24.

9. Heb. 13:5; Deut. 31:6.

10. Matt. 18:12.

11. "Reckless Love."

Acknowledgments

1. Quoted in Lauren Dockett, "Fair Play at Home," *Psychotherapy Networker*, November/December 2022, https://www.psychotherapynetworker.org/article/fair -play-home. See also Eve Rodsky, *Fair Play: A Game-Changing Solution for When You Have Too Much to Do (and More Life to Live)* (New York: G. P. Putnam's Sons, 2019).

DR. CAMDEN MORGANTE is a licensed clinical psychologist with nearly fifteen years of experience as a therapist and college professor. She owns a private therapy practice focusing on women's issues, relationships, sexuality, trauma, and spirituality. She is a writer, speaker, and coach on purity culture recovery and faith reconstruction. A frequent contributor to *Christians for Biblical Equality*'s blog, Camden won their writing contest in 2019 for her first article, "5 Myths of Purity Culture."

Dr. Camden combines her personal experience growing up in purity culture with her professional experience in mindfulness, emotion regulation, and somatic-based therapies. Through mind-body integration, she offers her clients and online community strategies for healing their faith from toxic beliefs.

Dr. Camden lives in Knoxville, Tennessee, with her husband and their daughter and son.

Connect with Camden:
DrCamden.com

DrCamden.Substack.com

@drcamden

@drcamden

@drcamden

@doctorcamden